CAN THE WORLD AFFORD

AUTISTIC SPECTRUM DISORDER?

of related interest

The Complete Guide to Asperger's Syndrome
Tony Attwood
ISBN 978 1 84310 495 7 (Hardback)
ISBN 978 1 84310 669 2 (Paperback)

The Imprinted Brain
How Genes Set the Balance Between Autism and Psychosis
Christopher Badcock
ISBN 978 1 84905 023 4

From Isolation to Intimacy
Making Friends without Words
Phoebe Caldwell
With Jane Horwood
ISBN 978 1 84310 500 8

The Girl Who Spoke with Pictures
Autism Through Art
Eileen Miller
Illustrated by Kim Miller
Foreword by Robert Nickel, MD
ISBN 978 1 84310 889 4

Autism Heroes
Portraits of Families Meeting the Challenge
Barbara Firestone, PhD
Photographs by Joe Buissink
Forewords by Teddi Cole and Gary Cole and Catherine Lord, PhD
ISBN 978 1 84310 837 5

CAN THE WORLD AFFORD
AUTISTIC SPECTRUM DISORDER?

Nonverbal Communication, Asperger Syndrome and the Interbrain

DIGBY TANTAM PhD FRCPsych

Jessica Kingsley Publishers
London and Philadelphia

First published in 2009
by Jessica Kingsley Publishers
116 Pentonville Road
London N1 9JB, UK
and
400 Market Street, Suite 400
Philadelphia, PA 19106, USA

www.jkp.com

Library of Congress Cataloging in Publication Data
Tantam, Digby.
  Can the world afford autistic spectrum disorder? : nonverbal communication,
asperger syndrome and the interbrain / Digby Tantam.
      p. cm.
  ISBN 978-1-84310-694-4 (hb : alk. paper)
  1. Autism. 2. Nonverbal communication. 3. Asperger's syndrome. I. Title.
  RC553.A88T37 2009
  616.85'882--dc22
                                              2008045295

British Library Cataloguing in Publication Data
A CIP catalogue record for this book is available from the British Library

ISBN 978 1 84310 694 4

Printed and bound in the United States by
Thomson-Shore, 7300 Joy Road, Dexter, MI 48130

To my dearest, wisest, Emmy van Deurzen

Contents

Acknowledgements

Many people have influenced me during my career and have therefore contributed to this book. Those people who have contributed most directly include Jon Borus whose NIMH fellowship grant supported me during my initial reading about nonverbal communication; John Wing who first suggested that Asperger syndrome might be a disorder of nonverbal communication; Lorna Wing who taught me about Asperger syndrome in my first years of research; Uta Frith whose supervision introduced me to academic rigour at its best and who has proved an inspiration throughout my career of scientific psychology; my fellow supervisees at the MRC Cognitive Development Unit including Peter Hobson, Alan Leslie, Tony Attwood, and particularly Simon Baron-Cohen with whom I have had inspiring discussions recently in Cambridge.

Discussions with colleagues at the University of Sheffield and within Sheffield Care Trust have helped me to hone my views. They include Sean Spence, Sobhi Girgis, Myles Balfe, Chris Blackmore, and Tony Benning. Colleagues in the Developmental Psychiatry Unit at the University of Cambridge who have helped in a similar way include Tony Holland and especially Michael Lombardo in the Autism Research Centre, who has contributed considerably to my knowledge of recent neuroimaging.

I am grateful to the University of Sheffield for granting me sabbatical leave, to Adrian Grounds for introducing me to Darwin College,

Cambridge, to Tony Holland and Simon Baron-Cohen for providing me with office accommodation in Cambridge, and to Peter Jones. Having a Cambridge base has been an important spur to me developing some of the ideas in this book.

It is more than usually true that I have learnt from my patients and their families, and I am grateful to them all for their patience as they helped me to understand their predicaments better.

Finally, I would not have been able to write this book without the intellectual and emotional companionship of my wonderful wife, to whom I dedicate it.

*I*ntroduction

This book has had various working titles. At one stage, I thought to call it 'Things unsaid' to emphasize that it was about what language usually leaves out. After that, it had the title 'Nonverbal communication, autistic spectrum disorders, and the interbrain' because I wanted to give my coinage of that word, the interbrain, more prominence. I have, in the end, reverted to my first title, 'Can the world afford autistic spectrum disorder?' The title is deliberately provocative, and perhaps misleading although health economists have shown that the cost of autistic spectrum disorder (ASD) to society is very high, not least because many adults with Asperger syndrome are blocked from being economically productive. Often this is not because they are unwilling, or even unable, to work but because society does not create—'afford'—the opportunity for them to do so.

The 'world' in my original title was a reference to a perspective originated by the Estonian biologist, von Uexkull. The behaviour of an animal, he argued, cannot be understood unless you consider the environment, the 'Welt' or world, in which that behaviour is displayed or, to put it another way, what the animal's world affords in the way of the animal behaving. This is an idea that has taken root in a substantial philosophical and psychotherapeutic 'existential' tradition.

Von Uexkull posited three worlds: physical, psychological, and social. My colleague, Professor Emmy van Deurzen, has added a fourth (van Deurzen, 2002): the spiritual. Although the physical, psychological, and spiritual worlds of people with an ASD syndrome may be different from those of other people, these differences are largely the indirect consequences of the very substantial difference in the social world of a person with ASD.

We all need collaboration from those around us to create our own social world. It is, as one might say, a co-production. Many people with autism think others are unwilling to act as collaborators in their creation of a social world, or even that other people try to deny them having a social world at all, through bullying for example. It is true that shunning or marginalizing someone diminishes the area of his or her social world, but whether or not someone has a social world at all depends on something deeper than that. Consider the analogy of the spiritual world. A person might have built their spiritual world on their participation in a particular religious community. Being banned from this community, as may happen to a Christian who is excommunicated, may result in a spiritual and emotional crisis. But it does not take away the excommunicated person's awareness of, or capacity for, spirituality. In fact, the effects of being excommunicated will be substantially less for someone who lacks spiritual awareness than who has it.

Phenomenologically orientated philosophers, such as Heidegger, propose that ontology should not start with a consideration of self or individual at all, but of 'being', which is 'there' in the world (Dasein). This perspective is not dissimilar to that of the Chicago school of symbolic interactionism.

There is no doubt that many neurotypicals experience themselves at different times as individuals, for whom the personal world predominates, and as members of a social group, for whom the social world is dominant (Heidegger calls this state 'fallenness' because it is as if we have fallen from being self-aware into a kind of unreflecting absorption with the people around us). People with an ASD may be able to describe themselves as members of a group, have as we might say an intellectual grasp of this, but the experience of being taken over emotionally and even spiritually by a social group is mainly a neurotypical one. Although a person with an ASD is actually embedded in a social group—they are, after all, someone's child—they may not ever experience themselves as 'fallen' in the Heideggerian sense.

Perhaps there is a strength in this. It is being fallen that opens neurotypicals up to being members of a crowd, of being passive followers, followers of fashions and trends, of being and doing all of the things that make human beings into what some people term 'social animals'. Notwithstanding these undesirable consequences of being a 'social animal', many neurotypicals might argue that there is too big a price to pay for the separateness of being a person with ASD. There is loneliness, a feeling of being left out, of being different to everyone. 'Falling in' with other people has, in English, a different sense to that given to it by Heidegger. It means meeting new friends, being part of a group again, regaining that feeling of belongingness that comes from what is sometimes called (for example by Merleau-Ponty) intersubjectivity.

Psychotherapists and counsellors are the people we mostly turn to when life seems miserable, blocked, or frightening. Much of recent psychotherapy theory has assumed that being denied intersubjectivity—or close personal relationships, which is how many psychotherapists and social psychologists put it—is the basis for becoming miserable, blocked, or frightened in response to the everyday stresses of adult life. Two approaches have come to the fore in psychotherapy recently, cognitively based ones and attachment theory. Cognitively based approaches take a short-term view. People get miserable because they think wrongly about things, and if they think more positively their depression or anxiety will dissipate. Attachment theorists take a longer-term view. Misery or anxiety, they argue, are more likely to happen if a person is perilously embedded in their social world, or as we also may say, the person has weak 'attachments' to others.

Bowlby, the founder of attachment theory, based some of his ideas on ethology, and on the work of von Uexkull's successors who explored the social world of animals. He—and they—often turned to metaphors about adhesiveness to explain how animals interacted to make a social world. Bowlby himself used the metaphor of bonding, as well as attachment. Cohesion is the metaphor that is often used by people who have studied human groups. Sociologists write about 'ties' that bind people to each other, or the links between people.

The discovery of ASDs originated in the 20th century, the century that saw some of the worst atrocities in history, in which whole social groups were targeted for annihilation. It was a century of unbridled nationalism which marked the practical consequences of the death of God, that Nietzsche had announced already in the 19th. It was a century in which the best, and the worst, of individuals' capacity to immerse themselves in social groups was manifest and it is in this context that ASD itself stood out—a condition that prevents someone from falling into the social.

It was also a century that saw massively enhanced possibilities of communication between people, and consequently of people being able to influence each other across the whole globe—the global village as McLuhan described. Team working replaced individual genius. The manager who led the team, the accountant who made sure that it remained solvent, and the lawyer who dealt with disputes became dominant over the innovator or the creator. This collectivization of society is what exposed people with an ASD as having a hitherto unrecognized disability. But what is it?

The manager, the trend setter, the marketeer, the publicity agent, the celebrity, the politician, the satirist, the celebrity—many of those, in other words, who occupy the roles that our society extols—have one skill in common, along with the skills that each of these challenging roles requires. They must all be aware of cultural and social trends. They must, as we say, 'tap into' the Zeitgeist. They must have honed their intersubjectivity to a level which gives them access to the hopes, desires, fears, and expectations of millions. In this book, I shall argue that all of these disparate people are able to use a kind of direct interconnection between people which I call the interbrain, by analogy with the internet. The successful politician has the insight to drop the issues that will not be important in the election, and to pick up those that will. How does she or he know which these are? Not on the basis of their gravity, but using the interbrain. Knowing what will be on the brains of the voters.

Once we have a concept of the interbrain, the emotional and social experience of people with an ASD becomes much more understandable if, that is, we assume that their interbrain connection is weak or easily interrupted—if, as we would say of the internet, they have a low bandwidth connection.

The internet is maintained by connections between computers. Some of it is mediated by wires or cables, but some of it is wireless, for example the connection between my laptop and my router which is mediated by a radio wave. What could be the human equivalent of the wires, or the radio waves, that link computers in the internet?

The psychologist, J.J. Gibson, developed the theory that the world lets us know how to use it, it 'affords' our use of it, but only so long as we have the innate ability to approach it in a certain way. This it does by providing 'affordances'. Affordances are a bit like pointers, hooks, guides, directions, but they work without us having to think about them. A well designed door handle affords our use of it because its shape 'just naturally' makes a person want to put their hand at exactly the right spot, and its curves make them want to press it down or up or sideways, whichever is the right way to actuate it. Finally, a really well designed door affords either a push or a pull: no more feeling foolish trying to push open a door that was meant to be pulled!

The door handle and the person using it are linked, not because the door handle sends the user any information, unlike the server communicating with my computer, but because…well, what? Gibson says that the door handle 'affords' us to grip it comfortably in one way, but not another. A child might say that the handle 'wants' to be pushed down and not pulled up. All neurotypicals, and not only children, are inclined to attribute a soul to things they interact with, something that people with ASD do not do. This animation mainly expresses itself in what Brentano called 'intentionality', or the attribution of purpose. So, under extreme stress, a neurotypical might say that a door handle that is not user friendly is 'trying to stop him getting out of the building'.

The interbrain, I will argue, is composed of brains (obviously, but it is important to note that I am not describing the kinds of connection that might occur between minds) linked by the wireless communication of intentions and not information. So the door handle only affords correct use by a person who has a normally shaped arm, with normally powerful muscles, and a normal amount of vision, and who has previously used a door handle.

I am going to argue that the action that affords the interbrain is not a movement that turns a handle, but a communication—specifically a nonverbal communication—that changes another person's mood.

An impairment of nonverbal communication is the fundamental disability in anyone on the autistic spectrum, and many of the other hypotheses about the causes of ASD—central coherence, for example, or theory of mind—are either secondary to it or associated with another neurodevelopmental problem which affects only a proportion of people with an ASD.

These ideas are not new. I have written about them before, as has Katherine Loveland. In 1991, she applied Gibson's affordance theory to autism and has developed these ideas in several subsequent papers (Loveland, 1991b, 1993, 2001). She considered a deeper level, of 'social' affordance. Just as physical objects can afford the right way to use them, people can afford the right way to interact with them. She speculated that the fundamental problem of ASD was that people with an ASD did not recognize this and so often found themselves not knowing how to interact, or suffering noncomprehension or embarrassment because they did not interact the right way.

Many carers of people with autism, and many people with an ASD themselves, are aware of the difficulty that they have in interpreting what are often called social cues. One example of this is failing to pick up the cue that another person wants to change the topic of the conversation. Social cues are often nonverbal. So the cue that a person is getting bored with a conversation might be that they begin to shuffle, or try to capture the eye of someone else in the room. The difficulty in picking up on social cues is therefore rightly seen as a consequence of a more general difficulty that some people with ASD have in interpreting nonverbal communication, for which there is now considerable research evidence, including some papers on which I collaborated.

Nonverbal communication is often thought of as being a kind of signalling system. So a beckoning gesture means, 'Come here', an eyebrow lift (possibly the most universal of gestures according to Eibl-Eibesfeldt) means 'I'm surprised to see you' or 'I'm surprised at that', and so on. Signals have a message, and many can be replaced with an utterance. Some nonverbal communications are less signal like, and do not convey a specific message but still give socially useful information. Rubbing the nose indicates embarrassment, for example.

Many of the latter type of nonverbal communications may be subliminal in that they may influence us, but without us being aware of even seeing (or hearing, or feeling, or smelling) them. Loveland's idea was that there were a particular important class of these that subliminally influenced another person's attention and so afforded what the other person should pay attention to. She went on to argue that people with autism do not seem to be influenced by these subliminal nonverbal communications as much as others, and that this results in the difficulties in social interaction that are so characteristic of all the ASDs.

Let's consider an example of how this might work. It's an office party. Janice and Suzanne are having a *sotto voce* conversation about Jim, who is standing near them. Simon joins Janice and Suzanne, who look briefly at him, and then look at Jim before resuming their conversation. Janice says, 'He's an old goat. He pushed himself up against me in the kitchenette the other day and when he didn't say anything, I said, "Sorry, am I in your way?" and he said "No dear, you're fine where you are".' Simon says loudly, 'Who's an old goat?' and it seems as if the whole room goes quiet, and everyone looks at him. Janice says, scathingly, 'You are such a jerk' to Simon, who knows he's done something wrong, but not what.

If John had joined the conversation, and if John unlike Simon was neurotypical, he would have spoken as softly as Janice and Suzanne because their soft speech affords a soft reply. He would have gazed at Janice and Suzanne when he first started talking to them, because nonthreatening gaze at the eyes affords a return of gaze and his gaze would have been 'picked up' and 'transferred' to Jim when Janice and Suzanne glanced at him. Without having to think, he would have known that Jim was the object of Janice and Suzanne's attention because he had become the object of his attention too, when his gaze was moved onto him. In affordance terms, other directed gaze affords mutual gaze, and gaze away following mutual gaze affords gaze following.

John would not have to have interpreted these signals from Janice and Suzanne. He would just have to be open to the affordances that they provided, or at least that is what Loveland argued.

As it happened I had come to a similar conclusion about gaze and gaze following in adults with Asperger syndrome more or less simultaneously (Tantam, 1991, 1992) as had Simon Baron-Cohen. There was also closely similar work being conducted by Sigman, Mundy, Yirmiya, and others at the University of California at San Diego.

I had previously argued that ASDs were primarily a disorder of nonverbal communication (Tantam, 1986, 1988)—a hypothesis first suggested to me in 1977 by Professor John Wing when telling me about his wife Lorna Wing's work. But at the time I first wrote about this the message-like quality of nonverbal communication rather than its subliminal influence (something that I was then, for example in Tantam, 1986, calling its 'burden') dominated the research literature. It is only in recent years that there has been a swing of interest towards the kind of nonverbal communication that has a subliminal influence. Lakin for example writes in a recent handbook of nonverbal communication that:

> Nonverbal communication conveys information automatically about our social relationships, emotions, prejudices, personalities, and expectations, as well as indicates existing levels of rapport or the desire to create rapport... Ironically, with more awareness of automatic processes, we should have a greater appreciation of the importance of nonverbal communication. (Lakin, 2006, p.72)

What the world affords to most of us is a structure, or a web of subliminal nonverbal communication that points us in directions to go, regulates our minds, indicates whether our beliefs have, or have not, social approval, and generally guides us. To use the analogy of artificial intelligence, neurotypical brains are less like standalone computers and more like computers that are continuously connected to the internet. Software upgrades arrive from a server somewhere and change our computer's functioning often without us being aware of it. Sometimes this is good, and sometimes bad. Another computer may read the contents of our own and change the information that it sends us accordingly, for example when we search the internet. Our brains are influenced in a comparable way. For example, we can be put off (without being aware of it often) by the frown on another person's face when we express an opinion, and our readiness to express that opinion again becomes less until, perhaps, we even change our opinion altogether.

On this analogy, the signal type of nonverbal communication is like a verbal communication, and both are comparable to a file on disk or thumb drive which I am handed and have to make a conscious decision to receive. The subliminal type of nonverbal communication is like the internet traffic that changes my computer without my being aware of it, which may not make an obvious difference at the time, but may diffusely alter what my computer can and can't do in the future.

The software with which it is loaded affords what a computer can and can't do, and upgrades, patches, or viruses that it receives over the internet will subliminally alter the software and so change what the computer is afforded to do. In fact, once I log on to a website, there may be software on the site that affords new functions to me: so being web enabled increasingly means being fully enabled in the IT world.

In this book I shall argue that people with ASD have some similarities with a computer that is not web enabled. Their brains, their 'computer', may be very powerful, but if its software is not continuously kept up to date and especially if it is not web enabled, it may have less functionality than a smaller, less powerful computer that is. Because the world does not afford people with ASD a place, because people with ASD cannot participate fully in the traffic of subliminal nonverbal communication, a person with an ASD, however intelligent and dedicated, will have greater difficulty in finding and maintaining his or her place in it.

I shall further argue that many of the problems of people with ASD come back to this difficulty in subliminal nonverbal communication, that is in detecting and using what the social world affords to neurotypicals. Like Loveland, I think that gaze affordances are particularly important, and I shall give particular consideration to them in a separate chapter, drawing on research carried out in the last 16 years, since my original hypothesis that people with an ASD had an abnormality of a 'gaze reflex' was propounded. Finally, I shall consider whether training in the use of nonverbal communication may benefit people with ASD, as one might expect if this could be a cause of the disorder.

But I will start with an overview of the current theories on nonverbal communication and how nonverbal communication shapes normal (neurotypical) social behaviour and, in a separate chapter, the evidence for it being impaired in people with ASD.

CHAPTER 1

What is nonverbal communication, and how does it affect us?

I am speaking to my wife on my mobile phone. Suddenly, I see my bus in the distance and I begin to run towards it. I've been telling my wife about the shopping that I've got and she unexpectedly interrupts me to ask what is wrong. I seem so out of breath. I explain about the bus, which by this time is about to pull away from the stop before I've reached it. As it does so, I give the kind of noise that I give when something has gone wrong. My wife says, 'I suppose you've missed it'.

This illustration shows how verbal and nonverbal communication are inextricably linked. It also shows that there are different ways in which both are used for communication. Peirce, the founder of semiology or the study of signs, proposed that vocalization and other behaviours could convey information about something because they were the natural consequences of that something. So, my wife detected my hyperventilation through my shaky voice and inferred from it that I was either upset by something or running. Semiologists—people who study signs—refer to the shakiness of my voice as the signifier and to what it signifies—that I am running—as the signified. The relation between the signifier and the signified in this instance is 'indexical', that is, having a shaky voice is an index, or natural consequence, of speaking while running.

Communication is usually defined to be an exchange of information involving acts or events, 'signs', and for the exchange to be the purpose of the act or event. The changes in my voice are signals to my wife of my running, but the purpose of my ringing her was not to let her hear these changes. So the irregularities in my voice prosody are not messages, and are not intentionally communicative. The world provides us with many signs of this kind, many of them requiring skill or experience for us to read. Signs which are readily interpretable may, however, become signals, that is, messages whose sign value is exploited by the person or animal using the sign to convey meaning. So dogs can tell something about another dog who has urinated in a particular spot from the smell of residual chemicals that act as signs, and can exploit this by themselves urinating in the same spot to leave their own chemical traces as a 'signal' for the next dog to come along. Similarly, human beings who are surprised raise their eyebrows without thinking: contraction of the frontalis muscle is one element of the involuntary facial expression of surprise. But a person may also use the eyebrow raise as an expression of recognition, as the nonverbal equivalent of 'Hi'. The connection with surprise is obvious. There is very often an element of surprise when we recognize a person for the first time in a place. The social use of the eyebrow raise, or eyebrow flash,[1] comes about through exaggerating this involuntary response to demonstrate to the other person that they have been recognized.

At the other extreme from indexical signification is verbal communication, i.e. speech and language.[2] Here the relation between the signifiers and the signified is 'conventional' or 'arbitrary'. There is no natural or necessary connection between the signifier and the signified as there is in other forms of signification like indexical communication. The connection between a word, the signifier, and what it refers to, its signified, is created by culture and can be completely arbitrary. For example, there is no natural connection between the English word 'he' and its signified, the 'he' of whom I am speaking, and no connection between 'he' and the French 'lui' other than that they both mean the same thing.

Speaking is not the only conventionally based communication. American (or British, or other countries') sign languages are also conventional as are simpler signals, like the signals used to communicate to crane drivers, or to send signals by semaphore. All of these are properly speaking 'languages' since all of them can be translated into words.

We are familiar with language and use it reflectively. We can weigh our words, rehearse an utterance in our mind using inner speech, and can even study language itself as something outside ourselves, as indeed it is, since it is a cultural product. We monitor our own and other people's language and when we or others make a mistake, we are aware of it and may correct ourselves, or them. One reason that we can do this is that language often names things, and we know if the name is wrong. Sometimes, though, language names things that only exist in the language itself. We can start out a discussion by stating, 'Suppose that there were currently a King of Bulgaria, what would...' and other people are able to go along with us, without assuming that our statement is simply nonsense.

Those people with autistic spectrum disorders (ASDs) who do not show any language delay often seem to have an unusually good grasp of these conventional properties of language, and like to play with them. They may make up words—neologisms—to name things that they consider important, for example particular kinds of traffic cones, or electricity pylons. They may also be taken over by language. A few people with ASDs learn to read unusually early (a condition sometimes called hyperlexia) and may become overinvolved with words to the exclusion of other age-appropriate interests. I once heard a radio talk about a traveller who ended up in a caravan at the end of someone's garden. The talk was being given by the owner of the garden, who clearly became fond of the traveller, even though the traveller had many difficulties that were highly reminiscent of Asperger syndrome. The traveller was referred to a psychiatrist locally, and attended the appointment but left before seeing the psychiatrist. It took some time to piece together why, especially as it was reported by the out-patient staff that the traveller had left the hospital in a fit of giggles. The reason, as it turned out, was that the traveller was due to see a psychiatrist called Dr. Maddox or, as the traveller heard it, 'mad docs'. Surely, the traveller argued impishly, he could not be expected to see a 'mad doc'?

Right and left brain, or something

Hyperlexia is reminiscent of other unusual aptitudes, or savant abilities, sometimes exhibited by people with an ASD, such as the ability to draw accurately at a precocious age. One outstanding example of this was Nadia (see Figure 1.1) who could draw amazingly life-like horses.

Nadia's drawings regressed once she began to communicate with others although there were other changes in her life at the time, including the death of her mother. It was suggested by Lorna Selfe (1977), an educational psychologist who wrote a book about Nadia, that her drawings changed to a more age-appropriate, child-like form because of the growth of her communicative abilities. Although this has been disputed, there are other cases where savant abilities have emerged when people have suffered head injuries or dementia. Even more intriguingly, Snyder and colleagues (Snyder *et al.*, 2006) temporarily put the front part of the left temporal lobe (the part of the brain dealing with language) of 12 normal volunteers out of action by repeated magnetic stimulation. The volunteers showed more ability of the kinds of tasks that savants are good at whilst their language centre was out of action than when it was not.

A possible explanation for this, and the other savant findings, is that our actions are the outcome of several pathways, which may sometimes have to compete with each other to be the ones acted upon. We often experience competition of this kind when we think of what comes into our brains—we speak of things 'vying for our attention', for example—but not so much about our actions vying with our attention. This is partly because we usually experience ourselves as whole or indivisible.

Each side of the brain is particularly linked to its opposite side of the body, but there is a large bundle of connecting neurones, the corpus callosum, that makes sure that each side of the brain can control movements on both sides of the body. In some people with severe and intractable epilepsy, the frequency of fits can be reduced if this bundle is cut, isolating the right from the left cerebral hemisphere. In a series of Nobel-prize winning experiments, Roger Sperry with various colleagues studied some of the patients after this 'commisurotomy' operation and found, unexpectedly, that although they had previously been assumed to be psychologically unchanged, they were not. Rather, it was as if each half of the brain had developed a degree of autonomy, and could act almost like a person in its own right. The reason that this had not been apparent may have been that the left brain was the one

Figure 1.1 A drawing by Nadia at the age of three. (Reproduced from Selfe, 1977 with kind permission from the author.)

that gave an account of what the person was doing, and would ratio-nalize actions taken by the right brain. Patient P.S., for example, was shown a snow scene in his left visual field (only apparent to his right brain) and a chicken in his right visual field (and so only apparent to his left brain). He was asked to pick out relevant pictures and with his left hand (driven by the right brain) picked up a picture of a snow shovel, and with his right hand (driven by his left brain, where the language centre is) he picked up a picture of a chicken claw. When asked why he had chosen these, he said, 'Oh, that's simple. The chicken claw goes with the chicken, and you need a shovel to clean out the chicken shed' (Gazzaniga, 2000).

Some of the split brain experiments do have direct relevance to ASD in that the dissociation of function shown by right or left hemisphere patients is also shown by people with ASD compared to neurotypicals. For example, the split brain studies show that voluntary or posed facial expressions originate in the left brain, but that either side of the brain may produce involuntary, spontaneous facial expressions (Gazzaniga, 2000). Clinical observations of people with ASD suggest that their abil-ity to produce voluntary facial expressions is unimpaired, whilst their spontaneous facial expressions are inhibited or otherwise impaired.

People with ASD are also impaired in their interpretation of facial expressions,[3] and this is particularly apparent when they are shown pictures of upright faces. Neurotypicals develop, after about the age of 12, a rapid method of scanning upright faces that increases the speed and accuracy of their interpretations, and the likelihood is that people with an ASD do not do this. Experiments in split brain patients local-ized this ability in the right hemisphere (Gazzaniga, 2000) and more recent functional magnetic resonance imaging has localized it further, to a specialized area of cortex, the fusiform cortex, towards the back of the brain.

One of the first neurological explanations of ASD was that it was a disorder of the right hemisphere, but this now seems unlikely, not least because modern neuroimaging techniques have not shown consistent evidence of more right-sided than left-sided abnormalities in people with an ASD.

The important message from the split brain studies is that they uphold the hypothesis that brain systems may compete for the use of effectors, or to put it with less jargon, the action plan that is sent to muscles before an expression, action or vocalization has to result in one, distinct expression, utterance, or action and this can only be achieved if other action plans are suppressed. Gazzaniga's review (*ibid.*) is much more eloquent about the left hemisphere's functions than the right hemisphere. It is clear what happens when the left brain gets control of the effectors because we are aware of what we are saying or consciously doing. It is less obvious to us what happens when our right brain gets the control.

One person who speculated about this was Sigmund Freud, a neurologist before he became a psychotherapist. He thought that there were two signalling systems, which he called primary and secondary processes. Primary process relied on signification by displacement or condensation, which are Peirce's indexical and iconic significations respectively. Secondary process is language based. Freud thought that the competition between these two systems normally led to conflict, with primary processes being 'repressed' and therefore denied access to expression.

Competition does not always lead to conflict, though. It can be resolved by sharing, or by specialization. Both apply to communication.

Sharing the channels of communication

Sharing works in this way. Most of what we say, or what we do, has several potential meanings. I have already pointed out that there is usually a burden, or emotional flavour, as well as a content to an utterance. So, for example, if you give me your bag to carry, I might say, 'This bag is really heavy' and whilst the content of this is straightforward, the emotional flavour of it might be, 'Surely, you don't need all this stuff' or 'How can you ask me to carry all this weight?' or 'I'm happy to be carrying your bag for you, but please be properly grateful because it's no lightweight matter' or even, 'Gosh, I don't know how you carried all this yourself, before I took over'. Which of these burdens (notice how my example has been unconsciously influenced by this word) is conveyed by a particular utterance will depend on the nonverbal, paralinguistic communication that accompanies my utterance. A smile will add a friendly emotional flavour and so make the burden of my statement more likely to be seen as friendly, too. A heft of the bag as I speak will increase the chance that you see that I am not borne down by the weight, and so on. If there is any tension between us, I may choose different words to ensure that you don't read a burden of hostility into what I say, since the emotional flavour between us might already be negatively charged. So I might say, 'Carrying this bag is going to meet my exercise target for today all right'.

What happens in my language centre before I produce the utterance 'This bag is really heavy' is likely to be that I have an internal narrative about the task of carrying the bag and at some point this triggers an utterance. What the rest of my brain contributes to expression is much less well understood, and I shall go on later to suggest my own hypothesis for this. But it is likely to involve the monitoring of my emotions and of my bodily state, leading to nonverbal communication of these.

If I want to communicate something, I do not have to choose whether to say it or to signal it nonverbally but can send the same message over several 'channels' at once. Sometimes there may be complete redundancy as when I beckon with my hand and say 'come on' at the same time. More often there is some specialization, for example my words and perhaps a gesture or a posed facial expression convey my intended meaning, originating from my internal narrative, and the tone of my voice or my facial expression may convey my emotional and bodily state (see Table 1.1).

Channels of communication

If I want to send a message to a friend, I might email him, text him, leave him a message on his Facebook account, phone him, write him a letter, push a message under his door, or just wait till I bump into him, and then speak to him. There are various channels of communication open to me, but which I use will depend on many factors.[4] I may choose to use all of them if the message is particularly important. Some channels are particularly suitable for particular purposes, or functions. Speaking to someone, for example, enables me to adjust my message to fit in with what I observe of my friend's receptivity, but texting him has the advantage that he will have a record of my message for future reference.

Table 1.1 Channels of communication.

Channel	Function
Voice prosody (pitch or volume of the voice; the pattern of stress across the phonemes or spoken syllables in an utterance; the tone of the voice)	Relative social status, e.g. dominance or submission
Body posture	Alertness/arousal/engagement
Gaze direction and head posture	Attention or interest
Face	Emotional expression
Proxemics (where and how a person positions themselves in relation to others) and touch	Interpersonal distance and relatedness
Gesture	Commentary on the production of speech, and whether the focus is on inner processes (gestures are directed towards the self) or eliciting understanding in the other (other-directed gestures)
Paralinguistic features, e.g. filled (ums and ahs) and unfilled pauses	

However, some parts of the body have become developed as organs of expression for particular purposes. The human face, with its prominent brows, a mobile brow, and a recessed nose with prominent nasolabial folds, has become a specialized organ of expression and of identity. The contrast between a nearly hairless face and the hairy neck enables the orientation of the human head to be seen from a distance, and so head posture is an important channel of information about the direction of attention. Some of the channels, and their functions, often considered by semiologists are shown in Table 1.1.

Darwin chose the face to study because of its salience in communicating emotion. Other channels of communication have other functional specializations, shown in Table 1.1. It is important not to over-emphasize the dedication of channels to functions. There is considerable flexibility. On the telephone, voice prosody becomes the only channel of communication other than speech, and people use a telephone manner to increase the range of functions that their telephone voice can perform. Using pitch can, for example, convey interpersonal distance: a soft voice indicates closeness, a loud voice indicating distance. Other adaptations occur. When people who are emotionally close are physically separated, for example at a crowded party, they may use frequent gaze at each other to indicate attachment (Kendon, 1967). When one particular function predominates, all channels may be pressed into service. Thus threatening displays in man and other mammals may involve characteristic facial expression (snarl), vocalizations (loud, deep), gestures and proxemics (threat gestures, getting closer to the other person), and gaze (staring gaze). Even words can be expletives whose only function is to express threat (interestingly, the split brain studies showed that the right brains of some people could speak, at least in one word utterances, independently of the fully developed speech capacity of their left brains).

People with an ASD typically find it much more difficult to pick up the burden of what other people say than the content. So if I was given the bag by someone with an ASD, they might respond to me saying, 'This bag is really heavy' by saying 'It's quite heavy, but it was more heavy when I carried it last week'. This might be a factually accurate response to the content of what I have said, but it ignores the burden and, as such, may well be given a negative, hostile interpretation.

Other levels of interpretation of an utterance might include clues about my own physiological status, about my level of attention, about all the things that we read into vocabulary and grammar, and also a whole range of pragmatic factors, such as whether or not my use of language is chosen to enable you to understand clearly or not, that is whether it is appropriate to your age, intelligence, social status, and to the context including the context of any earlier dialogue. Fortunately, only academics need to talk, or write, about all of these interpretations. We do not make many of them explicit, although we do react to them.

What is the specialized function of nonverbal communication?

The competition for effectors can be resolved, as we have seen, by sharing, that is by combining different messages in one communication. The availability of multiple channels helps with this, in that some channels may carry more of the content, leaving others to carry more of the burden. A famous example of this was provided by Ekman and Friesen (Ekman and Friesen, 1969).[5] They asked a volunteer to play the part of a psychiatric in-patient requesting home leave. He was told that he was to play the role of a patient who had been aggressive on the ward in the previous week, and he would have to lie about his suitability for leave. The subject was able to control his face so that it gave little away, and he largely controlled his trunk, but his anxiety 'leaked out' in his legs and feet, which moved about restlessly.

The face and the voice have become specialized in communicating social smiles or socially winning utterances, but the legs and the feet have not.[6] So what are they specialized for? Clearly it is important as one of the reasons for hostility towards people with hyperactivity is that they 'cannot keep still'. Presumably, too, the legs are one of the channels that specialize in communicating unposed, 'leaked', messages, the kind that may be more associated with the right, rather than the left, brain.

The channels that are particularly associated with high levels of language content are, of course, the voice but also finger posture, which is important in conventional signing and also in writing or typing, and those gestures (or 'emblems') (Efron, 1972) which can be translated into words,[7] for example the gesture for OK (see Figure 1.2).

Hand gestures like this are often used by people with Asperger syndrome, who may also be manually dexterous, as evinced by the ability of a substantial minority who are interested in war gaming to make and sometimes paint the detailed models used in the games.

To work out which channels might be specialized for nonverbal communication, and what their function is, we might do well to consider communication in social situations where talking is considered unnecessary or even superfluous. Candidate situations are worship,

Figure 1.2 The hand gesture for OK.

admiration, loving, speechless rage, terror, or being stricken by joy or grief.

The first thing to note is that these situations all involve emotion, and in most cases this is emotion in relation to other people, that is social emotion. The situations in which speech is not just temporarily lost but is otiose are ones in which the communication is focussed on creating or building a social relationship, whether that is with God or with another person.

People with an ASD often have particular difficulty in many of these situations, too. It is often distressing to other family members that someone with an ASD may not show any grief at the death of a loved one, although it may come out over several months that they do experience the loss keenly.

The channels that are particularly active in these situations are voice, used nonlinguistically (sobbing, crying, crooning, sighing, and so on), touch (beating oneself, stroking, cupping one's hands and so on), posture (there are characteristic postures associated with many of these situations), involuntary facial expression, and proxemics (getting close in loving, moving away in grief, alternating approach and avoidance in rage).

We might conclude from these observations that the function of at least some nonverbal communication is to express emotion in the service of mediating relationships with others, and that there has been some specialization of communicative channels to facilitate this, tantamount to the language specialization in the left brain that influences our use of voice and finger posture.

The extent of this specialization is much less evident than it is for language. Touch, for example, is an important channel for mediating affection, but other primates seem to spend much more time in mutual touching or grooming[8] than people do. A possible reason for this has been suggested by Dunbar (2004) who has argued that social chat has replaced grooming in human beings as a means of expressing and monitoring affiliation.

Chat does not replace touching or grooming in the parenting of human infants, although it may supplement it. Recent studies suggest that grooming of infant rodents not only has the soothing and stress relieving effects that would be expected by any human parent, but that it produces long-term changes in the expression of genes: it literally alters the rodent's genetics. There is suggestive evidence that similar effects can be produced by human touching (Kaffman and Meaney, 2007). This is not communication in the sense of the transmission of a message. There is no content. But there is a burden, an emotional meaning: you are safe, you are cared for.

Many parents report that their child with an ASD did not seem to like cuddling, and did not soothe when held as a baby. Parents often have to find other more direct means of relating to their children, like rhythmic and energetic physical stimulation, or engaging in repetitive games. It is likely that this is another area in which people with ASD, and their impaired nonverbal communicativeness, are unable to pick up parental signs of care. One of the consequences of being stroked is the release of endogenous peptide hormones, including endorphins. One possible explanation of deliberate self-harm, such as the biting, scratching, or pressing of the eyes that people with autism seem particularly susceptible to, is that it releases these hormones even more intensely than ordinary levels of stimulation. One possible explanation of the disposition to extreme self-stimulation in some people with autism may be the lack of the normal levels of endorphin stimulation that go with the specialized touch system of affiliation. This is also the explanation that is sometimes given of the increased risk of self-wounding by prisoners who are in solitary confinement: that they are cut off from the social contact of their own kind. If there really is a commonality between these prisoners and people with an ASD, it might be that both are involuntary social isolates, the prisoners because they have been sequestered as a punishment, and people with an ASD because their lack of nonverbal interchange cuts them off from those around them.

Iconic exchange

Figure 1.3 A common example of an iconic communication and its conventional translation.

'Icons' are signifiers that stand for signifieds because they resemble them.[9] International signs, such as the one for gentlemen's toilet (Figure 1.3), rely on similarity as the basis of communication. Iconic communication is one manifestation of the capacity to see a relationship between any two or more entities that appear to have a resemblance. Resemblances are very important determinations of animal behaviour. Copying of movement ('contagion') is apparent in herd-formation or flocking, when animals follow each other in movement, and courtship when male and females may copy each other's movements (think of dancing in humans) (Zentall, 2001). Animal species may also evolve to look like another species as a protection from predation ('mimicry'). In fact the influence of resemblance can be detected in almost every aspect of life, including our own thinking patterns, when we reason 'by analogy'. Seeing, and making use of, resemblance is one of the major themes of animal behaviour, and therefore the science of animal behaviour, or ethology.

I was once talking with a parent of a young man with Asperger syndrome who wanted to join the army. She said, 'I don't know how he would manage with the marching. He would always be out of step'. Then she paused, and said, 'But of course, he would say that he was the only one in step...'

This mother was aware that marching is an imitative activity and that her son would have difficulty in performing it. What he would do would be to arrive at some rule about marching, which he would follow even though others did not. In his mind, her son would therefore be justified in saying, 'I was the only one in step'.

Many people with Asperger syndrome do join the services, usually in a technical capacity. The clarity of role requirements often attracts them. In my experience, it is rarely a satisfying life though because the camaraderie which is so important a part of services life often passes them by. But there is no doubt that the drill is usually their greatest challenge. People with ASDs have problems with motor development because they have difficulty copying other people's movements or actions. This is one contributory factor to their awkwardness or clumsiness. Our motor performances are not just fitted to an intended goal. They also need to fit social expectations. The school cricketer may be criticized not just for not catching the ball, but for catching the ball in a sloppy way, or not throwing back neatly or even gracefully.

It is confusing when we consider imitation that at least three distinct activities are being considered. There is the involuntary 'falling into step' kind of imitation which is sometimes termed 'observational' although I prefer the term 'iconic' since, as I shall argue, it is the basis of iconic communication.

Iconic communication does not just mean copying, but copying the particular movement that is distinctive of that kind of activity. Adjusting the length of the pace and the timing of the feet hitting the ground is what is salient in marching while coordinating the movements of the arm and the trunk in space is what is salient in catching and throwing back at cricket. How a person knows which movements are socially salient is a theme that I will come back to many times.

Many parents rightly observe that their child with autism seems often to copy the worst behaviours of other children. By this they mean that at the age in which a young person desperately wants to have a social impact, young people with autism, who rarely feel that they do have an impact, may be drawn to antisocial behaviour that they see elicits a social response. They too may begin swearing or threatening other people because they see that, when other children do it, it has an impact.

This is a different kind of imitation from marching in step because it is intentional. It follows from observing but then thinking about something. It is the basis of what Albert Bandura has termed 'modelling',[10] in which we take other people as models for our own behaviour.

In everyday life, we also refer to children copying when they look over another child's shoulder and write down what the other child has written. Teachers object to this because they believe that the child who copies does not understand. There is a similarity with what some researchers call 'barking at print', which happens when children are taught to read 'phonically' by knowing what particular combinations of letters sound like, without knowing what the combinations mean. 'Barking at print' has been observed in some children with autism who may apparently read better than a child normally would at their age, but whose comprehension of what they read is well below that expected for their age.

A comparable case to this kind of copying is that performed by a scanner copying a document. The image that the scanner produces does not differentiate text from any other image. It produces a picture of the scanned document, but does not (unless it feeds into character recognition software) produce characters. The scanner does not understand what it is scanning as signs but only as shapes. Similarly, the tape recorder stores and reproduces voices, but does not understand what they say.

We might call this kind of copying, or imitation, mimicry. People with autism may be very good at this kind of mimicry—in fact, there is a parallel with Nadia and her drawings who seemed to be drawing what she observed without thinking of what she expected to see and so could draw much more expressively than a child of a similar age who interpreted what they were seeing according to their expectations.

AN EXAMPLE OF MIMICRY

In the early days of my research into autism, in 1980, I visited one of the first schools to be set up by the National Autistic Society, in Dartford. I was learning about autism, and so had been sitting in class-rooms watching what went on. It was lunch-time, and I was sitting in what I thought was a nearly empty classroom: only nearly empty because there was just one child at the other side, who was standing, head turned away from me, working with his fingers on something. I was therefore shocked to find that I was unwittingly eavesdropping on a rather horrible family situation in which a mother was berating a child for bad behaviour. Where could this be coming from? And how could I have had the lack of social awareness to have put myself in a situation where I could observe what was obviously intended to be a confidential exchange? Then I realized that the whole conversation was being reproduced by the boy on the other side of the classroom. Without any change in his posture, expression, and without interrupting his activity, he was mimicking a conversation that I had to assume was one that he had previously had with his mother. His voice when he was speaking her part was full of expression, and sounded like that of an older woman. He was effectively voicing, I thought, a sound that he had memorized as if he was a tape recorder and not an interpreter. In fact, I wondered whether reproducing it in this way was one step that the boy was taking towards interpreting what had been said.

What makes soldiers march?

Imitation is clearly a ubiquitous aspect of human, and even organismic, behaviour. But there is so much that could be imitated, what determines what we do imitate? The unnamed boy in my previous example mimicked a conversation that was clearly very negative so far as he was concerned. Emotional factors like threat probably influence the selection of what to imitate. Many children, including children with autism, like to imitate things that are threatening: dinosaurs and trains are common examples. These often become objects of fascination to people with autism, too.

When it comes to communication, we could say that we are disposed to imitate signs. So children with hyperlexia are not only precociously good at reading, they find themselves distracted by having to read things. So their eyes are caught and held by notices, or the ingredients on the backs of packets, and they find that they have to read them even if they should be getting on with something else.

Symbols, letters of the alphabet for instance, and stylized icons, like the sign for the Gents, proclaim themselves as being clearly artificial and therefore likely to exist for some human purpose, such as communication. But this is not true of naturalistic signs. How do we recognize these or, rather, what makes us recognize them?

This is a question whose importance cannot be underestimated, as it goes to the heart of what makes us human.

Let's go back to marching and ask, 'What makes men march?' One answer to this might be to look at the goal of marching, how marching changes people. Consider some reactions to marching. An observer might comment, on people marching well, 'They're a fine body of men'. A soldier might feel, having got caught up in the rhythm of marching, that 'It's great to be part of this unit'. Marching in time with other people creates a sense of identity with them.[11] In fact, marching is itself a form of identification. If I am marching in time with other people, I am identifiably part of a group with them. If I look across a crowded parade ground and want to know who is in, say, the Anglian Regiment, I might look at uniforms, or cap badges if I can see them, but if I know one person in the Anglian Regiment who is marching I can identify the others, who will be marching with him.

Marching in time with someone else is therefore a sign that I am at one with them in some way, that I am identifying myself with them. To use an analogy taken from the adhesive industry, it is a sign that I am part of a cohesive unit, that there is a bond between us. I might also say, if I want to stress the fellow-feeling that I experience, that there is an attachment between me and the other men of my unit. The glue analogy is apposite because if I am looking from a distance at the Anglian Regiment marching, turning, wheeling, and so on, the individual men are moving so closely together that it is as if they had an invisible connection.

The pathways in the brain that create this virtual connection have become much clearer since the discovery of mirror and canonical neurones in the brains of monkeys. These are neurones that are specific to a movement, but are active both when the monkey sees the movement and when it performs the movement. Although ethics does not often allow the insertion of microelectrodes into human brains (an exception is made when these recordings are required during neurosurgical procedures to remove damaged brain tissue), and therefore single cell recordings cannot be done in normally developed human brains, the evidence is strong that humans have mirror and canonical neurones, and that these are present from birth. There is also growing evidence that people with autistic spectrum disorders have a reduced population of such neurones (a recent review by Lepage and Théoret gives details of the research leading to these conclusions) (Lepage and Théoret, 2007).

J.J. Gibson anticipated the psychological consequences of having mirror neurones in his affordance theory, according to which a person interpreted, say, the function of a door handle not by looking at it but by grasping it and turning it in the direction that it seemed to want to go in[12]—the direction that it afforded. All of us will have had experiences where we used the mirror system to decode a movement. For example, if you are learning to dance, and the instructor demonstrates a step, many of us will automatically try to copy the step and say, 'Is that it?' before we can see in our heads what the step involves.

So when we see someone else marching, perhaps out of the corner of our eye if we are alongside them, the mirror neurones that we have that are specific to the movements composing marching are stimulated and our marching pathways are activated. We can inhibit them again, so that we do not actually march or we only make small movements as if we are about to begin marching ('intention movements' these are called) without actually marching,[13] but seeing someone else marching sets the initial phases of marching going in us—and so the theory goes we might only perceive that someone else is marching because we sense ourselves going through these initial phases.

Marching alongside someone is a kind of communication, but a weak one. On the other hand, facial expressions of the emotion are some of the strongest iconic signifiers. There are many differentiable signifiers of facial expression, perhaps an infinite number, and their appropriate use differs from culture to culture. Some people have argued in the past that facial expression varies from one culture to another, but studies of a great number of different world cultures suggest that all of them are different blends of a few facial emotions, perhaps six. It has been suggested that these facial expressions are actions that are wired into the brain although some emotional theorists disagree about whether the whole expression is the result of a wired-in action or whether there are smaller components.[14]

Many neuroscientists think that mirror neurones, or something like them, are involved in perceiving facial expressions, for seeing another human smile evokes an action tendency to a smile in a normal human viewer[15] which is part of the recognition of it being a smile that the viewer is seeing. This 'sympathetic' response also applies to other facial expressions, such as sadness. Our experience tells us that when we pose a facial expression, we begin to experience the emotion that goes along with this even if we were not feeling it before and experimental research confirms that this does occur. So there is a hard-wired brain pathway that leads from your feeling happy to you smiling, to me smiling back, and to me feeling happy: a hard-wired pathway to what is sometimes called the contagion of emotion.

Consider how powerful this is as a way of hooking people up. The philosopher Wittgenstein in his characteristic way dissolved the question that often troubles philosophers (and other people who sit in lonely studies pondering)—how can I know that other people exist— by arguing that he did not need to know, because he just found himself taking that attitude. Had he known about this kind of connectedness, he might have said, 'I just know that other people exist because I find myself experiencing the same emotions and the same states of mind that they do.'

People with an ASD or Asperger syndrome do not show this kind of involuntary responding (see Chapter 4 for a review of the evidence). One consequence is that this may lead to a lack of empathy. But another, and more fundamental, consequence is that they may simply not recognize the nonverbal signs that other people make.

What is a nonverbal sign again?

If I were to find myself marching alongside another animal—perhaps another biped like an ostrich—I might copy them deliberately, but I am not likely to find myself falling into step with them. And, as we have seen, if I am with another person, I find myself involuntarily smiling, or at least beginning to smile, when they smile. If I am with a wolf, or a chimpanzee, or a dog, this does not happen because my motor schema for a smile is not the same as theirs, and therefore my smile schema does not get sympathetically triggered by their smile. In fact, I do not recognize it and, unless I am a careful pet owner or a biologist, I may not even see a change of expression at all. Only some actions that another person undertakes correspond to innate action schemata in me.

These innate action schemata are not just in me, of course, but in every 'neurotypical'. So we can define a nonverbal signifier as an action, such as a facial expression, that evokes an involuntary imitation in another person because that person has the same innate motor scheme, corresponding to that action, as I do. It has been suggested that many of the very first signifiers are based on orofacial movements (Bertenthal and Longo, 2007) because those need to develop early in the infant in preparation for suckling as well as communication. Tongue protrusion for example is one of the actions that even day-old infants have been observed to imitate in adults.[16]

Tongue protrusion is recognized as a signifier by every child. Like most iconic signs it doesn't translate straightforwardly into language, because it refers to the action of spitting out food which may mean disgust, or anger, or a lack of hunger, or struggle. As it happens in European culture, it is regarded as 'offensive' and its use is suppressed. In Maori culture, as anyone who has watched the opening haka at an All Blacks rugby game will know, it is a gesture of challenge and threat which has become an acceptable element of the greeting between males.

Nonverbal signifiers are, as the developmental history of the 'stick your tongue out' signifier makes apparent, open to considerable subtlety and refinement. Signifiers become more subtle as motor control develops, and what they signify may shift: a process termed sliding by the original describer of 'signifiers' and 'signifieds', the linguist de Saussure. Doctors ask children to 'stick your tongue out' a lot, and so one could imagine that a child might actually respond to a mother saying, 'Do you know where we are going today?' by sticking his tongue out to mean, 'Yes, to the doctor's'.

But this is not a very likely 'slide' because sliding has to retain communicability. The child's understanding of the signifier includes knowing what can be changed without removing the signification and what is essential. Without thinking about it, we constantly make this judgement about whether or not another person has received our communication, and also indicate to them whether or not we have received theirs.

Consider the following illustration.

John is learning to play the piano and is working on a very simple piece but is still at the stage of having to think about every note. At the start of each of his lessons the music teacher sets going a metronome on top of the piano and John finds that distracting and annoying but is able to ignore it. As John's practice of the piece progresses, he begins to hit the right notes and there comes a day when the beat of his playing matches that of the metronome. At the next lesson his music teacher increases the rate of the metronome slightly and John's playing is no longer in time. However, the lesson after that John speeds up his playing to match the beat and the music teacher says, 'You're starting to get a sense of rhythm as well as playing the correct notes. Let's see how well you've mastered it' and then decreases the rate of the metronome and John is able to play the piece at that reduced speed.

The rhythm of the metronome and the rhythm of John's playing are iconically related. They resemble each other in their beat although not in timbre or other ways that are irrelevant to the significance of a metronome beat. At the point at which John's playing begins to be in time with the metronome, then we can say that the beat of the metronome has communicated itself to John although not with his awareness. He is not, therefore, in a position to vary his beat intentionally until some further lessons later when he becomes consciously aware of the link between the beat of his playing and the beat of the metronome, and at the same time becomes aware of the intentions of the music teacher in using a metronome. The beat of the metronome is an iconic sign from the music teacher to his pupil, 'This is how fast this piece should go', but communication is only established when there is a response from the pupil, albeit the unconscious one of actually playing in time to the metronome beat.

If the music teacher had said 'I want you to play at the speed that corresponds to the marking on this piece which you can see is Allegro, which means brisk', the music teacher would rightly assume that if his pupil was English speaking, he had communicated his instructions because the music teacher would have heard himself speak and would have known what he had said made sense. His student may have been ignorant about how to carry out these instructions and may say 'I know what your words mean but I have no idea how to put them into practice' but that's another issue. In the case of the metronome method of communication, the metronome's beat is not a sign of anything. A metronome set going in the absence of a pupil, or a teacher, means no more than the wind making a branch tap rhythmically on a window, so the communicative sign that corresponds to a word spoken by the teacher is actually the beat of the metronome plus a matching beat in the music being played by the pupil.

I think that it makes sense to think of the iconic or indexical signs involved in nonverbal communication as being made up of the contributions of the communicants involved rather than being an exchange between the communicants involved, as is the case with language. Take the example of a very young baby's smile. Doctors used to say that was just indigestion, and this seems plausible if the baby smiles but when the mother looks at the baby and smiles herself, either the baby does not look at the mother or the smile dies out from the baby's face. In these circumstances, if the baby's smile brightens when the mother looks and smiles, then parents should be forgiven for saying that doctors are wrong and that they know that their baby is smiling at them: that here was a communication between mother and baby. Or, consider Mark meeting his greatest work rival, Jim. Mark hates Jim, but Jim is oblivious of this and thinks that Mark is his friend. Mark and Jim pass each other in the corridor on Thursday, and Jim smiles genuinely. Mark does not smile initially, but then gives a weak and rather forced smile back. On Friday, just before they pass each other in the corridor, Mark is told that he has just got the job that he always wanted. When Jim smiles at him, Mark smiles back unthinkingly and before he has had a chance to control his effervescent high spirits. An observer on Thursday, asked to say what had gone on, might say, 'Oh, that's usual between those two, it's just a sign of how much they hate each other' but the same observer might say, on Friday, 'Oh, that's something new—let's hope it's a sign that they're finally burying the hatchet'. In other words, for the observer the signifier is the expression that appears virtually simultaneously on the faces of the people that she observed and the signified is their relationship with each other. It would be difficult to find out what the nonverbal communication of each other's smiles meant for the two enemies because they would have been busy talking to themselves about what the other person's smile meant. Rather like the music pupil who had begun to suss out what the beat of the music was and could consciously vary the speed at which he was playing a familiar piece, so all of us add on descriptions of what nonverbal communications that we receive mean, but these are verbally mediated responses to a nonverbal cue, and they require a longer time to formulate. Studies of people responding to pictures of a smile using accurate measures of the timing of the smile show that there is a rapid involuntary smile, which may be suppressed and only discernible by direct recording from the zygomaticus muscle, and that this may or may not be followed later by a posed or intentional smile. It is quite possible that enemy 2 might, on a Thursday, have replaced his scowl with a smile having thought that enemy 1 was trying to smile at him but it would be the very rapid, indeed nearly simultaneous smile on one face and scowl on the other that would be the sign of their enmity.

Signs of relationship

In the exchanges between Mark and Jim, the observer noted both smiling at each other on two successive days, but Thursday's exchange was of a genuine smile by Jim and a false smile by Mark, although Friday saw them both exchange a genuine smile. Thursday saw a discrepant interaction, and Friday a matching one. Two people who show matching iconic signs signal to observers that there is a rapport between them, and matching signals is important in establishing and maintaining close relationships. We can infer who is the principal carer of a child by looking at who the child smiles at, particularly if that smile is returned. At a greater distance we can infer that two people are connected if they exchange glances more frequently than would be expected randomly across a room. We show our relatedness to others by involuntarily mirroring their expressions of joy, sadness or fear. Conversely, we begin to put a distance between ourselves and other people if we do not mirror when we are expected to do so. Even in the short run babies show disengagement from their mothers if the mothers respond to their smiles by blanking their faces. As children grow into adulthood so face expressions become subtler and more blended. The task of demonstrating mirroring similarly becomes more complex, particularly in group situations where the contribution of our signifier needs to constitute different signs for different people when taken along with their different signifiers. Although using vocabulary and syntax might seem a much more challenging task than simply iconically responding or not iconically responding to another person, the task becomes much more complex in group situations and in situations where facial expressions become blended and ambiguous.

Many people with Asperger syndrome say that they can function on a one-to-one basis but as soon as they find themselves in a group or a new and unfamiliar social situation, they feel lost and in these situations their facial expressions will often diminish. Signs also become deeper. New relationship qualities like 'disturbed' or 'calm' or perhaps 'wise' and certainly 'experienced' enter in. It is difficult to provide an illustration and so I hope that the reader will have an intuition about what I am referring to, an intuition based on their own nonverbal competence or, as people sometimes describe it, their social intelligence or (sometimes in a slightly different context) 'street wisdom'. This 'feel' for the pattern of nonverbal communication is lacking to people with Asperger syndrome and I apologize to the reader with that condition, but I can give an illustration drawn from the previous example of the teacher and pupil, taking their relationship on another few months.

By now the pupil has become quite used to the metronome being turned on at the start of a lesson and has indeed become quite taken up with the whole notion of rhythm in music. So, at the beginning of a particular lesson the student starts to tap out the rhythm repeatedly on middle C before beginning the piece, and accompanies that by rhythmically moving his body in a kind of parody of a dance. The teacher will know from this that the pupil has really understood the notion of beat as a pure aspect of music and as a form of expression in its own way, and the pieces that the student plays will have greater expressiveness as a result of the dual emphasis on the melody and on rhythm and timing. But after another year the student may play, just to show off, the piece with the stress not on the first beat of the bar but on the second beat. This syncopation would give an inappropriate lilt to many pieces of music but in the particular piece that the student is playing it may give it a jazzy, literally upbeat, feel that may be an attractive re-interpretation of it. The teacher would certainly conclude that the student had now gained quite a considerable mastery of musical rhythm and that the student was expressing this by the nonverbal signifier 'syncopation'. Perhaps too the student might be expressing impatience with the strait jacket of the metronome. Without any of this needing to be formulated in his mind, a socially savvy music teacher may dispense with the metronome from that moment on.

Social influence

In infant development the observation that mothers and their babies mirror each other's emotional response is often termed 'attunement'— another musical metaphor that refers to two instruments playing in harmony or in tune. Attuned instruments of course play at the same frequency or at a harmonic of it, and they have the same beat. Beat in nonverbal communication is communicated by timing, and attuned mothers and infants, as well as mirroring their facial and postural responses more than expected by chance, also make meaningful movements in time with each other. For example, attuned mothers and infants, and it is speculated attuned interactants of any age, tend to shift their posture at the same time.[17]

Mirrored facial responses correspond to the same emotions being shared between two people. Attunement can therefore act as a regulator of relationship and emotional state. In infancy, where the mother is the dominant partner, her mood can communicate itself to the child and attachment theorists speculate that this is one of the processes by which anxious mothers may make their children more anxiety prone, and calm mothers may make their children more calm, and therefore secure. This is probably an over-simplification as other factors, such as the inborn, temperamental disposition to anxiety, may be shared in mothers and their biological children and it has been argued that it is this, and not attunement, that results in the well-established finding that there is a greater tendency for anxious mothers to have anxious children than would be expected by chance alone.

Almost all parents of a child with ASD will describe their frustration at not being able to capitalize on attunement as a means of soothing their child. They will describe the child's apparent inability to mould to them, their aversion to being touched or stroked, their lack of response to cooing or to other vocalizations that normally increase a child's security and therefore reduce fretting, and will also describe the alternative means that they found to regulate their child emotionally, often through mechanical rather than human means. Some children with autism will settle when they are driven in a car, for example, or others when they are repeatedly but monotonously stimulated by a flickering light or by rhythmic movements. Others, again, can be soothed by tactile stimulation but only if it is initiated by the child and does not amount to communication. Common examples of this are stroking silky or furry materials or twiddling hair. As the child gets older, and grows into adulthood, so the responsibility for emotional regulation falls more on the child or young adult themselves.

Every couple knows that there are times when one partner has to be able to assist the other in emotional regulation and that this may involve the same kind of soothing that children receive from their parents, but it also involves selective responding to complex signifiers. Distressed adults may respond with feelings of hurt, of anger, of defeat, of sadness, and sometimes even of relief or unexpected happiness to adverse life events. The emotionally skilled partner will know which of these responses to mirror. For example, mirroring the relief is often perceived by a partner as unsympathetic at least in the early stages of responding to a loss or a threat. In my detailed consideration of the co-construction of iconic signs, I made clear that attunement is not mediated by language.

People demonstrate, or do not demonstrate, attunement without having to think about it. Thinking about how to deal with situations is one of the common strategies that people with Asperger syndrome use to deal with socially demanding situations. This will not work for emotional regulation through attunement and being able to provide this kind of support for a partner may elude even the most able person with Asperger syndrome. Partners often describe themselves as becoming inured to this. They say, for example, 'I have learnt that I can always rely on him for practical support, at least if I tell him exactly what I want, and he is always kind and well-meaning, but he never seems to know what I need without me telling him, and sometimes even if I tell him he seems at a loss to know what to do.' For some couples, this lack of attunement may be enough to break the relationship, particularly when the unaffected partner does not experience their other half as being kind or well-meaning. Other wives or, more rarely, husbands say that they have learnt to live with this and do not expect this kind of emotional care. Some of these partners have come to think that their fathers (or more rarely mothers), too, had Asperger syndrome and that they had learnt to get by without emotional support from an early age.

Attunement and selective emotional responding can contribute to being good at influencing, or persuading, other people. They are part of the necessary skills for being a 'people' person and therefore for selling people something they didn't know they wanted (although not necessarily selling something technical that other people want), for being a negotiator, or for being a mediator. Persuasiveness is one of the social competencies that is particularly important in adolescence when being a member of a group is so important that the only way to be able to get what one wants is to persuade other members of the group to go along with it. For example, a teenager who wants to go and see a particular film is usually very unwilling to go alone because that would lead to them being seen as a 'loser', so the only way to get to see the film is to persuade at least one other friend or family member to go with you. People with ASDs usually have considerable problems in persuading other people to do things except by reasoned argument, which is usually of relevance to matters of taste such as going to the cinema or going to one nightclub over another. So many people with Asperger syndrome experience increasing social isolation in adolescence accompanied by a growing sense of their lack of influence over other people, and their social impotence.

Looking up to someone, or looking down on someone

I mentioned 'indexical signs' early on in this chapter only to ignore them in favour of iconic signs in the bulk of it. Iconic signs, as I have discussed, are particularly important in constructing signs of shared emotion and therefore of affiliative status. By affiliative status, I mean whether people are positive towards each other or negative towards each other but there are many other statuses of importance in a relationship; in fact, if we simply say status, we usually mean something about the power or authority relations between people, sometimes termed dominance or submission. Dominance is of crucial importance in many nonhuman primate groups. For example, in the temple monkeys of India only the dominant male gets to breed. Dominance is signalled by a highly evolved group of signs in primates. These 'displays' are mainly derived from indexical signifiers. Threat displays, for example, are often elaborations of the intention movements or initial phases of an attack. They include standing up straight, throwing out your chest, widening your shoulders, deepening your voice and so on. Submission displays, or appeasement, may be drawn from the intention movements or initial phases of sexual submission, for example smiling, lowering the head, or drawn from the intention movements or initial phases of guarding oneself against physical attack, for example moving the hands down to the genitals, which may be done repeatedly as in the movement for go slow, crossing the hands over the chest, lowering the eyelids or even shutting the eyes.

Status is much more multi-stranded in situations specific in human groups but even so it is still possible to work out which child in an infant class is the most popular, and therefore has the highest status, by observing how often they speak and, more particularly, how often other children look at them. High status children tend to feel more positive about themselves and high status monkeys have biochemical evidence of well being. One explanation for depression is that it is a state of extreme prolonged submissiveness.

As with affiliation, none of us explicitly learn these signs of deference but they are built in, like the iconic signs, and released when babies are exposed to hierarchical situations, which may only occur, at least if psychoanalytic speculations are correct, towards the end of the first year of life.

The signs of a status difference may be less extreme in humans than in other simian groups and more nuanced, but neurotypical adults are expert in using them, responding to them, and observing them; however, this is something that is difficult for people with an ASD to do. Hierarchies based on age with differences in facial appearance or on uniform may be some of the easiest to discriminate and only people with the more severe manifestations of ASDs may have trouble with these. Hierarchies based on the status attaching to different occupations or, even more subtly, the informal status of people are much more challenging and even people with mild Asperger syndrome often will have difficulty with these. Many people with Asperger syndrome rationalize this by saying that they are not impressed by the trumped up differences between people that society invents, or that they are natural democrats or egalitarians. Status differences are, however, considered by many to be an indispensable element of social structure which enable organizations, groups and even families to function. Being oblivious of them, as even adults with Asperger syndrome may be, can cause offence and sometimes can disrupt smooth functioning of groups or teams. Getting and keeping employment is challenging for many people with Asperger syndrome and this may be one of the contributory factors.

In fact, for many people with Asperger syndrome this problem begins even at the stage of a written application. Jobseekers with Asperger syndrome will describe writing sometimes 40 or 50 applications without even getting an interview and the same winnowing process seems to occur at interview, too, with people with Asperger syndrome who have all the paper qualifications and even skills necessary for a job finding that they are not appointed, and no very good reason can be given as to why not. Not responding appropriately to status cues may be a factor in this, although this is less likely to be explicitly formulated.

Older employers may still say 'He did not show proper respect' but more modern employers are likely to couch the issue in terms of effort. 'He could not be bothered to' is often said in relation to some aspect of an unsuccessful candidate's performance. Often this comes down to some trivial matter such as not having checked for typographical errors, not completing every box on a form, not answering the question that is written on the form but a slightly different one, and so on. In a neurotypical candidate this might be rightly interpreted as not showing sufficient deference for the process, the company, or the interviewers, but in someone with Asperger syndrome it may simply reflect their lack of awareness that selection panels expect deference and of an appropriate degree which is neither, to use vulgarities, *'dissing'* or *'brown-nosing'*.

Combining icon and index

Similarity, which we are here calling iconic signification, or entailment, that is indexical signification, had been recognized to be of special importance in conveying meaning even before Peirce codified semiotics.[18]

These relations, it now appears, have a neurological base. So-called canonical neurones are activated by manipulating an object or by seeing an object that can be manipulated. A particular neurone is specialized for a particular kind of manipulation. So there may be a neurone, or some neurones, that fire when I grip a racket that will also fire when I see a poker that I intend to use as a weapon, a stick that I intend to beat down weeds with, or a rolled up newspaper with which I am intending to swat a fly. The poker, or the newspaper, will signify 'grasping a weapon' because the activation of those particular neurones occurs when I do grasp something with which I intend to beat something else.

Icon and index may often be combined. For example, if I stand and look upwards fixedly in public, so long as it is in not too sophisticated a place, someone is likely to stop and copy my action by looking upwards too. A person who considers me beneath their notice will not imitate me, because the act of imitation—or identification—is a sign of closeness or at least interest from another person. But when I stand and look up and somebody copies me the significance of that gesture is less importantly the sign 'I am imitating you' but more importantly the indexical sign 'You are pointing something out with your eyes'. Pointing is an important way of shifting another person's attention and, as we shall see in the next chapter, sharing, shifting and withdrawing attention are all important functions of nonverbal communication in addition to the affiliation or dominance functions that are being considered in this chapter. Attention shifting and its wide-reaching implications for cognition is the topic of the next chapter.

CHAPTER 2

What is the importance of gaze and shared attention?

Most human heads are hairless and shiny on the upper side of the front and hairy and matt on the back.[19] Humans in areas of the world where there is less sun to reflect on the shiny bits have developed pallor instead. One way or another it's usually easy to tell which way a human head is pointed from the proportion of the contrasting front and back that is visible.

The human eyes have also migrated, like those of other great apes, to the front of the head. One advantage of this position is that it makes stereoscopic vision possible. Another is that it is possible for someone to know the direction of gaze of a person with whom they are in a *vis-à-vis*. In particular, this positioning facilitates knowing whether the other person is looking into one's eyes.[20] Just to make absolutely sure of this, there is a brain circuit that inhibits looking almost, but not quite, at another person's eyes.[21]

This brain circuit, like other components of nonverbal communication, does not seem to work as effectively in people with autistic spectrum disorder (ASD). Just in itself, this may be enough to make them uncomfortable conversationalists. If someone that one is speaking with looks at one's eyelid, or even one's ear, should you assume that they are looking at you, or that they are looking away? Either way has important implications, as this chapter will show.

Michael Argyle, a pioneering UK researcher on nonverbal communication, distinguished gaze and mutual gaze, the latter being when two people gaze at each other's eyes and so make eye contact. Gaze, according to Argyle (Argyle, Lefevbre and Cook, 1974), serves three purposes: to get information from a target on which we direct our eyes, to send signals to accompany speech, and to control the flow of conversation.

Speakers tend to concentrate on what they are saying and spend less time gathering information from their listeners: the reverse is true for listeners. Or, at least, the reverse is true for neurotypical listeners. Many people with an ASD look more when they are speaking than when they are listening. Gaze is also used, along with facial expression and gesture, to 'punctuate' speech, highlighting key points. Again people with an ASD seem to use fewer of these 'paralinguistic signals'. Finally, these two uses of gaze blend into the third: controlling the flow of conversation, or 'turn-taking'. It is impolite to speak when someone else is speaking, and yet we manage to speak in turns even when both participants are keen to talk, and less keen to listen. One way in which this is achieved is that the speaker looks up at the listener she or he chooses as the person next in turn and if that listener looks back, the speaker is likely to yield the turn to them. Turn-taking often goes wrong in people with an ASD too. In fact, one of the social problems mentioned by people with the mildest Asperger syndrome is that they tend to 'go on and on' in a conversation, often on a topic of their own choice, without letting other people have their say.

Mutual gaze

All of these signals rely on gaze at another person (I shall call this direct gaze for simplicity) having a special significance. One explanation of autism is that gaze does not have this special significance for them: that they do not have what I have called a primary gaze reflex (Tantam, 1992).[22]

Being specially aware of other people looking at us is part of our everyday experience. Think of a party. When a stranger looks over at me, and tries to 'catch' my eye, I am likely to give this particular attention. In fact, feeling someone's eyes on me triggers a kind of alarm, which may set off particular emotions, like pride or shame. I may stand up straighter, or slouch more. I may become flustered, or more polished. So many and varied are the consequences of what Sartre calls 'the Look' that they occupy many pages of his most influential book of philosophy, *Being and Nothingness* (Sartre 1969).

Up to now in my party scenario, I have probably been observing the other person's gaze out of the corner of my eye, or even made use of a convenient reflective surface to observe it. I now have a choice. I am drawn to look directly at the person looking at me, and neurotypical infants do so, which is what I call the primary gaze reflex, but I can inhibit this and I may choose to do so, depending on what I think might happen when our eyes meet, and sometimes lock.[23]

If I am a commoner approaching the throne of an autocrat I know that I must keep my head bowed and my eyes lowered because to do otherwise would be to challenge the king and to commit lese-majesté. Nonhuman animals seem to live by this rule. Any mutual gaze is a bid for dominance, and therefore a threat. The dominant animal stares down the submissive one and if the two animals do not accept each other's status, their eyes lock and they may fight.

That may happen in people too. Nurses in casualty are taught that a patient who stares at them is a potential threat, and that the first thing to do is not to stare back. One reason for an increase in staring in casualty is that the patient may be trying to reclaim dominance against the overpowering tendency of the setting to make them submit. When there are no such conflicts, between social equals—and that is potentially anyone in a democracy—gaze has a new, and emergent, function. Like the other examples of iconic communication considered in Chapter 1, mutual gaze—or the imitation of looking at the other person—can be a sign of closeness.

So when someone tries to catch our eye at a party, we have to think whether or not they want to signal closeness or challenge. Our judgements about this are biased by our own mood, by the atmosphere, and by our expectations. It is well known that many people with an ASD do not look directly at another person's eyes. This may be no more than the lack of inhibition of looking near another person's eyes mentioned earlier, but there is another school of thought that considers that people with autism *avoid* making eye contact because they experience eye contact as challenging and that eye contact disproportionately provokes fear, rather than friendliness.

This hypothesis is supported by the first generation of studies measuring the time for which children with autism looked at other people (O'Connor and Hermelin, 1967). These showed that children with autism looked as long at other people's eyes as did neurotypical children, but that they did it in shorter bursts and at unusual times, as if there was something avoidant about it. This was consistent with the views of Tinbergen and others that autism was a kind of anxiety disorder, and that gaze avoidance occurred in order to avoid threat. Modern versions of this theory have focussed on the amygdala, which has often been found to have abnormalities in people with autism which would be consistent with it being hyperresponsive to threat. A recent study by Dalton *et al.* (2005) confirmed that direct gaze, even at a familiar face, activated the amygdala and was therefore presumed to be experienced as a threat by someone with an ASD.

There is no doubt that ASDs and anxiety are intertwined, but less evidence that anxiety causes autism. One point against the anxiogenic theory of autism is that there are other common psychiatric conditions in which eye contact is avoided because of anxiety: childhood shyness and social phobia in adulthood are examples, but these are not associated with the kinds of communicative problems that people with an ASD have.

Another argument against fear being the cause of ASD is that although there is a reduction in mutual gaze between people with ASD and the people that they are interacting with, some people with an ASD show the reverse pattern. They stare. This particularly happens if a person with an ASD is told that they must try to look at other people more. Paradoxically, it is the other, neurotypical, person who may show gaze avoidance in this situation, as they find the sustained eye contact uncomfortable. People with ASD who do stare will sometimes say that they find looking at other people makes them feel anxious, but that they have taught themselves to over-ride this.

Clearly a staring gaze represents as much of an impairment of mutual gaze as the avoidance of eye contact and the best explanation of the impaired gaze in people with an ASD is one that can explain both the avoidance and the excessive use of eye contact, which the fear hypothesis cannot.

A *third* hypothesis, which combines elements of both the failure of the primary gaze reflex and of the anxiety hypotheses, might also explain how human beings have been able to develop a use of eye contact to convey intimacy as an alternative to the use to convey threat that is so widespread throughout mammals and birds.

If we go back to considering the party situation, and whether or not we raise our eyes to the stranger looking at us, i.e. whether or not we want to take up their signal, our action is likely to depend on whether we think it is an invitation or a challenge. Normally we do not need to work out which is which. We just have that feeling because other social cues act as disambiguators. If the other person is genuinely smiling (the Duchenne smile mentioned in the previous chapter), we might assume that the bid for eye contact could be interpreted as 'You look nice, I'd like to get to know you'. If they stare with a neutral expression, especially if there is a lack of smile lines round their eyes which are wide open and therefore 'hard', their bid for eye contact is more likely to be interpreted as 'Go away, you're not welcome'. If we want to engage the person looking at us in a friendly way, we will meet their eyes; if not, we will avoid them. If we are not prepared to be faced down by a challenger, we will meet the threatening gaze, but if we don't want to risk getting into a bad situation, we will not.

If all of this is what actually happens, and there *is* some research evidence for it, gaze behaviour will be influenced by our ability to read the meaning of other people's gaze using other expressions as disambiguators.[24] This involves combining information from at least two channels of nonverbal communication, and this probably occurs in a particular area of the brain, the superior temporal sulcus: an area that we will come back to in a later chapter.

How would this explain gaze avoidance in ASD? There is substantial evidence that people with an ASD are impaired in their ability to read facial expressions, as summarized in the previous chapter. So they may be less able to use facial expressions, or other cues, to disambiguate direct gaze. Admittedly, there is very limited research evidence on this, but if this is the case, then it is likely that a person with an ASD would react as if the proffered eye contact were challenging since this seems to be the default condition in mutual gaze. A person with ASD's inclination would be to avoid eye contact, but an increasing number try to offset this by a conscious effort, having been told that other people react against someone who does not meet their gaze. Looking at someone else does not obviate the problem of determining whether the stare evokes a threatening response from the other person or a friendly response. Since most of us break off mutual gaze when we start to feel it is threatening, not knowing whether it is threatening or not is likely to make a person with an ASD maintain direct gaze for longer than is usual or until the other person breaks off the eye contact. So people with ASD are fated not to get direct gaze right so far as others are concerned. They either avoid direct gaze, or they make direct eye contact and maintain it to the point that other person concludes that they are staring.

To summarize, avoidance of eye contact in people with ASD may be caused by anxiety, which I think is unlikely; it may be caused by the absence of a primary gaze reflex, and a lack of salience given to another person's direct gaze; or it may be caused by the assumption that direct gaze is always a challenge. My own research suggests that both of the latter may occur, and this may be because people with an ASD do not all have the same kind of nonverbal impairment.

'You don't see *me* any more'

The world we communicate with nonverbally is very different from the world that we talk about. In fact, the two are formally incommensurate. We cannot put into words more than a fraction of what music means to us, any more than a composer can translate into programme music anything more than a sequence of impressions that accompany a narrative.

We met this theme in Chapter 1, when I described the experience of psychologists testing people with split brains as almost as if they were dealing with two people. It will come up again when we consider how difficult it is for people with an ASD to describe how they differ from neurotypicals. Since I shall be referring to it often, I shall give it a name: non-narrativity.

There is a more everyday name. It is unintelligibility or, *tout court*, nonsense. Imagine a couple whose intimacy has gradually faded. For months, perhaps, one partner (more often than not, the female partner, but not always) has felt that something was missing. One day, a small event prompts her to really think about what is going wrong and after a lot of tears and soul-searching, she tells her husband that the problem is that, 'You don't *see* me any more'.

Men often tackle relationship problems as, well, problems to be solved. So they want to analyse the problem, work out the cause, and then find a fix. Wanting to analyse the problem, many men might feel their wife's formulation of it to be unintelligible. Surely she cannot mean he doesn't look at her? He is always being asked to comment on her clothes, or her make-up. And if he looks at her, then of course he sees her, he's not blind. So he may ask her to explain. 'Give me an example', he might say. This may or may not be possible, because his wife's feeling that her husband does not *see* her is just that: a feeling.

Often this kind of conversation ends in a row, in which the husband concludes that his wife is talking 'nonsense'. He is half right. She is trying to put into words what is effectively non-narratable, but he is wrong, and she is right, in thinking that there is a real and potentially marriage-wrecking problem.

To explain what I mean, we need to take social interaction forward from the cocktail party situation, in which we might first meet a new acquaintance, to the situation in which there has been repeated interaction and a relationship has developed. The establishment of a relationship means that there is an emotional charge associated with meeting the person with whom I have a relationship.

There is an emotional charge meeting anyone, of course. It is connected to the alert that is associated with meeting someone's gaze: sometimes it is called the shock of recognition. There may also be an emotion associated with routine meetings. The news vendor on the corner that we see every day, the fellow traveller on the bus or train whom we recognize, and all the other people we meet that we recognize but hardly know are contributors to our daily routine. If they are absent, we miss them. People with ASD miss acquaintances of this kind even more than neurotypicals. Both neurotypicals and people with ASD do not much differentiate familiar people and familiar objects in their routine world. We miss a building that has been knocked down, or the model of a bus that has been replaced by a newer one as much as we miss acquaintances like the man on the train. We—neurotypicals and people with ASD, both—are equally likely to become emotionally attached to the familiar.

People with an ASD often have difficulty in separating out the concept of acquaintance from that of friend. Quite often they will ask, 'What do you mean by "friend"?' or 'How does one make a friend?'. Part of this is the idiosyncratic emotion with which I invest a friend. Each friendship has an emotional flavour left by previous meetings. Friendship means having a shared history in other ways, too. But another thing that happens when someone becomes a friend is that they take on an independent existence in my mind. A phantom of them, sometimes called a simulation, continues to exist in me. The simulation provides me with expectations: that I will hear from them at Christmas, for example, or that they will ring me as usual at the weekend. When this does not happen, I become worried and take remedial action.

Many people with ASD do not seem to have these prompts. Mothers will say sometimes that, although their son has a good friend that he has known for years and meets regularly, it is she who has to remind her son to ring up the friend. Sometimes this is described as people not knowing the 'rules of friendship'. Although some people have formulated such rules, they belong to the narrative domain, and not to the life of the emotions to which nonverbal communication, and our internalized friends, belong. They often fail in their application—we describe that as applying the rules slavishly, without using common sense or empathy.

We still need to be guided by a simulation at what is sometimes called the 'micro' level of socialization, that is, the sequence of social interactions in which our relationships are played out. If our housemate leaves the sitting room for a long time just when his favourite programme starts, or if he sits near the door when he usually sits by the fire, we find ourselves wondering what's up. This is part of what the aggrieved partner probably meant when she said, 'You don't see me any more'—that her comings and goings, and what they disclosed about her emotions, had ceased to be noticed by her husband.

People with mild Asperger syndrome may have this inner sense of another person too, but it is often much less well developed. They are les likely to 'see' their partners or indeed their parents in this particular way. Quite often couple therapy turns around whether this lack of 'seeing' is the inadvertent consequence of an incapacity or whether it is due to being taken for granted through negligence or self-preoccupation, which is often perceived as much more hurtful.

If a wife says to her husband, 'You don't see *me* any more', with the emphasis on the me, she is probably referring to the kind of simulation failure that has just been considered. But if she says, 'You don't *see* me any more', it's likely to be a different issue, and one more directly related to individual acts of gazing.

The absence of the other's gaze

So far, I have considered looking at someone else independently of whether or not they are looking back, and looking at someone else who is already looking. But what about looking at someone else expecting them to look back, but they do not?

Once we have established the capacity to simulate others, then we can simulate their looking behaviour. So when someone is not looking at us when we expect that they will be, it is an event. Probably all of us can remember events of this kind. They are usually associated with occasions when we strongly expected other people to be looking. It might be that we have done something embarrassing or stupid to draw attention to ourselves, or, contrarily, we are proud of ourselves. We might have just won a prize at school and feel how pleased our parents must be, or we are dressed up to the nines. We look around to our significant other and find that they are looking somewhere else entirely. Sometimes there is relief in this, but more often disappointment.

We do not require much of a simulation of the individuals in these situations. Being looked at is an expectation associated with the situation itself, and of the self-conscious emotions linked to it, like shame or pride.

The reverse is true of everyday situations. It only becomes an event if our housemate does not look at us when we are leaving in the morning, or when we come home at night, and if we have a strong simulation of them under usual conditions, and if our simulation does 'look' at us in this situation. The event has most impact when a situational discrepancy and the failure of a strong simulation are combined—for example when a person we are very close to fails to look at us when we meet them after absence. We might feel disappointed or surprised as we did at the prize-giving, but we also feel concerned. So when we look briefly at our partner across the room, but we fail to catch their eye, we seek a reason why. More often than not we search their face for clues. We *see* them. So when the wife says to her husband, 'You don't *see* me any more', she is probably saying something about his lack of apparent concern for her.

When people with an ASD attentively look at another person's face, it is often with a kind of intensity and searchingness which suggest a high degree of concern. Many people with an ASD become strongly attached to one or more person, and spend considerable time seeking reassurance that this attachment is reciprocated, and therefore safe. This may be through repeated questions or through keeping the other person in sight and under examination, or both. In fact, a proportion of children with what is called 'attachment disorder', who show these patterns of anxious attachment, may have an ASD. The tragedy is that *seeing* someone means exchanging gaze. Without this people with as ASD might not know they are *seen*.

Gaze and attention

I introduced the word 'attentively' at the beginning of the previous paragraph because that is the third reason that a person does not look at someone else: that they are not of interest. A wife who bitterly contrasts the frequency with which her husband looks at her with how often other people do is likely to be suggesting that he is no longer interested in her.

The wife is basing her deduction on her use of gaze to indicate not only relationship quality but focus of attention. With a certain degree of self-reflectiveness, neurotypicals can use this cue to obtain considerable information about another person. We can note the member of our committee who is looking out of the window, and is therefore not attending. Or we can observe that our nephew always seems to look at a particular train set when we pass the toy shop, and deduce that he would really like that as a present. In fact if that glance is associated with the disappearance of a frown or a worried look—if, that is, it is

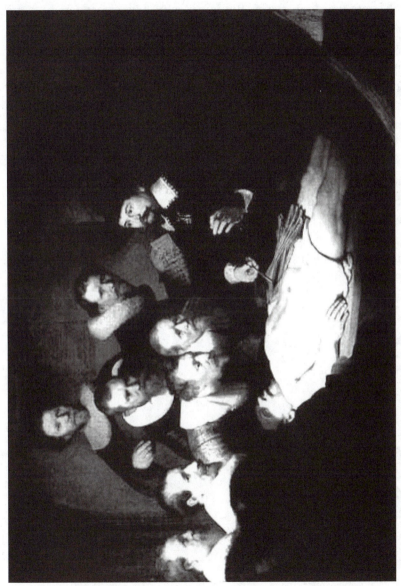

Figure 2.1 The Anatomy Lesson of Dr. Nicolaes Tulp. Reprinted with permission from Royal Cabinet of Paintings, Mauritshuis, The Hague.

associated with the clearing of his brow—we might say that his eyes 'lit up' at the sight.

In *The Anatomy Lesson of Dr. Nicolaes Tulp*, Rembrandt gives each of the protagonists in the picture a different axis of gaze and we are able to infer a different object of attention for each which, interestingly, allows us to think that we know something about each of their mental states and even to guess, from the 'liveliness' of their gaze, at their intelligence. The reader might want to guess at which member of this group will become the most famous scientist. Arguably it is Jan Swammerdam,[25] who is depicted holding a book or a sheet of paper, just to Tulp's left. He was the first to apply the newly invented microscope to insect metamorphosis and morphology, which he described in detail in several famous books, including the *Bybel der Natuure*.

Simon Baron-Cohen has used very simple schematic drawings to show that neurotypical children can make use of the apparent direction of gaze of cartoon figures to infer what the figures might be attending to, and therefore what they are interested in, and so finally what they want (see Figure 2.2).

Figure 2.2 What Charlie wants.

Interestingly enough, this kind of lack of concern is rarely complained about by the relatives, carers, or partners of people with an ASD who are often curious about other people's emotions, possibly because they often lack the confidence that they know what they are.

What happens when one's eye is caught?

If someone catches my eye, it might be swallowed up in a smile, it might be tossed back with a snarl, or it may be…turned on to something else.

Gaze in primates can be a signal of interpersonal relatedness like other iconic and indexical signs, but it may also be a pointer.

Possible support for this comes from one study of adolescents and adults with Asperger syndrome that Chris Cordess, David Holmes, and I carried out (Tantam, Holmes and Cordess, 1993). We made video recordings of a brief conversation between our participants with AS and neurotypical volunteers, and between neurotypical participants with social difficulties and volunteers. We counted the frequency of communicative behaviours in a face-to-face interaction. There was a reduced tendency for people with Asperger syndrome to look at the other person's eyes when the other person was communicating, whether by speaking, by head movement, or by gaze. A more recent study also adds support. Participants in this study with an ASD did not alter how much they looked at another person's face when it was showing emotions although neurotypicals did (de Jong, van Engeland, and Kemner, 2008).

This suggested that eye contact was not maintained by our participants with Asperger syndrome, suggesting that it may be of no particular significance for them, although there was no evidence that they avoided it either. This kind of noncommunication may lead to the other person becoming more forceful, and even threatening. So the association between a lack of eye contact and threat may still apply, but it will be the lack of eye contact that causes the threat, and not the other way around.

A pilot study[26] that I carried out with two colleagues (Dr. Ceri Richings and Dr. Gina Rippon) was designed to try to distinguish between the anxiety avoidance and the gaze reflex failure hypotheses, but the results were equivocal, with some participants' reactions supporting the one hypothesis, and the reactions of other participants supporting the other.

I have called this second reason for a lack of eye contact, a failure of the primary gaze reflex. I called it a reflex because there is mounting evidence that even neonates orient to another person's eye region and that there is a greater than chance occurrence of 'eye contact' (if that is the right word to use before the 'contact' has actually developed) or at least mutual gaze from birth.

So a third hypothesis to explain why people with an ASD avoid mutual gaze combines elements from the first two. This hypothesis goes something like this. Because a person with an ASD lacks the ability to combine information about facial expression and gaze (this was part of the evidence for the lack of the primary gaze reflex) then the emotional valency of mutual gaze cannot be disambiguated and the infant assumes that it is a threat (since this, after all, is the most primitive meaning of eye contact) and therefore avoids it. Some slight evidence for this hypothesis comes from clinical work. Many people with ASD who have taught themselves to maintain eye contact do so for long periods of time to the point of discomfort on the part of people interacting with them. It is as if, having been told that they should make eye contact, they cannot take account of the expressions of discomfort on the face of the other person any more than they may have been able to take account of smiles.

Why is mutual gaze so important?

The reader may be wondering why I have given so much emphasis to eye contact. Sure, it plays a very important role in negotiating dominance or submission, and it is the major signal of closeness or desired closeness when two people are beyond touching distance, but that does not seem to be enough.

That eye contact is so very important is suggested by the interest that even neonates have in other human eyes (Frischen, Bayliss, and Tipper, 2007), which must indicate the presence in the brain of a 'reflex' as I have previously termed it. Congenitally blind children still turn their heads in the direction of a human voice, but they cannot know that they have established eye contact. Congenitally blind children are known to have delays in their social development and may indeed be at increased risk of developing an autistic disorder.[27] The absence of being able to make eye contact does therefore seem to have a substantial developmental impact. Children who are brought up with minimal affectional contact may seem to have an autistic-like disorder, but this can be reversed by later caring. So the developmental impact of congenital blindness would seem not to be a consequence of the inability to express warmth or dominance through mutual eye contact. And this is exactly as one would expect, not only because there is no reason that parents of congenitally blind children should be expected to deprive their child of warmth or even of learning about social status, but also because there are many other signs for warmth and dominance that do not rely on gaze, for example touch and tone of voice.

So the reader may still be left wondering why eye contact is so important. And the reason is another reflex that emerges in the primates: gaze following and its corollaries, pointing and pointing with the eyes.

Gaze following

Vultures, circling high above the African plain, are not just looking down at the ground for potential food; they are looking across at their neighbouring vultures, possibly some miles away, and when one of their neighbours flies down they fly to the same spot, which means that, within minutes, not just one but a crowd of vultures is surrounding the wounded or dead animal which only one vulture spotted originally. Meerkats, whose head posture, and therefore gaze, is particularly easy to see because they stand straight up if alarmed, orientate to each other's head posture so that if one alarmed meerkat looks round until it spots a predator on which it fixes its gaze, neighbouring meerkats quickly look in the same direction and obtain information about the predator, too. Human beings are no exception and indeed develop specific gestures to indicate attention, which include putting a hand on the forehead to shade the brow and pushing the head forward on the neck, cupping the ear to point it in the direction of sound, and of course pointing itself with the outstretched arm and extended index (pointing) finger. If it is not possible to point with the arm, for example if we are lying on the beach and are too lazy to lift ourselves up, we can point with our legs or even our shoulders and other people will follow.

The most highly developed pointing system in visually driven animals is, however, gaze. Stand in a street in a small town, where odd behaviour is not immediately put down to intoxication or mental illness, and therefore blanked out, and stare upwards fixedly. As I noted earlier, it is likely that other people will begin to stare upwards too, sometimes stopping to do so but more often doing so furtively before moving on. There is an instinctual reflex, which I have called the 'secondary gaze reflex', to follow another person's gaze to its apparent destination. Gaze following of this kind is highly developed in the great apes[28] and also in two orders of birds, the Corvidae (crows) and the parrots. Intriguingly both of these birds are remarkable in another way, too, in that they are very able mimics and can be taught human words, with the mynah bird from the crows, and the African grey parrot from the parrots, being the champions. Crows and parrots have eyes on the sides of their head but have developed the gesture of pointing one eye at an object they are scrutinizing and so their access of gaze can be inferred from the orientation of the flat of their heads, helped, perhaps, by the crest of feathers that many parrots and crows have. Crows, like the great apes, derive information from the direction of gaze of a conspecific. For example, a crow or a parrot can take account of a barrier that might be in the line of vision of a conspecific even if it is not a barrier to their own vision.

There is a clear allusion to gaze following in expressions like 'seeing another person's point of view' or 'sharing her vision' although we use these words metaphorically, not literally. When we say 'seeing another person's point of view' or we say 'I saw it from her perspective' or 'I tried to put myself in her shoes' we are referring to our belief, or intuition, that we have experienced what the other person is thinking or feeling and that is different from our own thoughts or feelings.

As the expression 'seeing another person's point of view' suggests, there is an added step to gaze following before it becomes perspective taking. This step involves working out the intentions of the other person, why they are looking in that direction or what they are looking for. Sometimes this will literally involve seeing the point of another person's point of view, in that if our eyes do not see something obviously of interest when they arrive at the apparent destination of the other person's gaze, our eyes will travel back down the direction of that gaze to the other person's face and scrutinize it looking for clues.[29] If they are frowning in concentration, we might conclude that they are not gazing at anything outside themselves at all but gazing inwards, perhaps solving some sort of problem. We can make other important inferences from expressions like joy, surprise, fear, anger and so on.

People with autism are able to work out what another person can literally see from the direction of their gaze, and can take account, like other people, crows and nonhuman primates, of the effect of any obstacles to the other person's sight, even if they can see round them themselves. But people with autism do have great difficulty, as parents and carers or partners know only too well, in seeing another person's point of view in a metaphorical sense. Research into why this is has blossomed in recent years, building on a particular aspect of gaze that distinguishes humans from other primates, at least other primates reared in the wild.

Human beings deliberately show things to each other. To do so, they have to make sure that they catch the other person's gaze, and can select from a variety of channels, including vocalizations and utterances, to make sure that they do. Showing also involves not just directing another person's gaze, again using whichever channels are the most effective for doing so, but showing the person in such a way that what the other person looks at will appear phenomenally the same as what the showing person is seeing (Deak *et al.*, 2008). In other words, people show others not just what is apparent in the world, but what is in their 'mind's eye'. This leads on to being able to know what is in another person's mind, and to one of the capacities that is included in what is currently called a 'theory of mind'. What we see with our mind's eye may be very different to what we see with our eyes.

But research into 'theory of mind' had a tremendous fillip when Uta Frith saw that the set up of a study, conducted by two primatologists, Premack and Woodruff, to understand whether monkeys had a mind's eye view of things, could be applied to human beings. The best illustration of the paradigm is probably its application in the first test of children conducted by Uta Frith and her then PhD student Simon Baron-Cohen.

Figure 2.3 The Sally-Anne test of theory of mind. (Reproduced from Frith, 2003 with permission from the illustrator, Axel Scheffer.)

In this test, a child is shown two dolls, Sally and Anne. Sally puts a marble into a covered object, such as a basket, and then is removed (see Figure 2.3). Anne then takes the marble (or rather the experimenter moves Anne and pretends she is taking the marble) and puts it into a box. Sally is re-introduced and the child is asked, 'Where will Sally look for her marble?' Children who have developed a theory of mind—this occurs some time after 18 months in typically developing children—will say 'in the basket' because they know that Sally had last seen the ball there. Younger children, and children with an ASD, will say, 'In the box', because that's where they last saw the marble.

This first paper was co-authored by Alan Leslie whose paradigm for the difference between what a person sees in their mind's eye and what they see with their actual eyes was based on an observation of one of his children, then aged one. Leslie's son held up a banana one day and began speaking into it. Alan Leslie could see that his son was mimicking a telephone conversation with pauses in between utterances as if his son could hear somebody on the other end of the line. His son was also looking at him and smiling, as children do when they are playing a game with somebody. So Alan Leslie knew that this was a game of pretend in which his son was pretending that the banana was a telephone. To make this game work Alan Leslie's son had to have in his mind's eye what the banana looked like and also its resemblance to a phone, and had also to know that his father would also have that resemblance in his own mind whilst at the same time seeing the banana was a perfectly ordinary fruit. Alan Leslie's son had not only grasped that the banana was an icon of a phone because it was curved like a phone and because it could be held to the ear like a phone, he also had to be able to use the icon to create a phone in his father's mind's eye without the phone being actually present in what his father could actually see.

A lack of pretend play was a well-known feature of autism at the time, although in practice it is, as my description has indicated, a complicated concept that relies heavily on the intuitions of an observer. Many people with Asperger syndrome, for example, do play, although their games are much less likely to involve active collaboration with other people. Many people with Asperger syndrome also show inventiveness and creativity, for example in drawing, musical composition, or in writing stories, or in making up words of their own (neologisms).

Alan Leslie's paradigm theory of mind, pretence, has had less research application than the Premack and Woodruff theory of mind paradigm, or variants of it. Nor is it entirely clear whether or not pretend play is a kind of theory of mind demonstration or whether it is a manifestation, like theory of mind abilities themselves, of other cognitive changes. It is notable that children's social behaviour seems to change very considerably from 18 months to three years, with a much greater interest and awareness of peers, the development of language, and in most children the onset of temper tantrums and the discovery of negation and the words 'no' and 'I won't'. Some of these changes from the age of 18 months onwards do seem to relate more directly to theory of mind; deception, lying, and charming, all of which toddlers are capable of, are all based on a firm grasp that the mother can believe one thing and the child another.

Theory of mind tasks require an understanding of the effects of the passage of time and therefore the nature of memory, although lying and charming do not necessarily require this as liars may embark on a 'barefaced lie' in which the truth is clearly known to the person that they are lying to but they seek to replace the truth with a lie. Some kinds of lying may therefore only require that a person can tell when they are succeeding. Pretend play does not require awareness of the passage of time either, but does involve, as I depicted in my reconstruction of Alan Leslie with his son, a combination of several social cues, first to indicate joint attention and then to signal 'this is a game'. So it may be that integration, or the lack of it, is an important determinant of whether or not an activity is understood to be a game and understood to be pretence.

The case of blindness

One obvious objection to the repeated allusions that I have made to gaze specifically, and visual sensing more generally, being important in the genesis of autism is that there are rare conditions in which a person is born so lacking in sightedness that they are not able to pick up on even high contrasts such as the one between the iris and the whites of the eyes, and so cannot recognize direct gaze or read even the boldest of facial expressions. If it were true that autism were caused by problems with gaze, why would not people who are born blind have an ASD too? Stereotyped movements, which involve some degree of rhythmic self-stimulation, are common in people with autism, in people who are in solitude, and in people who have been born blind, where they are called 'blindisms'. It used to be thought that blindisms had a different cause to the stereotypies associated with autism but it is now thought that people born blind are much more likely to develop ASDs than people who are born with normal sight, and that blindisms are comparable to the stereotypies in other people with autism. But there are some people who are born blind who do not develop autism, indicating that gaze is not essential for normal social development and that there must be some other means of communicating emotion and intention. Emotion can be communicated by tone of voice and the voice can also give information about whether a person is looking directly at you, or whether they are looking away.

Showing

Lots of babies point including babies who later on turn out to have autism, but pointing has two purposes, which are sometimes described as imperative—'I want that'—and declarative—'Look at that'. Imperative pointing is a signal, a piece of nonverbal behaviour which need not be communicative. It is hardly different from reaching for something beyond one's reach and one can easily imagine that if a carer always passes whatever it is that baby is reaching for when they make the attempt to grasp it on their own, the reaching movement would be reinforced and become established as an agreed signal. Indeed, there is a transitional stage often seen in children with more severe ASD in which the child may alternate the pointing sign with taking the parent's hand and moving it, and sometimes that parent, to the object in question.[30] Declarative pointing is a device not for getting something but for redirecting another person's attention, hence its inclusion in a wider range of behaviours that have been called 'joint attention behaviours'.[31] Older children may accompany it with a vocalization such as 'look' or 'ooh' in order to first attract the attention of the other person to himself or herself[32] so that they can then redirect that attention to what it is that the child is interested in.

One of the rewards of redirecting another person's attention is that one has mastery over the other person and indeed this is recognized by applying terms that are ordinarily used for money to attention: people pay attention, or they bid for it, and if this is unwelcome, they are said to be seeking it. Children who are institutionalized do not use declarative pointing because they have learnt to expect that the reward is not there. One may suppose that this awareness of being able to control another person's behaviour through communication first comes about through the child's burgeoning awareness that their movements are imitated by a carer—something that all carers seem to do, and in such a spontaneous way that this might rank as another kind of reflex, and that when a mother imitates her baby it is because she has released her normal inhibition on these reflexes. In fact some mothers may make some self-effacing comment to another adult about why they have failed to inhibit this primitive response, saying something like 'She brings out the baby in me' or 'You have to get down to their level, don't you'. Babies and their carers both enjoy playing games involving showing or joint attention and these may well be important practice for later, and more complex, bids for other people's attention, which form the basis of a wide range of social skills including entertaining other people, negotiating or bargaining with them, or keeping them interested more generally.

The intrinsic reward of 'showing games' means that a lot of practice in demonstrating things to another person occurs. But practice does not explain how a baby knows when they have succeeded in getting the other person's attention on what they have been shown, or how they communicate to another person that they have registered what they are being shown.

Just before I wrote this, I watched a mother and her child, who was possibly three, walk up their garden path whilst their neighbour was coming out of the adjacent front door. It was the kind of terrace where there were no gardens or garden fences to speak of, and the two adult neighbours caught each other's eye and the woman who was going out crossed over to talk to the mother of the three year old. The three year old began to wave to the neighbour who was looking directly at the mother and so did not see her waving. She did glance around, as people do, scanning her environment for threats, but did not see the little girl whose face probably fell below the scan, which would have been at a height suitable for adult faces. The little girl carried on waving, obviously wanting to attract the neighbour's attention, but perhaps (and here I am committing the sin of the poorly trained anthropologist and adding my own meaning to the scene) did not want to intrude on what was becoming a lively conversation between the two grown-ups. She did, however, take a small pace towards the neighbour and turned her body towards her so that she was now gazing directly at the neighbour whilst continuing to wave. The neighbour, perhaps being alerted by the movement, or by the more direct gaze, turned her gaze on to the child and her face showed pleased surprise. Then she waved back, at which point the little girl stopped waving immediately.

This little girl had at her disposal various devices for drawing the person's gaze to herself which included body posture, her own gaze, and the use of movement and gesture, which she combined in a decorous and nicely brought-up sort of way. Having drawn the gaze the little girl wanted to make sure that she also had the attention—in other words that the neighbour's mind's eye saw her as well as her actual eye. During the first quick scan of the environment, she had on her the corner of the neighbour's eye, her peripheral vision, which was enough to sense a movement later on in the interaction, but may not have resulted in the little girl being in the neighbour's mind's eye. The girl seemed satisfied that she was in the neighbour's mind's eye when the neighbour gave an expression of pleased surprise, which was exaggerated as the neighbour realized how long the little girl had been bidding for attention, and by the neighbour copying her gesture, that is in formally recognizing it as a sign of greeting. Joint attention, at least in older children, would therefore seem to involve being able to interpret direction of gaze in combination with facial expression, just like pretend play.

Declarative pointing and employing joint attention signals have both been shown to be impaired in people with ASD. Adults with Asperger syndrome can be observed still to have difficulty in coordinating gaze and gesture. Gestures are used for different reasons, one of which is to assist the production of speech. Gestures sometimes fall into the same rhythm as speech. People who are tongue-tied may use gestures to fill the pause, perhaps twirling the hand over and over as if trying to unroll a carpet, and gestures may have a paralinguistic function in adding emphasis, with some chopping gesture accompanying forceful or domineering statements. Gestures may also be used iconically when language does not seem to be enough. The movement of a boat on the sea may be demonstrated by a gesture, for example, as may a shock with a gesture to the heart, or sweeping gestures intended to encompass some unspeakable totality.

Placing one's spread fingers on the chest to indicate shock is particularly interesting because it is a kind of response to the state about which people say, 'It felt as if my heart was going to jump out of my chest'. The spread fingers seem to reinforce the chest wall so as to hold the heart in. Gestures that are linked to a state of being can only be communicative if other people have some direct apprehension of that state of being. While that seems unlikely at first as we all feel ourselves to be separate from other people, at least in our bodies, I will argue in a later chapter that our bodies, or at least our brains, may be connected. So we can know what the other person means when they splay their hands on their chest, although the gesture may make our vague apprehension of the other's distress stronger and more focussed.

People with an ASD use fewer gestures. My clinical observation is that there is little if any reduction in the gestures that assist speech production but that the reduction is mainly in those gestures that are used when speech will not do. When these gestures are used they are not presented within the natural visual field of the other person and they are not accompanied by the kind of sharp gaze of the other person's eyes which means 'Look out, something important coming up' and are a bid for increased attention.

Scan paths

Our ability to recognize faces, or to read facial expressions, signs of age, and signs of weariness or illness in another person's face improves steadily throughout our childhood. From about the age of ten or so we have settled on the strategy that we use, which is sometimes called configural processing. We use the angles and distances between key parts of the face rather than searching for identifiable features. There are two consequences of our adoption of this strategy. The first is that the configuration is much harder to interpret when the face is upside down. So we have difficulty in recognizing people if they are, for some reason, looking at us through their legs. But we are also not put off by accessories or 'paraphernalia' as they are called by the psychologists who do these studies. Whether or not someone has a hat on, is or is not wearing glasses, or has or has not grown a beard don't much affect our ability to recognize them.

It seems that people with an ASD are slower to adopt configural processing, and are more thrown by paraphernalia. This is assumed to be the cause of many people with an ASD not being able to recognize facial expressions of emotion if they are blended, muted, or brief. That reduction in face reading ability is further assumed to be a major contributor to the lack of empathy in people with an ASD. Another consequence of seeing paraphernalia is that many people with an ASD will report finding faces confusing, and some say that there is just too much information, too much detail, and that they get so lost looking at another person's face that they can only do so at a glimpse.

The underdevelopment of configural processing for faces in people with an ASD means that their brains do not develop a specialist face interpretation centre in the fusiform cortex, as neurotypicals do.

But why should people with an ASD be impaired in this way?

One theory (Schultz *et al.*, 2003) is that it is simply practice. Since people with an ASD do not look so much at another person's face when that face is expressive, they may have many fewer opportunities for practice than neurotypicals. The practice effect seems to explain, too, how people learn other special discriminative skills—the one that is often cited is chicken-sexing. Chickens lack external genitalia and it is difficult if you are a human to tell male from female chicks before they have developed their adult plumage. But when people buy pullets they want to buy hens. So someone needs to tell them apart, ideally on a production line and quickly. People do learn to do this, but cannot say what exactly they are looking for. It too is a configural recognition.

One problem with the practice explanation is that practice works well when there is feedback but cannot work without. I can practise singing a scale, but if I am tone deaf and if there is no-one to tell me whether or not I am singing the right scale, I may be getting more and more used to singing the wrong notes. Although we may sometimes get feedback about our judgements of another person's age or emotion, this is not common and it may anyway come long after we have looked at their faces.

Adopting configural processing co-occurs with developing limited facial scan paths when looking at another person's face. That is, when an adult looks at another person's face, unless they have been invited to make a wider scan—for example by someone saying, 'Do you see anything different about me?'—they will scan from one to the other, and up and down to the philtrum. People with an ASD do not adopt this strategy however but scan the face much more widely.

It has been suggested (Pelphrey *et al.*, 2002) that the development of the narrower scan, which does cover the main angles and distances that are used in configural processing, is what enables neurotypicals to improve their face recognition, and that the lack of this rapid scan strategy is what prevents people with an ASD acquiring the same level of skill.

But this still leaves the question, how do neurotypicals learn this better scan path, and why don't people with an ASD learn it, or learn it as quickly?

There is no known answer, but I have a hypothesis. What if that is one more way in which gaze following transmits other people's knowledge to us? If I am standing with my teacher or my parent whilst they are talking to someone else, I am likely to look backwards and forwards between them. I am sure that this is how it is, because I can remember doing this myself as a child. I am perhaps putting myself in the shoes of the adult, practising for the day when I will be grown up too. One way for me to do that is to try and look out of the adult's eyes, to look where he or she is looking. Perhaps that is how I learn to adopt the standard scan path for faces—by imitating other, older neurotypicals.

What the eyes don't see, the heart doesn't grieve over (co-constructing a world without the use of narrative)

The angles subtended by the moving gaze of one person's face on another are very small, and my ability to discriminate them when I am standing to one side is likely to be limited. Perhaps that is not a plausible way for me to learn a facial scan path. But I think that imitating another person's gaze *is* likely to influence what I see around me. There's plenty that I don't see. It was only a few years ago that I discovered that every piece of street furniture has a number, for instance, and that was not because I noticed the numbers, but because I met someone with Asperger syndrome who was bothered that his local council often omitted one so that walking down the road, street light number 89 would be succeeded by street light number 91, and not 90. This offended his sense of order, and could cause an outburst.

We are not just taught what to look at by following other people's eyes, we are taught what not to look at—or, rather, we simply stop looking at things that do not attract other people's attention. This can be a drawback. It is easy to feel ignored when all the men in a group are staring at the prettiest girl, or when everyone is staring at the celebrity. But it also acculturates us into how other people like us see the world. If you are a stranger in a city, it's often upsetting how many piles of rubbish, graffito-ed walls, or characterless buildings are there. Live there for a while, become a native, and one's eyes take in the buildings that people are proud of, or the glimpse of the hills beyond that makes this particular street picturesque. In fact because one does not want to be like the tourists, one might *not* look at what they look at, and stop seeing the historic monuments or the world renowned sculptures that make one's city famous in the wider world.

Gaze and gaze following can have, as I hope that I have demonstrated, profound effects on our perceptions. In the next chapter, I want to consider how it, in combination with other nonverbal signs, amounts to a kind of wireless connection linking our brain to the brains around us, the 'interbrain'.

CHAPTER 3

What do people make of nonverbal communication?

The designers of our species set out to produce a being that might be capable of an order of mentality higher than their own. The only possibility of doing so lay in planning a great increase in brain organisation. But they knew that the brain of an individual human being could not safely be allowed to exceed a certain weight. They therefore sought to produce the new order of mentality in a system of distinct and specialised brains held in 'telepathic' unity by means of ethereal radiation. Material brains were to be capable of becoming on some occasions mere nodes in a system of radiation which itself should then constitute the physical basis of a single mind.

(Olaf Stapledon, Last and First Men, *1999)*

...at every moment there is in us an infinity of perceptions, unaccompanied by awareness or reflection... That is why we are never indifferent, even when we appear to be most so... The choice that we make arises from these insensible stimuli, which...make us find one direction of movement more comfortable than the other.

(Leibniz, Discourse on Metaphysics and Other Essays, *1991)*

It is normal to dream, and it is normal to communicate without words. In fact, we spend a considerable amount of our day doing one or the other. Both activities are much written about. One internet bookseller carries 12,345 titles on nonverbal communication, and nearly half a million in which the word 'dream' occurs. Yet both remain mysterious. No-one knows why we dream, and no-one can be sure what much of our nonverbal behaviour is for, either.

There are other similarities between the two activities. Both are linked to creativity. Many artists attribute ideas to dreams, and there are some famous scientific examples, too, for example that of Kekule, who imagined the carbon atoms in the benzene ring joining hands and dancing in a round. Dance and much of music is purely nonverbal. Poetry and the visual arts, although often drawing on language and symbols, have elements that cannot be reduced to a verbal description. This is another similarity, too. Some dreams are described as thought-like and can be put into words easily. Others are described by researchers as 'dream-like' and elude verbal description. As we have already seen, some nonverbal communication is speech-like, but much is not and, like dream, is incommensurable with speech.

This is not to say that speech and nonverbal communication are incompatible. A substantial element of 'paralinguistic' nonverbal communication is tied to speaking or listening. Our understanding of utterances or written statements benefits from the adaptation of the linguistic code to the particular needs of the listener or the reader in an exercise of perspective-taking that originates, as we saw in the previous chapter, from gaze following.

Dreams do not stop when we wake either, although we pay them less mind. The imagery which we use to embellish what we say or write draws on fantasy or imagination, and perhaps ultimately therefore on dreams. It's not all a one-way street. Vocalizations like 'oof' or 'um' contribute to nonverbal communication, and words appear regularly in dreams as objects, although we are rarely speakers in our own dreams.

Much more has been known about dreaming since the routine use of the encephalogram has enabled researchers to wake people at night during periods when dream-like dreams are most likely. What has emerged is that dreaming goes on throughout the night. Contrary to our hopes when we put our heads on the pillow, the mind never stops working.

Similarly, the routine use of video and sound recorders has shown that nonverbal communication does not occur in discrete packets, but is continuous. We make signs even when we are alone. Think of getting the car into the garage, when it is already full of clutter. Or think of threading a needle. Is there a gesture that comes to mind? Many people will push their tongue between their lips when they are doing something like this, one of the signs that infants apparently produce and an obvious icon of pushing something through a narrow place. Neurotypically, our facial expressions do not disappear when we are alone, either, and we still gesture, at least towards ourselves (think of slapping your forehead with exasperation).

'Mystery mining'

A great deal of writing about dreams has been about what dreams 'mean'. People who seem to be expert in this, dream interpreters, have played an important role in culture. Jews, Christians, and Muslims all include stories from the Pentateuch in their sacred book and so are likely to be familiar with the story of Yusuf and his meteoric rise in the service of a Pharaoh because of his ability to interpret the Pharaoh's dream about kine and sheaves of corn.[33] Other dream interpretations have also been accorded a pivotal role in history.

Dream interpretation has similarities with a modern statistical technique called 'data mining'. Data miners take some large body of data collected for some other reason, such as the copies of card payments by people in supermarkets, and apply multivariate statistical analyses to extract patterns that may be of use to the supermarket. For example, one Midwest grocery chain found that most people did their weekly shopping on a Saturday, which is when men bought nappies (or diapers) and also beer. But men also came in on Thursdays to buy fewer items, which often included nappies and beer. The shop used this information to put the beer display closer to the nappies, and also to increase the cost of both nappies and beer on a Thursday (example taken from Anderson[34]).

Many of the books on nonverbal communication or 'body language' are based on methods of extracting and interpreting patterns that are similar to those of dream interpretation and of data mining. To stress that there is an interpretative step involved, and in recognition of these similarities, I shall call this interpretative approach, which some call hermeneutic: 'mystery mining'. The best-selling book on nonverbal communication, *I Can Read You Like A Book* by 'interrogator' Greg Hartley, is an example of mystery mining. Hartley or his publisher explains the title by stating that being in business, journalism, law enforcement, or medicine requires the skill to read other people like a book, as does having children, being in a relationship, or even looking for a relationship. So the book promises the reader that:

> Step-by-step, you will develop the same skills the best interrogators and detectives use to assess spies, criminals, and witnesses. As part of the process, you will observe some of the most famous people in the world... You'll discover what emotions these politicians, pundits, and stars are leaking through their body language and facial expressions, and what their answers (or non-answers) are really saying. (Hartley and Karinch, 2008)

Reading the book, the blurb seems to suggest, will reduce the uncertainty and complexity of nonverbal communication to a message that can be read, just like reading this page. In the process, the reader can expect the salacious thrill of peaking into the private lives of celebrities who will be revealing their secrets unknowingly to the reader who has learnt to interpret them.

This promise (the former one, and not the latter) may sometimes be attractive to people with an autistic spectrum disorder (ASD) because it counteracts the confusion that many of them feel in the face of the unspoken and it also suggests that they need no longer feel the powerlessness that this confusion often leads to. But, like dream interpretation or even data mining, there is an incommensurability between the burden of nonverbal communication, or how nonverbal communication wordlessly affects us, and the interpretation of nonverbal communication, or what we can say about it. This means that deliberate interpretation will always be open to error. Reading the face of a person is not like reading the face of a watch. It's much more like reading the weather: chancy, easily influenced by wishful thinking, and not rule bound unless one has access to satellite pictures, a very large computer, and a network of monitoring stations.

Another problem with the 'I can read you like a book' approach is that there is a reliance on what 'leaks out' when a person is trying to control their nonverbal communication. As we have seen, there is good evidence for leakage but no evidence that what leaks out is more truthful than the information provided by the rapid intention movements or transient expressions which are inhibited and do not progress to slower and more overt communication. These communications are taken in by the brain since they may be acted on, but they are too rapid to be taken in by a process of conscious attention. So the assumption that what we can consciously attend to, can 'read', is the 'real' message seems questionable. In fact, research on detecting deception suggests it is plain wrong.

I can always tell when he is lying

Using leaked cues has become the focus of research on mystery mining in nonverbal communication to detect lying or deception. It is of considerable commercial interest. Paul Ekman, who was one of the authors on the original leakage paper, has developed a successful consultancy training police and other state officials how to detect liars. In the UK, many insurance companies are trialling voice analysis software that claims to be able to detect lying in the voice of people making insurance claims over the phone.

Ekman in fact repudiates the use of leaked cues, arguing, as I just have, that there is no reason to consider them more veridical. He bases his approach on teaching people to be better at evaluating micromovements. Neurotypicals can all do this, albeit subliminally, and intuitively base their judgements of whether someone is or is not lying on these movements. But, as Ekman points out, people rarely find out when their judgements about lying are right and when they are wrong. In fact, Ekman thinks that people often try not to find out and so 'in social life, people unwittingly collude in maintaining rather than uncovering deception' (Ekman, 1997, p.104). Practice can improve skill, but only if the correct way of doing something is reinforced and the incorrect way of doing it is inhibited. So by avoiding finding out whether or not the prediction that someone is lying is true or false, most people are also avoiding improving their skill at detecting lying.

Part of that skill involves focussing on some micromovements and ignoring others. According to Ekman, most people simply get overwhelmed with information and thus are distracted from focussing on the transient cues that are most informative. He trains people by providing information from one channel at a time, for example the voice, and by giving immediate feedback about whether the raters have been right or wrong.

Why people with an ASD do not lie, and why they may sometimes smile inappropriately: an aside on the unreliability of mystery mining

Transient expressions are a kind of micromovement. They are difficult, if not impossible, for neurotypicals to inhibit, but, clinical experience indicates, are less likely to be shown by people with an ASD. This might make people with an ASD more fluent liars than neurotypicals but most people with an ASD are known for their honesty. There may be two reasons for this. The first reason may be that many people use gaze as their main means of detecting lying. Looking straight at someone else is, in their view, a mark of honesty. People with an ASD find it very uncomfortable to look straight at someone else, particularly when that someone else has a stern expression as people often do when honesty is in question. This is not the only nonverbal behaviour that confuses neurotypicals, especially those who pride themselves on their ability to detect lying. Many people with an ASD smile when they are anxious because smiling is a submissive gesture, and they want to show their lack of threat. It is a conscious smile and therefore unaffected by whether or not a person has an ASD, but people who observe it often interpret it as 'devious' and involuntary, the leakage of what they take to be triumph at 'getting one over'. 'I saw you smile,' an irate teacher might say, 'don't think you can fool me. Don't be too quick to assume you've got away with it'. So many people with an ASD have the experience of being suspected of lying even when they are telling the truth that most conclude from this that it is best never to lie even if they believe that they could do so, and get away with it.

The second reason that many people with an ASD choose to tell the truth is that they lack empathy. Empathy provides reasons for lying and also the ability to lie well. Telling the unvarnished truth to other people can often hurt, and this impact is normally minimized by the nearly universal practice of 'white' lying and of being economical with the truth because when we hurt others, we feel hurt ourselves. Empathy is required to be able to lie well so that one can adjust one's lie according to how it is being taken by the other party.

People with an ASD are more willing to be dishonest in nonsocial situations but may be inhibited by their exacting and concrete interpretation of good behaviour or of legality.

There are a minority of people with an ASD who may lie a lot, and sometimes so fantastically that their lies are hardly believable. They tend to have less impaired nonverbal expressiveness than those with an ASD who are unflinchingly honest, and so are less likely to appear to be lying to other people because of their lack of mutual gaze. Their lack of micromovements is, as I have already suggested, an advantage. This group includes people who have an atypical form of Asperger syndrome which I will describe in detail in the next chapter. People with atypical Asperger syndrome often lack an ability to judge the consequences of what they do, and it is this that makes their lying easy to detect in the long run if not in the short term. Telling a lie is not for most people something that one can do, and then forget about. Telling a lie involves remembering who one has told the lie to, so that one can repeat it again, and so that one can ensure this person can be kept away from people who know the truth. The lie may spawn other consequences, and need other lies to support it—and so on. A reckless person will tell a lie without thinking because they do not anticipate these cognitive[35] and social costs (these are sometimes collectively called 'cognitive load'). Most people who do anticipate consequences find lying stressful, partly because of these load factors, but also because of the performance demands of suppressing leakage, and because lying may conflict with strongly held values (leading, some researchers think, to 'emotional stress').

Why doesn't lie detection work?

Many US courts, Government agencies and an increasing number of employers in all parts of the world use lie detectors in apparent confidence that they do work. These are machines that pick up the effects of stimulation of the sympathetic nervous system, including a fall in the skin's electrical resistance, that are the consequences of small increases in sweating that are not consciously detected by others, but possibly may be smelled.[36] But, as Ekman pointed out in the reference given above, we rarely place confidence in subtle signs that we cannot detect consciously. We do however place sometimes undue weight on machinery. So an increase in sweating if it is measured by a machine is a sign that we defer to.

Lying does create anxiety in most people, including people with an ASD, and does induce an increase in sweating, but then so do other emotions. But this is not the main reason for the unreliability of the lie detector, but that it is an interpretative, mystery-mining procedure. It detects anxiety, and that is interpreted as an indication of lying, but that is an interpretation. The sweating causes the polygraph needle to shift but lying does not cause the sweating, although it may be the reason for it. There is always the potential for error when we attribute reasons, for the same reason that there is error when we put nonverbal expressions into words.

The English novelist G.K. Chesterton has given a fictional example of the failure of a polygraph test in the Father Brown story called 'The mistake of the machine' (Chesterton 2007). In this, an English aristocrat, Lord Falconroy, disappears shortly after he arrives in the United States. His murder is suspected and a dishevelled man is found near the scene of his disappearance and is suspected of the deed. There has been an escape from a local prison, and the Deputy Governor arrests the tramp assuming him to be the escaped convict and the murderer of Falconroy. His suspicions are confirmed when the tramp is shown the word 'Falconroy' on a card and the polygraph demonstrates a strong positive response. It turns out that this response, and the anxiety underlying it, is because the tramp *is* Falconroy, and not the murderer of Falconroy. The tramp has certainly run away, but not because he is afraid for his life but because, before he became Lord Falconroy, he was a petty criminal in the US known as Drugger Davis. He was afraid of his criminal past catching up with him. The convict had escaped for a quite different reason than to kill Falconroy. He planned to elope with an heiress, which it later turns out he coincidentally had.

Performance and nonverbal communication

Knapp (2006) is in little doubt that nonverbal communication does have a special link to relationships and to emotion.[37] One instance of this is that we try to manage our nonverbal expressions of emotion, in response to cultural expectations if for no other reason, by focussing on our gestures, facial expressions, posture, and so on.

I have argued that our nonverbal communication is mostly unintentional and even automatic. But the fact that we do not fully know what we are communicating need not stop us from trying to improve on it, any more than a pianist may not know the meaning of the music that she is playing and yet will try to make her interpretation as effective as possible. We may enhance nonverbal communication by increasing our body's communicative capacity, for example in our choice of clothing, in the use of skin and eye colorant, or in our use of artificial eye lashes to enhance signals of submission. Mostly, we can practise and improve our performance of nonverbal expressions. People with an ASD may try to enhance their nonverbal communication too, although their empathy problems can make it difficult, and sometimes impossible, for them to know what to enhance.

But what are we enhancing when we try to be better communicators?

The first known training in nonverbal communication was provided by Sophists like Empedocles, itinerant teachers and philosophers in ancient Greece who specialized in teaching the technique of rhetoric, or public speaking. Their commitment to the relative nature of truth, a fashionable view nowadays too, led to 'sophistry' becoming a dismissive term, but the study of rhetoric took root in classical culture. Its touchstone was persuasiveness. A good argument was one that won the other party, or the jury in a law court, over. Nonverbal communication played an important role in this.

Studied persuasion does carry with it the implication of trying to get away with something, of sophistry. Cicero, one of the great Roman exponents of rhetoric, made a practice of bringing wives and their children to court in their meanest clothes, with their faces smeared in ash as if in mourning, so as to extract the greatest advantage from the husband they were suing.

But persuasion is also an essential social skill in bridging potential conflicts between people. Without it, coercion or noncooperation would be much more frequent as they are for people with ASD who, lacking in persuasiveness, often find themselves either submitting in or, more much rarely, forcing others to submit, or being excluded from informal social activities.

Collaboration as a function of nonverbal communication

Persuasion is one aspect of collaboration, literally people working together, but a term which might be applied to all kinds of cooperative activities.

An important aspect of collaboration is timing, of being in the right place at the right time. Collaborators may need to do something simultaneously, or 'synchronously', or to do one thing before or after another person has done something—'serially'.[38] Lifting a heavy object with other people is an example of synchronous activity. Conversation is an example of a serial activity, and as we saw in the chapter on gaze, eye contact plays an important role in maintaining orderly turn-taking.

The interchange of eye contact between turns is just one instance of a 'timing' signal which, detailed analysis of social interaction suggests, occur continually at the most detailed or 'micro' level of analysis or at the macro level. Timing in mother–infant interactions is now considered the basis for learning to turn-take in other situations, and for providing the basis of speech. Other aspects of social interaction rely on timing to make the 'inter' part of 'interaction' work. Otherwise, we would each be performing social actions on each other without any interchange.

Iconic signs are used as timing signals. We may begin a social exchange with a handshake, and we often terminate it with a handshake. Second by second analyses have suggested that postural shifts also act as timing microsignals. These studies have also suggested that people with autism may be impaired in either emitting or responding to such timing signals (Condon, 1996).

At a more macro level, adequate timing is an expectation that we have in any social exchange. If we are stopped by an acquaintance in the street and our exchange is too brief, we may wonder about our, or more likely their, brusqueness and lack of interest. If it goes on too long, we will feel uncomfortable and try to give more and more signs that we want to be elsewhere. How do we know what is too short or too long? It will depend on when we last saw the person, if we have news to exchange, if they or we are or are not preoccupied, their social status relative to us, and so on. Of course we do not compute all of this. Instead, the social exchange throws up timing signals which we respond to with more or less accuracy. People who ignore them are at risk of being seen as very self-preoccupied or uncouth.

Disposing appropriately of time in social situations is very challenging for people with ASD and one possible explanation is that they do not receive or do not emit timing signals. A common example of this in practice is exemplified by William, whose father described how leaving the house for a family outing would go:

William of course would want to know days beforehand where we were going, and when. He would start packing long before the rest of us, but then we would all be rushing around getting ready and I would be telling him that it was time to finish his packing, but if anything he seemed to get slower and slower. He just can't see how we are all getting more and more het up, and rushing. Then as we are leaving the house, he'd say, 'I can't go without my usual shoes' and his mother would say, 'You don't need those, there's no time' but he would insist on getting them. So despite getting ready for hours, and worrying about being on time, we would all arrive late.

The beat of the drum, the pace of the dance

The frequency of timing signals can vary. Some people are languid, and their beat is a bit slower. Some people are energetic or driven, and theirs is faster. So long as other people can adjust, it doesn't matter to the interaction although people whose timing seems exactly right do come across as elegant in their social interaction, just as dancers who fit the music's rhythm perfectly are more elegant.

The variability of timing, like the selection of parts of icon to signify, are an expression of creativity and sophistication so long as the synchrony, or the matching, works. If the variation is too great, or too inconsistent, there is a breakdown and the interaction fails.

One reason that slight variation is possible is that rhythms get entrained. A driven person drives up the rhythm of those around. A languid person seems to infect others with languidity, too. Entrainment affects very fast rhythms, like those in brief interactions, in circadian or day length rhythms in which the biological rhythm of a 25 hour day gets entrained by the social adoption of a 24 hour day, and in even longer rhythms. Rhythms may affect more than we know. Women who live in the same household and who are still having menstrual cycles find that these cycles become synchronized so that the menses of all the women fall on the same day.

People with ASD have rhythms too, but because of the lack of synchronicity of timing signals, these may not become entrained with people around them. Take Roger, a highly intelligent university student who would study flat out for 30 hours and then sleep for 15. He would sometimes be asleep all day, sometimes for half a day and half a night, and just occasionally all night and into the morning. He had a girlfriend who loved him, and this mattered to him, but she had a normal circadian rhythm and so often slept without him, or had to go shopping or to lectures without him. Roger was willing to consider trying to change his pattern, but it did not naturally come to him to do so, and it looked as if this would eventually break up an otherwise promising relationship.

Psychiatrists are familiar with the problems of people whose lives have been torn up by mental illness. One of the many consequences is that the activities like work or even family life that would have normally filled up the day are stripped away. In these circumstances people often wish for 'more structure' in a day which can otherwise just drift by with nothing achieved and nothing enjoyed.

Structure is provided to us by collaboration, partly through planned timetables like the time one has to be at work, but mainly through the rhythms of the social world. These entrain our own innate rhythms and become a part of us. My wife and I like to stay in France, but find shopping there a problem. Not that the shops themselves present any difficulties, or even getting to them. It is just that our daily rhythms have lost their entrainment with French shop opening hours (although these were also the hours that shops used to open when we were children). So we often find that we do a morning's work and are ready to go shopping just when we realize (sometimes belatedly) that the shops will shortly be closing for the usual long French lunch. Were we to live in France, no doubt our rhythms would become entrained by the French rhythm of two cycles of work in a day, morning and afternoon, and not one as in the UK and we would stop arriving at a shop just as it is about to close.

The lack of entrainment in people with an ASD leads to many everyday problems. Some people simply lack structure and spend long periods gazing into space, or following someone else around in the hope of distraction. Other people with Asperger syndrome may fall back on timetables to create structure, and their day becomes organized into chunks of time dedicated to an activity. To undermine this often seems threatening to people with an ASD who resist change, and may become anxious or angry if change is sprung on them. The emotional reaction may be no different to that of anyone else who feels wrong-footed by a sudden and unlooked for turn of events. It is the fact that it is unlooked for that seems inexplicable to others who have, without knowing it, matched their own preparations to the rhythm of others and so arrived at the point of departure at the same time, and ready. Yet their family member with Asperger syndrome has not been able to coordinate his efforts despite worrying for days and starting early.

Collaborative attention

Working with other people, in fact doing anything with another person collaboratively, requires the ability to focus on the same task or issue; it requires joint attention. Animals may jointly attend to a stimulus that has importance to both of them: a snake or a hawk, for example, will get the attention of all the baboons in its vicinity. But collaboration requires getting another person's attention on yourself—so that one can issue instructions, for example, and signal that one is ready to receive them—and also being able to redirect other people's attention to some part of the job that requires attention.

Gaze is one of the most used channels for signalling joint attention, and for redirecting attention, too, as described in the previous chapter. But, unlike language, where there may be just one statement that conveys a particular thought, engagement does not rely on any particular channel of communication or even any particular signal. It is an interconnection between two or more people which may be established by gaze, but also by imitation, or by vocalization. And the token that engagement has taken place is a quality of that interconnection, which may often be signalled by imitation but is not limited to any defined signal.

Having to learn a new motor skill by copying someone else doing it exemplifies the importance of attention. Imagine learning to tie a tie. Dad (most likely) is demonstrating. He is perhaps standing in front of the mirror. His face shows his concentration; his legs are restless because he is keen to show a perfect tie-tying performance; perhaps he makes a mistake and says, 'No, that's wrong. Don't do that' or he says, 'It's very important that you get the length right'. What does he mean; the length of what? What movement is he cancelling, when he says, 'No, that's not right. Ignore that'? How important is the colour, or the texture, or the length of the tie itself? Does it matter that Dad has taken his wrist watch off? Does it matter that Dad runs the tie through his fingers before he starts? Or that he runs his finger round his neck beforehand? Could this mean that he is checking if the tie is twisted or does it mean nothing at all?

Somehow neurotypicals know what is important about this complex process of observation, but many people with an ASD do not.

Tying a tie or a shoelace may remain impossible for them until they are in their teens. Many parents find that their child can learn by backward chaining more effectively than by imitation. In backward chaining, the parent performs the action until the very last element, which he or she asks the child to complete. In the case of tying a tie, this would be putting the tie through the loop and pulling it tight. Backward chaining is a counter-intuitive process that makes the action that completes the task stand out. Copying a movement from the beginning, on the other hand, means working out which of the elements of all the things that the person is doing are the ones to copy. It is not running the tie through one's fingers, but it is running one's fingers around the tie as it is looped round the collar, to check if it is twisted, for example.

Knowing which action components of a complex sequence of actions to copy would require knowing how to do the action unless, somehow, the action components were 'bracketed off' (to use a phenomenological term), so that we know which components were essential and which adventitious. Cues from the person demonstrating can indicate what must be attended to, and so what it an essential component.

Infants, for example, who are learning to copy a motor task use their general knowledge about what is likely to work plus alerts from the person that they are copying about what to attend to.[39] These may be vocalizations indicating that the next action is important, points to what element of the action is important, or gaze flicks to the body part that has to carry the action out. Neurotypical children can blend this input into a kind of action grammar that enables them to 'parse' the action that they see into identifiable units. Without this kind of parsing, copying an action becomes impossibly difficult as indeed it often seems to people with an ASD.[40]

Hidden in plain sight

I have argued that our conscious awareness is made up of what we are conscious of—what we can reflect on—in our awareness, and that there is a considerable amount that we may be aware of, but not conscious of.[41] I have further argued that what we can become conscious of in nonverbal communication is mystery mined from a continuous traffic of nonverbal signals, and that this interpretation may be quite wrong.

I gave an analogy to this in Chapter 1, when the left hemisphere of a split brain patient said that they had pointed to the image of a snow shovel because chicken houses needed cleaning out because the left brain had been shown a chicken and had been unaware that the right brain had been shown a snow scene.

Detecting deception is an important task which confronts many of us regularly. As Ekman was quoted earlier in this chapter as saying, it seems that we rely on our conscious awareness to do this despite our conscious interpretation being no better at detecting lying than chance would be. If we learn to detect transient movements of particular communication channels we can improve. But we are not conscious of these—we need to be conditioned to respond to them—and few people trust them.

But if we appear not to use nonverbal communication very reliably, what is it for? My answer has been that it is to knit together collaborative action. Even that seems quite a narrow purpose. Yet as we shall see in the next chapter, there are whole brain regions that become specialized in dealing with nonverbal input—perhaps as much of the brain as is dedicated to language processing, a communicative activity that seems to affect almost every action.

If, as I have been suggesting, the fundamental impairment in an ASD is a disorder of nonverbal communication, how come this can affect people in so many ways that the ASDs are known in the US as 'pervasive' developmental disorders?

In an analogous consideration of what dreams are for, sleep researchers identified periods of sleep in other mammals which were comparable to the rapid eye movement (REM) sleep during which dream-like dreams are most likely to occur in people. Cats who have a characteristic electroencephalogram (EEG) change called 'sleep spindles' during their analogue of REM sleep can be deprived of it by being made to sleep on a small island in a pond. When they lose muscle tone during REM sleep, they fall into the water and wake up. Cats who are sleep deprived in this way become emotionally disturbed and, eventually, die. Human beings have much more variable responses to sleep deprivation, but these may include psychosis and, possibly, death. Clearly dreams, or the brain's activity during dreaming, cannot just be auguries or processing emotional residues. One influential hypothesis is that dreams are a by-product of periods of synaptic remodelling when the brain is making and breaking connections between neurones, and between groups of neurones. Dreams occur during downtime for networking.

Could there be a similar function for nonverbal communication? Could it be that all the functions that I have written about so far in this chapter can be subsumed under a general function of networking, but networking not between neurones inside the brain, but between individual brains? It is my belief that there is.

The interbrain

The internet is composed of cables linking boxes together which amplify or convert the code in which packets of information are transmitted. Our own computer at work or at home connects to one of these boxes, either by wire or wirelessly. It is possible to set up a home network using wireless connections only but there still needs to be a box, a router, to transfer the signals. Alternatively one can connect computers up through a direct radio or infrared connection, but this is less flexible.

My idea of the human to human connection is that it is wireless, since it is mediated by nonverbal communication, and that it requires no special box. Before the development of telecommunications, connection was limited to line of sight or range of hearing. But the media which propagate imagery also propagate nonverbal communication, and so much wider brain to brain connection has been possible since then.

The internet is a means of exchange of information that can be digitized. Nonverbal communication is iconic, or indexical—analogue to use a now outmoded term. But with the evolution of computer viruses and malware, we now know that the internet can alter our computers without our intending it and, because many of our computers are now set to automatic download of new versions of software, our computer's own functions are continuously being modified by their connection to the internet.

That being in contact with someone else can alter my mood or my attention will not seem a new idea to the reader, I am sure. We all recognize of course that people are connected with each other in some way. In fact, I have just used the term 'connected' knowing that a reader will take this meaning for granted. We use many terms for this. We call people we know 'contacts', we have a social 'network', we 'bond' with others or become 'attached' to them.

Many of these connections are created and maintained deliberately. Even those that are not, like our emotional bonds to others, are open to our introspection. We also know who our contacts are: we set out sometimes to make a new contact, and know how to do that. I am making contact with my computer now, by typing these words into it. But I am not aware of the contact that my computer is making through the internet. It could even be running a malware program, called a 'key logger', which is sending the characters that I am typing to be recorded by another computer without me knowing. The contacts that my computer is making are not in my awareness; they are direct computer to computer contacts.

What I am suggesting is that the contact that we have with others through our nonverbal, or, perhaps more precisely, our nonsymbolic communication is not open to our awareness in the same way—I have made this point several times—but that it is constantly influencing the activity of our brains 'in the background' just like the internet connection has the potential to alter the settings of my computer. In order to bring out this special sort of automatic, nonintentional connectedness, I shall coin a new term for it: the 'interbrain'. It is not an original idea. Something like it was proposed by Olaf Stapledon, the writer who is sometimes termed the father of science fiction, although he imagined it to be a development of humanity in the future, and not something already here. The development has become a science-fiction reality though, often involving the physical incorporation of machines, which provide the intercommunication: hence cyborg, or simply borg, as the commonly used term for human multibodied, super-organisms.

Susan Hurley's description of horizontal modularization has similar features to my interbrain model particularly as it is formulated in the 'shared circuits' model in which 'subpersonal' modules were coupled together by resonance. Hurley tragically died of breast cancer before her description of this was published (Hurley, 2008). Related models are 'situated cognition' (Clancey, 1997), 'distributed cognition' (Hutchins,

1995) and 'extended cognition' (Clark, 2005). All of these ideas may have been anticipated by Leibniz, the 18th century philosopher and mathematician whose reference to the unconscious, and possibly also to the interbrain, is a heading to this chapter.

To make a case for the existence of the interbrain, I will need to establish that this kind of automatic networking actually does occur; I will need to establish that nonverbal communication could mediate it; and I will need to deal with some of the obvious objections, for example that people alone do not seem to be so different from people in company.

So for the rest of this chapter, I will focus on the notion that social networking is more than acquiring a useful group of friends and acquaintances, but requires in addition something much more like the networks that increasingly link our computers together.

Intuitions about society and the interbrain

Many of us have experiences in which we feel so connected to other people that it is as if we are all part of something larger and with its own goals or destiny. We may also feel this in relation to nature. So it is not directly the product of our nonverbal connection with others.

If we were connected at every important level with other people, we would stop thinking of ourselves as separate organisms because our activities would be directed not by our own goals, but the goals of the Borg. If many PCs are sufficiently tightly connected together they stop behaving as interacting individual computers, and become a super-computer. Clearly each of us is not so closely connected to our neighbours and the accumulation of different experiences and emotions keeps us further apart. Our minds may therefore be quite disconnected, even though our participation in the interbrain—if such exists—means that our brains are more tightly coupled to those of other people.

The intuition that there is another side of human experience, in which we are cells in a super-organism rather than self-determining individuals, has repeatedly surfaced in philosophy and literature. During the European enlightenment the bee hive was often taken as an analogy of the state, and of the interconnectedness of citizens whose individuality was less important than their labour. In the last century bee hives and ant societies have been routinely considered by biologists to be super-organisms and the individual bees themselves as super-cells within that organism.

Sociologists have similarly sometimes thought of the family or society itself as the autonomous unit that they study. Durkheim showed that the economic and religious climate in a whole country could influence the behaviour of individuals. He proposed the category of altruistic suicide—of which a modern example would be the terrorist suicide bomber—to cover people who thought that their own lives were less important than the continuation of their society's identity and so gave their lives for a nation, a family, a cause, or a sodality (Durkheim 1970).

Group therapists sometimes feel as if the people in the group that they are assisting have fused together in a kind of network, sometimes called a matrix, in which ideas and emotions circulate around like signals resonate between transistors in a radio. Some therapists even address the group, and say, 'The group is thinking...' or 'The group is feeling...' Drill sergeants think of masses of soldiers similarly. They will shout, 'The regiment will march. By the right, quick march...' or 'Platoon, "shun"'. Priests offer prayers on behalf of 'this congregation'.

Are cells not organisms?

The possibility that we are cells in a transpersonal organism is recognized in a number of theoretical perspectives, too. 'Intersubjectivity' is a term coined by the philosopher Merleau-Ponty and applied to child development by the psychologist Colwyn Trevarthen for something that many fathers have noted: that mothers and babies seem to share each other's mind. Winnicott said of this phenomenon, 'There is no such thing as a baby. Only a mother and a baby' (letter, published in Rodman 1987). There is in fact a field of study called transpersonal psychology which deals with the psychiatrist C.G. Jung's ideas that we tap into autonomous ideas or 'archetypes' which pass across individuals and even generations.

Jung's ideas may seem far-fetched to some. Some might dismiss his ideas along the lines of it being a fact of biology that a body equals an organism equals a mind. Biologists are less certain themselves. We carry within us many cells which are not human, but we rely on them for digestion, and to repel infections. Some of them have actually fused with our own cells and their DNA is now 'ours'. Biologists would therefore consider that the human body is less like the single organism that was once taken for granted, and more like a community of organisms.

Slime moulds provide an example of a community of organisms that metamorphose into what can only be called a single, multicelled organism. Slime moulds are single cell organisms for most of their life cycle, but when population density reaches a certain point, they stop becoming repelled by the chemicals secreted by other slime moulds and become attracted to them instead, which leads them to clump together. When a sufficient mass of cells are formed, some turn into tubular structures, others turn into supports. Consequently a structure is formed very similar to that which we would perceive in mosses as a single organism. This has a fruiting body, as does a moss at one stage of its life cycle, and the individual slime moulds attached to this turn themselves into spores which are propagated.

For slime moulds to stop being individuals and become cells in a larger multimould individual, an efficient means of communication is required. A similar problem arises in human development when multicompetent 'stem cells' need to turn into bone cells, or brain cells, or whatever is required, and then migrate to their correct positions in the embryo. This they do under the influence of chemical gradients, and when these fail as they do in Rett syndrome, which is one of the pervasive developmental disorders, learning difficulties and autistic-like symptoms result.

Bees use nonverbal communication, the 'waggle dance', to exchange information about food sources, scent, and taste to modify the activities of the hive that require a queen. Mammals, including humans, use scent as a means of bonding to and then recognizing offspring and possibly, by extension, sexual partners. The scents trigger the release of peptide hormones that switch on or switch off (that is, alter the expression) of genes and result in long-term changes in production of the chemical transmitters that allow one neurone to stimulate another.

If chemical signalling is conserved, as it obviously is, why not nonverbal communication? Actually, there are nonverbal signs that all mammals can recognize: the snarl, for example.

Cybernetic parallels for networks mediated by nonverbal communication

Computers that have wireless contact with other computers or intelligent machines may use several methods of communication: infrared, Bluetooth radio signals, or WiFi microwave connections. The computer has to detect a signal from a receiving device, and also generate its own signal. Then the two machines need to 'handshake', that is, to send a signal backwards and forwards that enables them to recognize a common protocol so that each can communicate with the other. Now that there is so much potential for the transmission of viruses and malware, an additional security step is usually interpolated here. Then the computers need to split the bandwidth available and allocate it to either uploading or downloading information.

How might this work for people? First, there has to be a carrier 'wave'. In cybernetics that might often be a radio wave. In human beings, nonverbal communication can play a similar role and, as in computers, different carriers are available in that there are different channels of communication which can take over from each other. Handshaking requires that each person catches the attention of the other, although not necessarily conscious attention. This, as we have seen, may be one of the functions of the brain's considerable investment in gaze recognition and signalling. Security may be achieved by nonverbal communications about, well, security—security in the sense of 'secure attachment'. To put this in more prosaic terms, matching of nonverbal signs which indicates affiliation or liking may be the signal that information can be exchanged, for example by maintaining gaze or by approaching the other so that information can be more readily exchanged through subtle voice cues, by touch, or by scent.[42]

Matching can also take account of cultural variants in that the two parties to a potential interaction may 'handshake' if they can match the same variant expression. This might explain David Hume's observation that we can most easily sympathize with those who most resemble us.

How about negotiating uploading and downloading? In the last chapter, I mentioned that some social psychologists now preferred to use Freed Bales' term 'Upward' or 'U' for dominance because it allowed other dominance related statuses, like status itself, to be incorporated.

Bales' term for submission was 'Downward' or 'D'. There are rapid means of communicating both U and D nonverbally. Could these work as a means of signalling Upload or Download? It is certainly the case that dominant individuals, or individuals in authority—U individuals, in other words—expect to speak more, and to be listened to when they speak. So they do seem to do more uploading. D individuals, on the other hand, are expected to be guided, advised, to follow along, to be instructed, to listen, and to...well, download.

Implications for ASD

I make these proposals here because my experience of working with people with ASD suggests to me that the explanation for their social impairment is not that they have particular and specifiable problems in social processes, but that they are—as people with ASD sometimes say—cut off from other people. People with Asperger syndrome are not completely cut off. They can and do make contact through language. But some people with autism, who also have little or no usable language, may be cut off altogether unless energetic efforts are made to create a communicative bridge through some other means, such as the use of simple, arbitrary signs. The behaviour of severely autistic people can be similar to that of people who are kept in complete social isolation. Both groups may develop motor stereotypies, rituals, and extreme self-stimulation leading to self-harm, for instance. This may be because a person with severe autism experiences the world as if they are completely alone in it, in a way that neurotypicals cannot comprehend because of their interbrain connection.

An obvious objection

If being cut off from nonverbal communication has such a profound effect on people with Asperger syndrome, why does being alone not result in a comparable, albeit temporary, effect on everyone? One reason might be that being connected is most important during early development when people are most actively learning, and when habits and beliefs are being formed. Children reared in orphanages where there is a complete absence of anything but physical care do have many features that resemble children with an ASD. But adults with an ASD still experience being cut off behind a 'pane of glass' as some of them say.

There is some reason to think that long enough isolation may produce psychological deterioration even in adults although this may take a mystical or psychotic turn, rather than an autistic one. For example the lone sailor Donald Crowhurst wrote this in his log before his disappearance and probable suicide: 'The Kingdom of God has an area measured not in square miles but in square hours. It is a kingdom with all the time in the world—we have used all the time available to us, and must seek an imaginary sort of time.'[43]

It has to be said that solitary people are not so obviously different though and, if my theory is correct, they should be. Unless, that is, there is some alternative to a wireless connection. There is in a computer. You can set your connection to download pages that you visit so that they are stored in a special memory—the 'cache' or hiding place—so that if your computer is offline, you can browse the cache as if you were browsing the web. Of course the cache is limited, but it can store important information that one needs over and over again.

If human brains had a cache, this might explain why being offline—being solitary—has such a slight apparent effect. It is a difficult speculation to test because our tests for the impact of the interbrain are themselves not well developed. However, there are existing theories that pose something similar. The conscience is, for many religious people, something like a cache that can be used when out of contact with spiritual guides. Psychoanalysts suppose that our images of our parents get taken into our minds and memories as 'internal objects', and some of these become incorporated into the super-ego, which provides us with a kind of inner parent. Finally, the development of theory of mind has led some people to posit that we create the ability to bring other people to life in our minds through an inner narrative or simulation so that we can anticipate how they might react before we carry out any planned action.

Simulations are related to the imaginary friends that gregarious children create, and with whom they have conversations which may include rehearsing plans. In my experience, many people with an ASD have imaginary friends, too, and even imaginary enemies. Sometimes the friends and the enemies fight, and this can lead to a diagnosis of psychosis particularly when the person with the ASD describes these imaginary figures as 'voices'.

Imaginary friends are rarely embodied. When one asks a child who has one what they look like there is a pause and one feels almost certain that the child is making up an appearance that was not needed before. Simulations are embodied, indeed may be purely embodiment, in that they are made up of the gestures and expressions of the other person—exactly what one might expect to find in a nonverbal cache, in fact.

Cache

There is some overlap between my proposal of a cache and what is often termed working memory. Working memory is a temporary store, like the random access memory of a computer, which keeps information that one might need temporarily. It is sometimes called a scratch pad because it is used rather like a jotter on which one scribbles a phone number that one has to ring. Being interrupted and knowing where one was up to when one can go back to the task, looking at a blackboard, looking away, and then knowing where to look back to are all examples of the uses of working memory. Keeping track of the time, having a background idea of what's in the bank when one passes a shop window, prioritizing are all more complex tasks that are semi-automatic and probably require working memory. Impairments in working memory in people with attention deficit hyperactivity disorder (ADHD) may be associated with impairments in impulse control, for example when people do something that turns out badly and say, 'I just didn't think'. Not thinking may extend further to not thinking about how other people will be affected by one's actions: how hurt they will look once they find out, for example.

If people are there one can check out their immediate reactions to an action, or the suggestion of an action. If they are not there, the cache would provide one way of trying out an action mentally and seeing the other person's reaction in the eye of one's mind. The absence of a cache could be one reason that a person says, 'It didn't occur to me that anyone would be really upset if I did that'.

CHAPTER **4**

What is the evidence that impaired nonverbal communication is the fundamental problem in autistic spectrum disorder?

The social animal is always led to majority conclusions, going with the flow, following the crowd. The Autistic thinker comes to his/her own conclusions and does not care if they are not socially acceptable. All progress has come through being unafraid to differ in opinion from the majority, look at Galileo, and Einstein.

Nonetheless I do not seek out isolation deliberately. I do need others to exist and many of my troubles seem to come from being rigidly independent. We are all interdependent whether we are aware of the fact or not and if each of us persists in being the centre of our own existence we are all doomed to suffer at each other's hands.

(Arnold, 2003)

The fox knows many things, but the hedgehog knows one big thing.

(Attributed to Archilocus, 680–645 BC)

Every human being is unique, but if it were not a solecism, I would say that my experience of people with an autistic spectrum disorder (ASD) is that they are even more unique than anyone else. Patterns do begin to emerge once one has met and got to know enough people with an ASD but it is this diversity that is the most striking at first. In fact, it is this diversity that first set me thinking about the extent to which neurotypicals conform from an early age, and I remembered Rousseau's adage that, 'l'homme est né libre, et partout il est dans les fers' (Rousseau, 1962). This literally means, 'man is born free, and everywhere he is in irons' but 'irons' is often translated as chains so that my image was not of people being hobbled by leg fetters, but somehow being linked together by an endless chain to which we become attached when we are born and from which we only escape when we die. The chain may be a fetter, like the leg irons, but it also keeps us going in the same direction as everyone else, and at the same pace. People with an ASD are not, I imagine, chained. They are free but they are also outside of the system. They can diverge from the norm, and many of them do, but the price that they pay is that they are not part of the solid mass of the group.

The point that I have been making throughout this book is that although neurotypicals may not be connected to each other by a chain, they may be connected by the interbrain. That network facilitates collaboration of many kinds. In childhood, the main collaborative task of mother and infant is to enable the infant to become emotionally secure and so move towards autonomy and the realization of a loving relationship. Even earlier than that, perhaps, there are other collaborative tasks that mother and infant have to perform even though we do not observe them. Birth is one example. Birth requires adaptions in the mother, but also that the foetus fold her- or himself in just the right way to make passage through the birth canal as easy as possible. One element of this is 'lie' and 'presentation' so that the right body part which points downwards into the pelvis when birth begins. The position of the foetus is influenced by uterine contraction and by foetal movements, and correct presentation presumably requires some signalling between the two. So even being born is a collaboration.

Collaborations that the growing child has to negotiate include extending relationships to other carers, making relations to peers, and of course learning. Neurotypical children may be connected to each other and to their parents and other adults via the interbrain. It is demonstrably true that they are therefore constantly attuning to and being influenced by communication with the parent. Some knowledge can be acquired (I would argue that it is downloaded from the inter-brain) without the child even being aware of it happening. For example, a girl of three in a shoe shop might already know what kind of shoes she wants because she has been attending to the shoes that other girls wear, and has particularly attended to those of a girl she knows who seems popular. A boy of five who looks out of the window and sees that it is frosty may very likely know that he must select different clothes from the cupboard and dress up warm. It's just common sense, his mother might say, but he is drawing on what he has seen other children wear in similar circumstances, or even what the children are actually wearing that he observes out of his window.

Both the girl of three and the boy of five are likely to be conforming to the styles of dress preferred by their peers because of their interconnectedness. A girl of three or a boy of five with an ASD is much less likely to have a preference, or if they have one, it is much more likely to be to continue to dress as they have always done. Moreover, they may wear shoes that other people find odd because they do not conform to what is expected in their culture, or they may wear clothes that seem to others manifestly unsuited to the prevailing weather.

My explanation for people with an ASD being more unique than is usual (if that were grammatically possible) is that being disconnected from the interbrain means being disconnected from these conformist influences: from the chains that I imagined neurotypicals are entrained by. But this is to leap frog over what I want to do in this chapter, which is to convince the reader that an impairment in nonverbal communication generally, and more specifically an uncertain or absent interbrain connection, is the fundamental impairment in ASD.

Factors to keep in mind

There is no doubt that many people with an ASD do not just have one difficulty, but several. Some who have a chromosome disorder or any other known physical cause of their ASD may suffer from other consequences of the physical condition; epilepsy, for example. Epilepsy is a nonspecific sign of neurological disturbance and perhaps as many as a quarter of people with an ASD have had a fit at least once. Some have fits much more frequently and may suffer the consequences of this.

Then there are a number of developmental problems that may or may not be the consequences of the fundamental impairment. Dyspraxia or developmental incoordination is very common in people with Asperger syndrome. It probably results from impaired coordination of different parts of the brain, for example information from the cerebellum about where the whole body is in space not being combined with information from the motor cortex about where the arm is going next in an action sequence. An adequate level of coordination will obviously be required to combine hand, head, and gaze direction and, as we have seen, this might be required to indicate attention. So dyspraxia could be the cause of the failure to connect to the interbrain that I am presuming is the basis of autism, or it could be a consequence, because we learn coordination partly by imitation and for this we require an intact nonverbal communication with other people.

Speech itself involves both verbal and paraverbal elements. The latter are more like nonverbal communications in that they cannot be reduced to a message, but are linked to the maintenance of the speaker–hearer network that ensures collaborative turn-taking, and joint attention. But speech also involves the coding and decoding of language, and language does not require a network for communication, only a shared knowledge of the language code. It therefore seems right to distinguish language use from other forms of communication, and indeed there appears to be parts of the brain that are dedicated to language. Some developing children have specific language impairment, just as some have developmental dyspraxia. Children with specific language impairment may have no difficulty communicating nonverbally but are still slow to talk or to understand others talking.

Children with autism are also slow to talk and to understand talk. This was once thought to be their main communication problem, but another view, currently held by some, is that they have the fundamental impairment in communication that other people with an ASD do, and a specific language impairment in addition.

Other developmental problems associated with ASD clinically include problems with hand coordination and writing; with orientation in space and finding one's way; with coordinating right and left (which can lead to problems in learning to dress), sometimes considered to be form of dyspraxia; with numerical calculation; and with spelling. It is one of the paradoxes of ASD that some people with ASD are very skilled in just these areas too. For example, there are some children with an ASD who teach themselves to read even before they can speak, and show a precocious grasp of spelling and grammar (hyperlexia).

Getting back to the fundamentals

There is general agreement between parents, people with an ASD, and professionals that the core of the ASDs is some kind of social impairment or social impairments. However, there is very little consensus about what a social impairment is. Take for example Tariq (not his real name, and his details have been amalgamated with those of other young men).

Tariq was suspected of having Asperger syndrome. He had been in trouble since he was eight when he had started stealing from his adoptive parents. At ten his obvious intelligence was enabling him to find devious ways of outwitting the school authorities who seemed powerless to engage him in education. Attention deficit hyperactivity disorder (ADHD), poor impulse control, and personality disorder were all considered by psychologists and psychiatrists who saw him, and it was undoubtedly true that if Tariq saw something he wanted, he felt that he had to have it. He also found it difficult to keep his attention focussed on school work, although he was an excellent sportsman and could concentrate on a ball or the movements of the opposing team. He had many acquaintances and one close friend with whom he drifted into a series of crimes. This intensified after he was excluded from a private secondary school after only two weeks. They made him feel like a prat, he said. At about this time, his parents consulted a psychiatrist who told Tariq that his mother was from Pakistan, but that his father had been white, a stranger to her, who had raped her after a party. This was new information to Tariq; to be half-white felt to him like a contamination. He had been brought up by adoptive parents who came originally from Pakistan, both of whom were devout Muslims. His father was a doctor and also a part-time Mullah at the local mosque.

Tariq liked the feeling of having money in his pocket and could also find a girl who was impressed by his cars and his money, but Tariq felt embittered that they always wanted him to go straight and the relationships always broke down whilst he was in custody, which began to be more often than he was on the street. His parents gave up on him, and he lived in a series of hostels and on the floors of the houses of acquaintances. He hated drug users with a passion, but began to use cocaine himself because it made him feel 'invulnerable'. He always managed to get on with his fellow prisoners, but had only one friend, the one that he had met at school and with whom most of his crimes were committed.

When I met Tariq, he was very personable and seemed to be making an open and honest attempt to give me an impartial account of his life, although when I looked in the hospital notes he had made clear before he met me that his aim was to get transferred to a psychiatric unit. He told me of his anxiety and of his sudden low moods which had led him to cut himself on several occasions, and also to take overdoses. He described himself as a caring man, who sometimes cried at news stories about children being hurt. But he said that his victims were faceless and he did not feel upset about their suffering. I asked him about hurting his mother, and he seemed not to have thought about this. He did say, though, that he had never been able to tell a woman, neither his mother nor a girlfriend, face to face that he loved her, although he had said it in letters. Tariq had the occasional temporary unskilled job, and claimed to have enjoyed them, but they had usually lasted only a few days. He was extremely tidy and fastidious about his appearance and had demanded a cell on his own as he found it intolerable to share with an untidy cell mate. Tariq was knowledgeable about the latest fashions in men's clothes, and a substantial proportion of the profits from the thefts that he committed went on new clothes.

Compare Tariq with Simon. Simon was also adopted, and was told that his mother had been unable to look after him from the moment he was born. His father had been married to someone else and not willing to leave his wife. Simon had read before he could speak, had screamed when taken to play group, and had never been soothable except by being fiercely and repeatedly rocked. He had struggled throughout school where he didn't seem to know how to behave, and where he had been bullied. His refuge had been in Postman Pat videos, which he had watched repeatedly. He had never had a close friend either in childhood or in his teens.

At the time that I met him, he had left school with a good A level in scripture in which he had taken a particular interest (his mother was a vicar) but had not been able to get a job subsequently. He had gone through a period of marked anxiety in his early teens, and this had returned for a while after leaving school. However, he had become a verger at his mother's church and as a result he had started mixing with people in the church and seemed to have become more confident. Even so his parents had to remind him to shower or to change his clothes. There would be a battle over replacing them, as Simon found it very difficult to choose any clothes for himself, but refused to wear anything that his mother bought unless it was identical to what he had before. His father had once stepped in and thrown all Simon's old clothes away so that his mother could replace them. Simon had screamed as if tortured and had then flown into a rage and attacked his father who had to go to hospital with a suspected broken leg where Simon had kicked him. The family contemplated prosecuting Simon for assault but decided not to. This had never recurred, but his father thought that this incident indicated that Simon had little feeling for anyone else but himself although his strong sense of right or wrong held him back from harming another person under normal circumstances. Simon had never had a girlfriend, and said that he did not want one. His parents did not know much about his sexuality although they suspected that he sometimes masturbated when taking the long showers that he was known for in the family.

And compare them both with Roger. Roger had shown many of the same developmental abnormalities that Simon had, which Tariq had not, although all three had temper tantrums when they were two. Roger had a special interest although his was in model cars which he would line up, and then push across the floor so hard that they would often get damaged. Like Simon he would play alone but he did have some short-lived friends, although these friendships would always end in tears and never lasted more than a few weeks. Roger went through a period of having a very monotonous voice and lacking facial expression, although this seemed to improve as he got older. He had problems with multiplication at school, unlike Simon who was excellent with numbers, and he had some degree of dyslexia. Roger was hampered by his inability to plan and often turned up at school having done the wrong homework, not done the homework at all, or bringing in the wrong books. He got picked on by the teachers and by many pupils, but there were some who treated him in an apparently friendly way and cajoled him to do things for them, things that always turned out to get Roger into trouble. Roger tried to hang on to these friends though and would give them his lunch money and then began to steal from other children to give to them.

At 14, he began to get into more severe trouble and his parents warned him to be more choosy in his friendships, but Roger always said that his current friend (they never lasted long) was absolutely trustworthy and that he had learnt his lesson. At 15, he got into the habit of setting fires. One of these was serious and he was nearly prosecuted for arson but the police decided that prosecution would 'not be in the public interest'. At 16, his parents said that enough was enough. Not only was Roger bringing all sorts of people home, some of whom stole valuables from the house, but would disappear for several days at a time. He had dropped out of school, and had been sacked after three days in the one job he had taken. His parents thought that they could tolerate all of this if Roger had ever seen their point of view, or why they were so upset about the turn that things had taken. But he seemed incapable of empathizing with them, or with anyone else. The final straw was that his parents found out that Roger was in the habit of lying about his family, apparently in order to win sympathy or respect from his friends. Some of these lies were so unlikely that it was nearly certain that they were disbelieved, but even so they were still hurtful. He told one friend, for example, that his mother beat him; another that his father was a convicted gangland leader; and a third that he had had sex with his own sister. Roger often said that he would like a girlfriend, and would sometimes say that he had one. He had lived with a married woman some ten years older than himself for about six months after leaving his parents' home, but he had not had a relationship since.

Clearly Tariq, Simon, and Roger are all socially impaired. None has obtained stable employment, or a stable girlfriend. All of them have very limited or no friendships and a strained relationship with their parents. But it seems that they are socially impaired for different reasons. Although Tariq has some difficulties with learning, which may be due to ADHD, and is impulsive, which some would see as a brain problem, his social difficulties are the consequence of alienation from his parents and the society in which he was brought up. Although he has very limited close friendships, this seems more to do with an inability to trust other people and he can confide in his one close friend. He is able to dispose of stolen property through a network of acquaintances, always manages to find a new girlfriend on his release, and has a canny knowledge of how to please such a girl, at least on the surface. He rubs along with other young men in prison, although he cannot tolerate too much closeness with them. He is street wise. Most people would say that Tariq has a lack of empathy. His criminality had created many victims, not least his own parents and probably a few girls who have become fond of him, too. He holds himself emotionally aloof from them by not thinking about them, or even blotting out their faces in his mind. He lives life in compartments: in gaol he contemplates a criminal future, out of gaol he just wants a nice car and sharp clothes. This capacity for 'dissociation' is what stops him really feeling for others, or indeed for himself. Tariq has never been abused like many people who go on to develop problems with dissociation, but he has to deal with lots of difficult to resolve discrepancies or conflicts in his life history. On the one hand he has had a privileged upbringing, but he has been adopted and not born to it. He is of mixed race, and half of him comes from a culture that he detests. He was not born of a harmonious couple but of a violent coupling, that was unwanted by his mother. Doing wild or antisocial things has been his way of achieving social rewards. Going the conventional route of study and slogging has never worked.

Although Tariq's story might have turned out differently if he had a different brain, if he had as we might say a different temperament, I think most people's intuition would be that it was his life experience that made him what he was. True, his ADHD, if that is what he had, would have made him less able to deal with some aspects of that experience but it was still the experience that had the major impact. Regrettably, his future experience—of gaol, of discrimination in employment and in relationships with law-abiding people because of his criminal record, of being thrown together with people who lived by crime—was likely to keep his feet firmly on his criminal path.

Simon and Roger's social impairment is of a different kind, just as they seem to be different from the normal run of young men. People who met Simon thought within seconds that he was odd or different. Roger did not seem to come across as being different quite so quickly, but anyone who knew him for a week or two began to sense it, and those who were minded to do so marked him out as an easy target for practical joking or exploitation. Both of them had experienced more than the usual degree of adversity in childhood, partly as a result of being bullied. But they had already seemed different as toddlers and this difference could not be explained by their inability to get on with their peers. In fact, it feels like a better fit with the facts to explain their difficulty with peers as being the consequence of their difference.

A difference between Tariq on one side and Simon and Roger on the other was that Tariq took charge of his life. He knew what he wanted in cars, clothes, and women. Another difference was that Tariq had made one good friend in his life, and they really were buddies. They got back together after every separation when one or other or both had been in gaol. They worked as a team, usually planning and undertaking burglaries or car thefts together, and they confided in each other.

Two current theories of autism relate to the differences just mentioned. Knowing what one wants, making choices even if within severe constraints imposed by life circumstances, these are aspects of what is called 'executive function'. Executive dysfunction is one possible explanation for autism. It is attributed to an impaired development of the frontal lobes, and so is a kind of neuropsychological explanation as are most contemporary hypotheses about autism.

Kanner, although not Asperger, suggested that autism might be a consequence of upbringing and this has proved a persistent hypothesis of all kinds of ASD, despite a paucity of supporting evidence. One reason for this persistence may be the kind of observation that I made, when comparing Tariq with Simon and Roger.

Neurotypicals, however disordered their social lives, are rarely friendless or, if they are, have rarely been friendless all of their lives. However, people with an ASD may never have what others think of as a close friend. In the past, this has been taken to be as an indication that people with an ASD lack emotional warmth or the capacity for intimacy, or both, and has been put down to a lack of a loving relationship with a mother or other carer in infancy. The theory that has come to seem the best in explaining this has been 'attachment theory', which starts from the observation that human infants seek the proximity of their mothers when danger threatens, as if they are 'bonded' or 'attached' to them by a virtual string.

Attachment theory has often been considered to be a psychogenic theory of ASD, i.e. to assert that ASD can be caused by purely psychological means, and does not require any underlying neurological abnormality. Psychogenic theories of autism were developed by psychoanalysts like Margaret Mahler and René Spitz. They have many moral implications for people, not least that they suggest that families are to be blamed rather than pitied for having a child with an ASD.

Bowlby, the progenitor of attachment theory, thought that children were preadapted to form a close relationship to their mothers, a view also held by another child analyst, Melanie Klein, who believed that the foetus had a 'fantasy' of the mother's breast.[44] A failure to bond could therefore be due to an innate failure of this inborn disposition to seek out the mother or her breast. So attachment theories are not always 'psychogenic'. Some assume that the autistic impairment is hereditary and based on altered brain function, but that its main effect is still on the emotional bond or 'intersubjectivity' of mother and child.

Anxiety and comfort seeking: is repetition fundamental to an ASD?

'Attachment' theories of ASD have received some support from studies of children raised in Romanian orphanages who show behaviours that are reminiscent of those seen in ASD. John Bowlby, the originator of attachment theory, had based his theory on the study of similarly traumatized children but from a previous generation, that of children orphaned by the death or forced removal of their children in the second world war.

Nico Tinbergen, Nobel prize winner in animal behaviour (and the brother of another Nobel laureate), had spent his war time years in Holland, and had experienced the horrors of the Nazi blockade of that province in 1944. He would, I am sure, have been familiar with the consequences of adversity. He felt strongly that ASD was a condition caused by anxiety in the child, and therefore potentially reversible.

Although few would now agree with him, the behaviours that children with an ASD share with the deprived Romanian orphans are also seen in children who have experienced severe anxiety, particularly in the absence of comfort to offset it. These behaviours all involve a measure of self-stimulation through repetitive movements like rocking; repetitive stimulation of the eyes through flicking; or repetitive and sometimes traumatic skin stimulation through banging, biting, or scratching. Repetitiveness and self-comforting can be discerned in many other activities that are characteristic of people with ASD: liking for routines, time spent ordering objects by size, by date of acquisition in the case of CDs, or by artist...and so on.

It may well be that anxiety plays a part in the genesis of these comfort behaviours in people with an ASD, too. But it is not necessary to assume that people with an ASD have been made anxious and comfortless deliberately to invoke anxiety as the cause of these repetitive behaviours. It would be sufficient, I think, for them to be offline from the interbrain and therefore cut off from the soothing and other anxiety regulation procedures that are integral to mothers caring for their babies.

Repetitive behaviours are also part of obsessive-compulsive disorder and the rarer developmental disorder of Tourette syndrome. It is often assumed that people with these conditions have something in their brains, perhaps the levels of neurotransmitters or their receptors, which predisposes to repetition. Some have argued that this may also be true of ASD and that repetitiveness is fundamental to the disorder. My own impression is that this is not so, but more research will be needed before anyone can be sure.

Both Tariq and Simon demanded order in their environment, but there was a different quality in that orderliness. Tariq wanted to look neat. He saw himself through others' eyes. Simon did not care what his clothes looked like so long as they were the same as they always had been. Tariq loved buying some new clothes so long as they were really fashionable. Simon hated buying new clothes, and had no idea about fashion. In fact, he would not have been able to choose new clothes at all, and relied on his mother to do it for him. What he wanted was to carry on as before. Many people with autism are 'sticky' in this way. They tend to bring conversation back to what interests them, and then carry on and on, or 'perseverate', with it. Less able people with an ASD may make a gesture or a movement and then repeat it, perhaps several times, a kind of motor perseveration.

Based on her experimental observation of this, Uta Frith proposed that perseveration could explain the tendency of people with an ASD to focus on details at the expense of the whole picture. In the animal analogy used by the Greek poet Archilocus which heads this chapter, they are foxes and not hedgehogs; to use the silvological metaphor which is currently more common, they cannot see the wood for the trees; or, as psychologists say, they are field independent. Uta thought that seeing the wood for the trees required a cognitive operation which she called 'central coherence' by analogy with semantic memory which is organized so that neurones linked to specific features refer to association neurones which are linked to more general features, and so on to abstractions. More central coherence means stronger association links with superordinate categories.

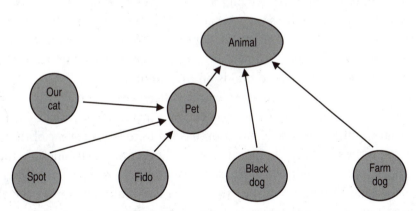

Figure 4.1 A hypothetical diagram of part of the semantic field, with the names of particular dogs being associated with the label for 'our cat' in a superordinate category of 'pet' and that being combined with other instances of dogs in the further, more abstract category of 'animals'. Strong central coherence means that thinking 'Spot' easily makes one think 'animal'. Weak central coherence might mean that the superordinate category 'animal' was rarely accessed.

Not seeing the wood for the trees is something that many people with Asperger syndrome are all too aware of. Here for example is what NeantHumain writes about his experience:

> **Perseverations** Aspies tend to take an obsessive interest in detailed things. It is typical for an aspie to take an all-encompassing interest in something for a few months and later become interested in something else after having already learned enough about the first subject. In other words, we aspies have 'weird,' nerdy interests and hobbies. (Kuro5hin, 2004)

Weak central coherence is one example of a theory which attributes ASD to a particular psychological dysfunction, or impairment of a particular module. People with autism do well on the Embedded Figures Test, a test in which a drawing of a shape is hidden as part of a larger shape, and they are able to spot this smaller 'embedded' figure more often than neurotypicals. But another way of looking at this is that they are less good than neurotypicals at seeing the whole picture, the larger drawing, or 'gestalt'. The areas of the brain that are active in the more general, gestalt perception in neurotypicals are not those associated with perception, but with training (Manjaly *et al.*, 2007). Perhaps then people with autism do not see the wood because they have not learnt to see it. One way that they might learn, that we all might learn, is by watching and then by seeing what other people see. In other words, strong central coherence is not a product of an autonomous brain module, but of a high bandwidth interbrain connection and exposure to other more experienced brains on the interbrain.

Modular theories like the central coherence theory of Uta Frith have contributed to the development of a psychological field called social cognition, whose exploration has led to the rediscovery of those parts of the brain which appear to be dedicated to social function, the 'social brain'. Many parts of the social brain were previously known as the emotion brain, or limbic system. But a feature of the new, social cognition theories of autism is that they take little account of emotion, and much more of what is sometimes called 'cold cognition', that is thinking processes that are devoid of emotion.

Emotionless thinking is rare in practice, but sometimes people with an ASD seem to be particular exponents of it although only if one ignores the kinds of things that people with an ASD do feel emotional about which may be a ritual, a place, a special belonging, an idea, a fascination, or an object invested with personality. One of the most prolific contemporary ASD researchers, Simon Baron-Cohen, has gone so far as to make the ability to think unemotionally as being the hallmark of having an ASD. He calls it 'systematizing' and thinks that all men tend to be systematizers, which accounts for the excess of males with an ASD over females. In a sense he is reproducing the old male/female stereotype which, as formulated by men, meant that they were logical but women were swayed by emotion in their thinking. Simon is aware of this, though, and also of the feminine rejoinder to this charge, which is that women have to think of the consequences to other people of what one thinks whereas men can imagine that it is possible to have abstract thoughts, with no implications for other people's conduct. So Simon contracts 'systematizing' with 'empathizing'.

If empathizing were the criterion of the particular kind of social impairment characteristic of an ASD, then Tariq would be socially impaired. He was conspicuously lacking in concern for the welfare of his victims, or of the family members whose lives had been disrupted by his antisocial behaviour. But I have argued that Tariq did not have an ASD and that he lacked empathy in many situations, but had empathy in a few, such as for his friend. Empathizing is a complex skill, not easily reduced to its components but, like appreciating music or fine wine, requiring many different skills and also a certain kind of emotional openness. Tariq was not emotionally open to empathy. In fact, he hid emotions from himself by means of dissociation.

One way of rescuing the empathizing theory of ASD would be to focus on one particular element of empathy that might be specifically impaired in autism, and that was the route taken in an earlier theory of Uta Frith, Simon Baron-Cohen, and Alan Leslie. According to that earlier theory, the empathizing deficits specific to an ASD result from a lack of a theory of mind, that is, the ability to know what someone else thinks about something, even if it is different from what you think.

One obstacle to theory of mind theories is that evidence of a theory of mind does not become apparent until after infants are 18 months old.

But parents often suspect their child of autism before this, on the basis of signs like gaze, moulding or rather the lack of the baby moulding to a person holding it, and on the child's attention.

Another problem is that many different developmental tasks have become subsumed under 'theory of mind'. These include perspective-taking; self-recognition; and inferring others' beliefs. Although all of these seem to develop at more or less the same developmental stage it is not clear that they are all variants of a single task. Inferring others' beliefs for example is language dependent. Children of hearing parents who are themselves born deaf have language delays, and the degree of delay is correlated with the delay in acquiring theory of mind skills. So perhaps theory of mind is tied up with the language problems that some, but not all, people with an ASD have and is not the fundamental impairment.

Infants with autism may become unusually attentive to repetitive stimulation like flickering light or shiny objects, but at the same time show limited interest in the kinds of social cues—mother's smiles, or human voices—that other babies orientate to. It has been suggested that this may be due to over-sensitivity to sensory input.[45] It is certainly true that later in life, many people with an ASD do show a dislike of particular sensations of touch or particular sounds that can lead to disabilities in themselves. For example, many people with an ASD have a very restricted diet, or faddy eating as it is sometimes called, which may be due to an aversion to particular food textures. Other people cannot bear certain textures of fabric next to their skin, or become anxious or upset if they hear particular noises, like vacuum cleaners or the chimes of ice-cream vendors.

Studies of these phenomena do not show that people with ASD are uniquely hyperacute in their hearing or touch, and often show that the same person with an ASD may be particularly sensitive to one stimulus, but unusually insensitive to another. It seems likely that the problem is more of attention and habituation. Many children find wool next to their skin itchy, but bow to the wishes of their parents and their culture, and wear woollen vests until they become used to them, or habituated. People with an ASD are less compliant in this way. But a larger problem is that people with an ASD may simply attend to some stimuli that other people ignore, whilst failing to attend to others. Many parents have suspected that their child with an ASD is deaf because he or she fails to respond to their name being called, sometimes quite loudly. This is a cue that neurotypical children orientate to strongly, and by the time adulthood is reached, neurotypicals can pick out their names being spoken from a noisy background with remarkable ability. The same child who does not respond to their name may respond to something in which they are interested, like a sweet being unwrapped, with normal auditory ability which may seem greater than normal when contrasted with their lack of response to social cues.

So the earliest signs noticed by parents that their child has an ASD are more likely to be those of unusual patterns of attention, rather than unusual sensory acuity. This has led to another theory about the fundamental impairment of ASD, the joint attention theory, which places considerable weight on the second gaze reflex and the ability of the child to redirect an adult's attention, or to have their own attention directed by an adult, on to objects or people of mutual interest.

There is strong evidence that babies with an ASD do have consistent impairments in joint attention. One very interesting recent study looked at babies at 14 months, at 24 months, and at 30 or 36 months (Landa, 2007). Some who were diagnosed as having an ASD at 36 months had shown signs of it at 14 months (early developers) but some were apparently developing normally at that age, and only showed signs at 24 months (late developers). At 14 months, when compared to the late developers and the babies who were not diagnosed later as having an ASD, the early developers made fewer attempts at attention redirecting using gaze, looked less often at another person when that person was smiling, and tried to get another person's attention less often. But at 24 months, the late developers now differed from the babies without an ASD in the frequency of these same behaviours, but no longer showed more of these behaviours than the early developers. So the development of an ASD coincided with the fall off in joint attention.

Joint attention theories of autism fit well with parents' experience of not being able to interest their affected child in things, and so of feeling that their child is in their own world. But joint attention theory needs to be stretched to accommodate some of the other observations, even of those made in the recent study just cited. For example a reduced use of gesture was another of the ways that early and late developers differed at 14 months, and both differed from normally developing children at 24 months.

Another theory of autism puts the problem even further back in infant development, and ties it to an even simpler kind of neurological function, that of imitation. As we have already seen, the importance of imitation as a means of communicating emotion or of learning new movement sequences is very important. It is what I have previously referred to as iconic communication, although that term stresses there is interaction involved, and not just passive learning. The importance of imitation has been given a boost by the discovery of specialized neurones in monkeys which fire in response to doing a movement or seeing a movement (the mirror neurones). I shall discuss these more in the next chapter. Parents' observations that their child does not mould or that their child does not look at them could both be explained by a failure of imitation. Moulding means that the infant makes the same shape with his or her body that the parents make with an arm so that the infant fits snugly onto the parent's side or front. Moulding is essential for the survival of infant monkeys who are carried on the mother's back through tree canopies. An infant monkey who did not fit well would simply get knocked off. Eye contact is also an imitative movement in that either the infant, or the parent, is imitating staring into the other one's eyes.

Imitation and joint attention both presume that infants give special importance to other human beings. An infant who imitated their cradle, or the dog who stared at a reflective surface in which they could see their own face mirrored as avidly as looking at another real human being looking back at them, would not be developing normally. So the Klein hypothesis that the normal development of human infants requires that they know the difference between people and things, and that the former have special importance, seems to hold. But this may not require the kind of thinking or emotional preparedness that Klein suggested. It might only need infants to have a primary gaze reflex, that is for infants to look preferentially at a human face, and then to narrow that down to the eye region of familiar faces. Or to put this in a more general way that infant brains are preadapted to connect to the interbrain.

Linking the theories together

It may be that some of the current theories of ASD are plain wrong, but that seems unlikely in that all have supporting evidence. It may be that some theories of ASD are actually theories about associated conditions. Dysexecutive syndrome, and the role of the frontal lobe in it, might be one of those, since dysexecutive syndrome occurs in other conditions, such as schizophrenia, dementia, and attention deficit disorder. The tendency to repetitiveness similarly occurs in other conditions, including severe social deprivation, and seems unlikely to be a fundamental impairment of autism itself.

This is not to say that research into theory of mind or into dysexecutive problems or the tendency to repetitiveness will turn out to be irrelevant or misguided. Knowing more about these problems has helped to understand many of the difficulties that a significant number of people with an ASD have. But these theories may not be the key to the fundamental impairment of the ASDs.

Some of the theories, like central coherence theory, the failure of intersubjectivity, or the empathy failure theory, seem to be quite distinct from the others. I think, and will try to show later in this chapter, that this might not be so. But the other theories seem quite closely linked: it can easily be imagined how a failure of imitation at a very early age could lead to a failure of joint attention at a later age (and how both could lead on to a failure of perspective taking which is an apparently language-free element in theory of mind impairment).

One way that most of the theories may be linked is to consider them pertaining to different stages on a developmental pathway. This would mean that there is one underlying impairment whose manifestation changes either because different developmental stages bring different aspects of social interaction into salience, or because each stage builds on the other. If an ASD was the result of a lag in development, then it would be the most recent developmental challenge which would be the one at which a person with an ASD would most obviously fail.

What do we need a single theory for?

Some scientists are beginning to question whether there can be a single theory of autism.[46] They have pointed out that each generation has a particular orientation to socialization and each generation has a theory of autism to match it. Perhaps, these scientists argue, the fundamental impairment of ASD could be the result of breakdown of several different psychological functions (and therefore several different pathways in the brain).

But we still need to have a clue to what has been called the enigma of autism. A clue to a puzzle doesn't necessarily tell us the answer but it puts us on the right track to find the answer for ourselves. Diagnosis might tell us what kind of puzzle it is, but doesn't give us a clue about how to solve it. In this respect, the diagnostic criteria provided in the most widely used diagnostic manual (the fourth edition of the American Psychiatric Association's Diagnostic and Statistical Manual, also known as DSM-IV) are not particularly helpful. They are strongly influenced by the triad of social impairments of Wing and Gould and by computerized methods of questionnaire analysis in which answers are weighted and combined.

To know how to cope with an ASD it is necessary to look behind symptoms to what is happening in the person's experience and in their mental processes. DSM-IV criteria do go beyond symptoms in that they require raters to interpret behaviour, but they stay pretty close to the symptomatic surface. Giving someone a DSM-IV diagnosis still leaves the task of explaining what the implications are, what it means in everyday life, to have an ASD.[47]

Why I think that being socially offline is the fundamental impairment of an ASD

In quoting from experts or people with an ASD writing about the manifestations of ASD, I have repeatedly referred to abnormalities of nonverbal communication like problems with the use of gaze to signal attention, diminished gesture, altered facial expressiveness or face interpretation and so on. To illustrate the point, here is what NeantHumain, whose website I have quoted from already, said were the main features of his problem:

> First of all, unlike autistic people, I did not have trouble learning to speak. However, I do have mild hyperlexia, which basically means a large vocabulary. Moreover, it is common for autistics and aspies to have some trouble lying, recognizing lies, and interpreting metaphors. The result is that most aspies are seen as literal and humorless.
>
> Like many aspies, my voice can sometimes sound monotonous and emotionless. Similarly, aspies are known for giving soliloquies about their favorite subjects, or *perseverations*, not always realizing how much they are boring the people they are speaking to.
>
> Aspies sometimes also miss facial expressions, body gestures, and implications. While I can often pick up on someone's emotional state from a quick glance at their face (and it has to be quick because, like most aspies, I have trouble looking people in the eye), I can often completely miss things or misinterpret them. Likewise, my facial expression is usually plain or uncontrolled. (Kuro5hin, 2005)

NeantHumain mentions almost all of the channels of nonverbal communication, and their uses, considered in previous chapters and says that he has problems with all of them. No doubt his perception of his own condition has been influenced by what he has read about it, but it seems unlikely that he would accord first place to impairments in nonverbal communication if these did not seem to be crucial to him.

My own research bears out what NeantHumain says. When I compared people with a diagnosis of an ASD and other socially impaired individuals, I obtained information about nonverbal communication during development from parents, and also made systematic observations of it. I also collected information about personality, about life style, about stereotypies and perseveration, about language and speech, about coordination: impaired nonverbal communication, whether reported by parents or observed by me, was the single strongest differentiator of the ASD and the other socially impaired group.

Other evidence that impairment of nonverbal communication is fundamental comes from the order in which the signs of ASD emerge. It would be expected that the most fundamental impairments would be the ones that are detected at the earliest age, and this is borne out by studies of babies who go on to have a diagnosis of an ASD. The editors of a special issue of the Journal of Autism and Developmental Disorders that published the results of 14 of them concluded that '…these studies collectively show, among other things, that early differences in joint attention, shared affect, verbal communication, and repetitive behaviours are common in infants and toddlers later diagnosed with ASD' (Yirmiya and Ozonoff, 2007, p. 9). The impairments of nonverbal communication, the differences in gaze, movement synchrony, and awareness of other people's smiles that were coded as impaired joint attention and shared affect preceded the impairments of verbal communication and overtly repetitive behaviour and are therefore the better candidates to be considered the fundamental impairments.

For me, the most convincing evidence that nonverbal communication is the fundamental impairment of ASD is how helpful people with an ASD and their carers find it to have this explanation. It seems to make sense of so many of their difficulties. My clinical practice is now to tell everyone that I see whom I think may have an ASD that I expect that they have a difficulty knowing what other people are thinking and feeling unless they are told. Furthermore, I say, a person with an ASD may also find that other people do not know what the person with the ASD is thinking and feeling, either. So useful has this been that if someone says, 'I think that I am good at knowing what other people are feeling' and their parents or spouse agrees, I think very carefully before making the diagnosis. Similarly if a parent says, 'It's not difficult to tell from his voice or his face what's going through his mind', I am reluctant to make the diagnosis unless the parent adds the rider—'but I've had to learn to do this, and someone who does not know him well couldn't do it'.

Why is nonverbal communication neglected?

It's not entirely true that it is neglected. There is a theory about ASD that it is due to 'nonverbal learning difficulty' (Rourke, 1988; Rourke and Tsatsanis, 2000), and this has many overlaps with the position that I am putting forward, although it does also presume that the cause lies in an abnormality of the right side of the cerebral cortex, which I do not.

One reason that nonverbal learning difficulty does not seem to me to be a completely satisfactory explanation is that it is not a theory of communication. It assumes, as many people do, that impaired communication is the result of an impairment in the communicator. We would not automatically make that assumption if verbal miscommunication was the problem. We might wonder first if the two people communicating were using the same language: this might, for example, be our starting point when a wife's depression turns out to be the result of marital conflict with her husband. It would not make sense to look only at her side of the marital dialogue and then find out what caused it. It might make sense to look at her and her husband's interaction and see what influenced her contribution to that, though.

How accurately an emotional expression is judged is not just a matter of the person doing the judging or the person doing the expressing; there is an element too of how well they click together or not. For example, in one study 24 students were asked to pose standard emotional expressions, which were photographed, and they then had to rate the photographs of everyone else. When the data were analysed some students were more accurate raters than others and some were more precise posers, but there was an additional 'dyadic' effect on accuracy. So the accuracy of a student rating another student's emotion was made up of the rater's overall accuracy and the poser's overall precision, and also how well that particular face communicated itself to that particular student (Elfenbein *et al.,* 2006).

My hypothesis about autism, which is not inconsistent with people with autism having different brains to those of neurotypicals, is that the focus of the problem needs to be shifted from looking at the brain itself in isolation, but to consider the function of the brain under the description of it being a node in a network of automatically but wirelessly connected brains. To use another analogy to try to bring home the implications of this focus, I invite the reader to consider the television in the living room. The commonest reason for people's televisions not working properly is not a fault in the receiver, but that the aerial is not adequate—or is not even plugged in. Similarly I am arguing that the fundamental impairment of autism is that the functions subserved by nonverbal communication fail because the wireless connection does not get established, and the signal does not get through to the set.

Simulations and caches: the difference between Simon and Roger

Having started out this chapter by emphasizing how different people with an ASD are from each other, I seem to have ended up by stressing their similarity. Admittedly, the similarity that I have proposed lies entirely in a communication breakdown, and communication breakdowns can occur for all kinds of reasons. A communication breakdown may mean that people increasingly go their own way, and so become more idiosyncratic. But there are differences between the two young men that I described, Simon and Roger, which seem more fundamental.

Simon struck almost everyone as different as soon as he met them. Compared to other young men of his age, he looked different, dressed differently, spoke differently, and spoke about different things. People did not seek him out as a friend and often rejected his friendly overtures. Roger seemed a bit immature to a critical eye, and perhaps his face was a little bit unlined for his age, and his eye a little less keen. But Roger was particularly concerned to fit in and generally did so... at first. It took a little while for his difference to emerge, and for others to exploit it. Simon had given up trying to deceive, charm or flatter people, even when he had thought of doing so. It just didn't seem to work. Roger did all of these things although in such an ingenuous way that his attempts inevitably worked against him.

It is possible that Roger does not have an ASD at all. There are similarities between Roger and people described as having antisocial personalities, impulsive personalities, or even psychopathy. But I don't myself think that he does fit these categories as well as Tariq does. Yet there is a bigger difference between Roger and Tariq than there is between Roger and Simon. Simon and Roger both share a common developmental history, with Roger being reported by his parents as having more of the symptoms of autistic disorder given in DSM-IV. In fact DSM-IV recognizes the existence of the pattern of symptoms that Roger displays and categorizes them under 'pervasive developmental disorder, atypical'. Other people have labelled these atypical cases according to whatever characteristic that they consider fundamental. Elizabeth Newson has termed them people with 'demand avoidance syndrome' because of their disruptiveness. She considers this is designed to break up social situations in which they feel at sea. I agree with this. Dorothy Bishop terms it 'pragmatic-semantic disorder' focussing on the malapropisms that are sometimes apparent in language and on the problems of social communication which, as it affects language, is termed a pragmatic impairment.

I used to think that the difference was that people with atypical ASD had problems in nonverbal communication that were largely confined in nonverbal interpretation and lacked the impaired nonverbal expressiveness that is characteristic of people with more typical ASD. What has struck me more recently is the association between atypical ASD, ADHD, and dysexecutive syndrome. The latter are disorders that have been supposed to be, at least in part, linked to a reduction in working memory. The lack of empathy of people with atypical Asperger syndrome is often cited as the problem that upsets other people the most. Although people with a typical ASD may also be described as having a lack of empathy, what that is attributed to may be different. People may say of themselves that they find it difficult to read faces, and therefore to know what another person is feeling. That is consistent with one theory of empathy, that it is a failure of emotional contagion, and it would be consistent with my hypothesis that ASD is an inter-brain connection failure. More rarely a person may say that although they knew how the other person was feeling, they had no idea what they were expected to do about it. This would be consistent with the theory of mind, or cognitive, approach to empathy. People with either or both of these empathy failures may try to offset them by being very sympathetic, for example like Tariq, crying at news items about the ill-treatment of children or animals. (Just to complicate matters, some people with an ASD become embittered about their treatment by neurotypicals and may actually laugh at ill-treatment or adversity of this kind, but this is rare.)

Roger was not particularly sympathetic, but tried to imitate the emotional reactions of those around him. He would show sympathy if that was the norm of the people he currently admired, but he may show Schadenfreude if that was the prevailing norm. His lack of empathy seemed to get to people particularly because it did not seem to arise from disability. His parents sometimes said that he could empathize if he was interested, but he was rarely interested. Here is what another young man, who had much more to lose from his lack of empathy than Roger, said about it. He would feel he needed a breathing space from his girlfriend, of whom he seemed genuinely fond and she of him, and would tell her that he wanted to go to the pub. She would ask, 'How long for?' as he had a habit of getting lost, and he would invariably say, 'About an hour'. William found the pub difficult if there was a group of people that he didn't know, but since it was a rural pub, he could usually rely on there being a few acquaintances only in the bar, and he could manage. Sometimes one would suggest that William would go back to his place and he invariably would. Sometimes he stayed out all night.

I asked William if he thought that his girlfriend, who was called Tracy, worried when he did not come back. He said that she did. I asked whether he thought about this when his friend said, 'Come back to my place' and William seemed perplexed. In discussion, it seemed to him that there was no continuity in his mind between how he was when he was with Tracy and how he was when he was in the pub.

Although we have all had some experience like this, many of us might consciously have to suppress what we had said to our partners if we were minded to do what William did. We would either have to suppress a mental image of what our partners would say to us, or would do, the morning after an unscheduled night out. We might most likely have to have quite a few pints or Bacardis and coke to help us to blank this out, but even so we would experience anxious anticipation that would inhibit us from accepting the invitation. At the very least we would phone up to try to persuade our partners that it was acceptable. William did none of these things. He never drank heavily, and although he had a mobile phone (which he often lost), he did not ring up.

What was missing for William was a continuous presence of Tracy with which he was in internal dialogue, just as a person might be with themselves. When this continuous presence is God, we might call it conscience. Tracy was not William's conscience but she was his mentor, and when he was with her he would often check things out with her. But when she was not there she was gone. Psychoanalytic psychotherapists might say that she was not 'internalized'. For William to empathize with Tracy requires him, according to theory of mind theorists, to have a theory of Tracy's mind, or perhaps a simulation. This simulation is assumed to be maintained even in the absence of Tracy: it is stored. But William could empathize with Tracy when he was with her, and paying attention, but when he was not, the simulation either melted away or at least it did not get evoked appropriately.

Empathy normally requires the capacity for emotional contagion or, as I would put it, connection to the interbrain, so that we are provided with information about what another person is thinking, through their gaze, and feeling, through mirroring their facial expressions or some other means of emotional contagion. Most of us do not switch off from another person simply because we are no longer in nonverbal communication with them, like William did. We can still see their facial expressions, or hear their tones of voice, in our mind's eye. Even if the image is very fragmented because we are not good visualizers or have poor vocal memories, we can still experience their emotions and how they would make us feel.

I have previously used the analogy of a computer and its wireless internet connection, and it might be useful to return to this for an illustration. Many browsers on the internet can be set to offline browsing which means that when the computer is wirelessly connected not only do we see the pages that we are surfing on the screen, the computer is also downloading them into its memory, in the background. So if our connection with the internet goes, the browser will look into this memory—or cache, because the pages are hidden away there—and bring up the copy that is stored there as if we had actually navigated to the page on a server computer.

My explanation, for which there is as yet little evidence, is that alongside our real-time experience of other people's emotions, thoughts, beliefs, and so on we are storing these experiences in memory, in a cache. So even when we are alone we are able to interact with other people, bounce ideas off them, or experience their emotional reactions but not through their real-time reactions but using their cached images.

So my explanation for William's, and Roger's, lack of empathy was that they had no cached store of other people's reactions on which to base their prediction of what other people were feeling. William had perhaps a limited cache. He would not forget what Tracy was doing when she just went upstairs, so he would follow her if she hadn't come down when he expected or pick it up if she became more than usually quiet. Roger did not. It was as if other people ceased to exist for him when he was not attending to them. This was one reason that he could not keep a friend. His mother had to remind him to phone them if they had not phoned him.

Caching clearly requires some degree of volatile memory. Cached pages may disappear when the computer is turned off and are not usually stored. So there may be a potential link between Roger's empathy problem and his attentional problems which do, so much recent research suggests, require working memory.

CHAPTER 5

*I*s an impairment of nonverbal communication a brain problem?

Alan glares at his son, Paul, who in turn stares fixedly at the table. His son is only 14 and yet he was home past midnight. Alan has gone from calm questioning through anger to rage trying to find out where he was and what he was doing. Paul has remained imperturbable. He was just 'out'. Now his father is fearing the worst: perhaps Paul is into drugs, and was arrested, or worse...what could be worse? Alan starts to beseech Paul, but Paul remains fixedly staring at the table.

Has Paul got an impairment of nonverbal communication, and is it a brain problem? The answer to the first question is probably 'no'. Gaze avoidance and lack of expressiveness particularly in adolescence is most often a sign of anger or anxiety or both. It is not an indication of a persisting inability to exchange gaze or show feelings. So we would not expect any abnormality in the brain, either.

Let's suppose that Paul continued to stare fixedly at objects over the next few days and weeks, and still showed a lack of expressiveness. Then there might be a question of whether he had somehow lost the capacity or competence that he previously had in nonverbal communication. A psychiatrist called in at this stage is likely to wonder at several possibilities. The first is that Paul's nonverbal behaviour is environmentally induced, for example a consequence of his very great fear of his father or, possibly, that he has developed a mental illness. But another possibility might be that he has suffered some kind of brain injury which has impaired his nonverbal competence. To check this out the psychiatrist may order some kind of examination of the brain, and the one that would likely be chosen is a magnetic resonance imaging (MRI) scan because it provides the most detailed view of brain structure of any current, noninvasive techniques.[48]

So far in this book, I have argued that ASDs are characterized by an impairment in nonverbal communication, but if this were due to some kind of environmental constraint, then it would be the environmental problem that was fundamental to the autistic spectrum disorder and not the nonverbal problem. There are still practitioners, particularly in France, who would argue that this is so—that the fundamental problem in ASD is the quality of relationship in infancy between the child and his, or her, carers. As in the hypothetical Paul, one possible refutation for this would be that characteristic brain abnormalities are found in association with impaired nonverbal expressiveness. An added bonus would be if they could be fitted into a general theory of how the brain might mediate nonverbal communication.

Brain structure, autism, and nonverbal communication

Suppose you are in the garden and you try to ring someone on your cordless phone. They pick up the phone and they can clearly hear you, but you cannot hear them. Where is the problem? In your phone? In their phone? It could even be that you are too far from your base station, that you are using too many phones in your house, that there is an exchange fault—the full list is only known to a telephone engineer. Telephony is a kind of communication and, as the example shows, communicative malfunction does not necessarily mean a hardware fault in either the receiving or the sending apparatus. So it is with the hardware of the brain and nonverbal communication. We are well short of understanding the whole communicative cycle,[49] and therefore can only sketch what the contribution of the brain[50] is to it.

We do know that there are some basic functional requirements for nonverbal communication, and for the interbrain, and I have already outlined them. In this section I will consider what is known about their neurological substrate.

Icons

Icons are one of the most important building blocks of nonverbal communication and, as I have discussed, their use requires one kind of copying or imitation. This kind, which I called 'iconic' in an earlier chapter, is involuntary and rapid. Sometimes this type of process is called 'automatic' or 'reflexive' to distinguish it from the type of 'voluntary' processing which we can be conscious of and influence, for example by focussing our attention. Voluntary processing is sometimes called 'deliberate' or 'reflective'. Most recent neuroimaging studies of the imitation of gestures have focussed on the voluntary imitation of gestures, and demonstrate activation in several brain areas, with an emphasis on the left, or dominant, hemisphere where the language centres lie. This is not surprising given that voluntary processing requires deliberate thought, and that normally requires language (Lee *et al.*, 2006; Tessari *et al.*, 2007).

Instructing someone only to observe a gesture or facial expressions blocks deliberate imitation, but not reflexive imitation. It has been argued recently that reflexive imitation occurs automatically because of the activity of specialized 'mirror' neurones are active both in perceiving and in initiating movements. Leslie, Johnson-Frey, and Grafton, (2004) gave participants videos of smiles, frowns, and finger movements whilst they were being MRI scanned. They subtracted fMRI activity during a verb generation task (which would activate left temporal areas) and a motor task (which would activate left parietal areas) and suggested that the remaining activation delineated a 'cortical imitation circuit' consisting of Broca's area, bilateral dorsal and ventral premotor areas, right superior temporal gyrus, supplementary motor area, posterior temporal-occipital cortex, and cerebellar areas.

A probable function can be attributed to several of these areas based on other studies. Broca's area is involved in the generation of words. The cerebellum coordinates movements. The posterior temporal-occipital cortex is involved in recognizing objects presented visually. This leaves the premotor and supplementary motor areas, and the superior temporal gyrus. The motor areas are the areas that are suspected to be richest in the 'mirror' neurones that fire when an action is perceived and when it is performed. The superior temporal gyrus is activated when the brain is called on to handle sequential, temporally distributed inputs or outputs.[51]

In a recent study (Pfeifer *et al.,* 2008), ten year olds were scanned whilst watching and imitating facial expressions. Activation of an area of the inferior frontal gyrus (the part of the prefrontal lobe adjacent to the motor system) thought to be rich in mirror neurones occurred in line with the finding of Leslie *et al.* There was also activation of the amygdala and the anterior insula. The amygdala is particularly associated with fear, and the insula with disgust. It has been supposed that activation of these two structures is one step on the route to empathy, in that doing something to harm or upset someone produces facial expressions in them which cause iconic imitation of the same expression in the person doing the harming or the upsetting who then experiences something of the medicine that they have dished out. Support for this came from this study since the degree of activation of the areas during the observation/involuntary imitation task was correlated with a measure of empathy.

A previous study (Dapretto *et al.,* 2006) carried out under similar conditions by the same team had found that young people with Asperger syndrome were able to imitate facial expressions as well as neurotypicals, but did not show the activation of the inferior frontal lobe. The authors took this to mean that people with an ASD lack mirror neurones in this area, and this 'may underline the social deficits'. Other teams accept that the inferior frontal cortex is involved in the pathway from imitating a facial expression to experiencing the emotion being imitated but consider that it is only involved in voluntary and not in reflexive imitation (Lee *et al.,* 2006).

Some autism experts dispute too the significance of mirror neurones in explaining autism. As I discussed in an earlier chapter, one possible explanation for the difference is that mirror neurones only get activated when a person sees something to activate them. Before interpreting a facial expression, which is where the mirror neurones come in, it is necessary to be looking at the face and at the right parts of the face, too.

All of the studies considered in this section identify similar areas in imitation: inferior frontal, premotor and supplementary motor cortex, and superior temporal areas. Mirror neurone proponents locate them in the first three areas, but not in the superior temporal cortex. This area is involved in integrating multiple sensory inputs in its role of handling sequential inputs particularly well, which would make it a candidate for linking gaze direction and mirror neurones, the kind of indexing function that I have considered in an earlier chapter is necessary for knowing what action is a gesture to be focussed on.

Gaze

In monkeys there are populations of neurones that respond to gaze direction and to head direction, but much larger populations respond to the direction of either head or gaze. These populations are different from those that use the eyes in face identification, strongly suggesting that there is a specific gaze detection system. There is evidence for a similar gaze detection system in people (Pelphrey, Viola, and McCarthy, 2004), or rather for three that usually work together: one that detects where another person's right eye is pointing, one that detects where a person's left eye is pointing and one that responds to the apparent direction of both eyes (Calder *et al.*, 2008). There is evidence, too, that this detection system is localized in the superior temporal sulcus (Engell and Haxby, 2007).

Using the same adaptation procedure used in the study just quoted, Calder and other research workers showed that two areas are activated by adaptation to eye gaze direction and presumably are involved in processing eye gaze direction, the anterior temporal sulcus and the inferior parietal lobule (Calder *et al.*, 2007). The posterior temporal sulcus is activated by both mutual gaze and gaze avoidance (Conty *et al.*, 2007; Lee, Dolan, and Critchley, 2008), and it has been suggested that it is involved in mediating the gaze/dominance system in which mutual gaze is perceived as a threat or a challenge, and gaze avoidance as submission. There is a case report of a rare lesion rarely confined to the right superior temporal sulcus impairing mutual gaze which demonstrates that mutual gaze requires this area of the brain to be intact (Akiyama *et al.*, 2006).

The inferior parietal lobule, at least in monkeys, has neurones that respond to actions rather than behaviours. For example, some might fire when a monkey grasps something to eat it, but not when the monkey grasps something to move it. Some are also mirror neurones, too, so that they fire when an action is taken and when it is perceived. In some sense, these cells differentially fire according to the intentions of the monkey (Rizzolatti *et al.*, 2006). fMRI studies of people undertaking economic games show that the inferior parietal lobule and the superior temporal sulcus also light up when the most difficult determinations of the other player's intentions are taking place (Polezzi *et al.*, 2008).

In the introduction to the book, I pointed out that one characteristically human (or possibly primate) approach to the world is 'animistic': to treat things, particularly moving things, as if they had 'souls', that is, intentions. People with ASD do not do this to the same extent, and it may be one of the important functional differences between neurotypicals and people with ASD. The whole of the superior temporal sulcus and the inferior parietal lobule, as well as an area of the frontal lobe, called the frontal operculum, are activated when people view animations of rigid shapes, but not when they are responding to false belief tests presented as stories (Gobbini *et al.*, 2007). The same team provide evidence that the frontal contribution is particularly relevant to facial expressions, and the parietal contribution to gesture (Montgomery and Haxby, 2008).

Many of the papers that I have cited in this section have been published in the six months preceding my writing this sentence. There is very rapid progress in this field and it would be unreasonable to expect closure. New methods of study, that are more sensitive to the interconnection of neuronal populations, will undoubtedly provide more relevant information.

However, there is a considerable convergence of evidence from different sources that:

1. There is reflexive processing of nonverbal communication.

2. It involves a mirroring like process, although it is not yet established whether or not mirror neurones are involved.

3. This mirroring process is consistent with what I have called iconic imitation, and constitutes one essential element of interbrain function.

4. The other elements, the first and second gaze reflexes, have also been supported by the studies that I have reviewed, and now rest on a substantial basis of research.

5. Their neurological substrate is the superior temporal sulcus, which is also involved in judgements about intentions, and in attributing animation to shapes.

6. The superior temporal sulcus is often activated during tasks requiring the observation of facial expression, and this may be related to the point that I have previously made about the interbrain—that gaze or more broadly attention is what chunks up our world into significant elements, including facial expressions and gestures.

Evidence for the cache

People do not necessarily behave differently simply because they have no nonverbal communication with others, but over a long enough period social behaviour does deteriorate. Similarly we do not normally act against a person's interests if they happen to be out of nonverbal communication if we act on behalf of their interests when they are in communication. People who do are, in fact, considered to have a deficit in their ability to empathize. One explanation of what fills the gap in another person's being off the interbrain is the theory of mind: this explains how I can, for example, imagine what my wife might think about something even though she is at that moment on a train to London. Normally, if I want to know what she thinks about something that has happened I would look at her, but if I am in Sheffield and she is just going through Derby, this would not be possible. But the knowledge still comes to me. Psychoanalysts might say this is because I have an internal object that corresponds to my wife. Simulations theorists would call it a simulation of my wife. I have called it previously a 'cache' of my wife.

When my wife is with me, her direction of gaze and her emotional state are important cues about what she is thinking—they are, as I have argued several times, two of the important connections in the interbrain network. So it is likely that cached information will be derived from brain areas that are activated by emotional faces and by gaze direction. One area that is common to both of these is the orbitofrontal cortex. It is active during mutual gaze (Conty *et al.*, 2007) and in face-processing, particularly the processing of familiar faces (Fairhall and Ishai, 2007). Selective damage to the orbitofrontal cortex in some types of fronto-temporal dementia, possibly involving the von Economo neurones that are specific to this area, results in a loss of social inhibition and a lack of empathy (Viskontas, Possin, and Miller, 2007).

Being scanned inside an MRI machine normally means being cut off from nonverbal communication, and therefore offline from the interbrain. Tasks requiring empathy judgements can only be solved by a person in the scanner drawing on their simulation or cache. So do such tasks provide any evidence for what part of the brain might act as a cache?

Is there neuroimaging evidence for the interbrain?

Neuroimaging results show that the brain has a system for iconic imitation (premotor and supplementary motor cortex)[52] and for responding to gaze direction in others (frontal operculum, superior temporal sulcus, inferior parietal lobule) but although these *could* be used as the hardware for the interbrain connection, I have not presented any direct evidence that they *are* used for this purpose.

It is difficult to find this evidence. The existence of language centres, interestingly occupying similar areas in the left hemisphere that the gaze detection system does in the right, was suspected because injuries to the left side of the head often led to an obvious alteration in speech and language. But an impairment in interbrain function would not be obvious. Nor is it easy to think of a task which would directly demonstrate interbrain function since much of what I suppose to be interbrain function is complemented by voluntary processes, too.

A new generation of fMRI studies has involved the use of two scanners, and simultaneous scans of the person in one scanner interacting in some way with the person in the other. So far, these interactions have mainly been determined by a task, usually an economically orientated one, set by the experimenters (King-Casas *et al.*, 2005). One consistent result is that the experiences of how another player responds in a game quickly leads to a 'judgement' of either trust or distrust in that player. I put 'judgement' in inverted commas because this is really a kind of thoughtful feeling or, at best, an emotional thought. The area of the brain that interfaces emotions, thoughts, and memories is the cingulate cortex (Phan *et al.*, 2002). It is also an area that is activated when making moral judgements (Greene *et al.*, 2001) and judgements about the self compared to the other (Frith and Frith, 2008), for example when playing a trust game in ASD (Chiu *et al.*, 2008) or in target detection (Shafritz *et al.*, 2008).

Changes in cingulate activation could be brought about in trust games simply by reflecting on how the other player is responding, that is, by intellectual calculation. If so, then there is no intersubjective, empathic, or reflexive element involved, and so no interbrain link. My own view would be that we use our feelings about another person—which are provided by the interbrain link—as well as our cold calculation of how they have been playing to judge whether or not to trust them. However, judgements that a person is sharing attention with us are, if my account is right, based on an active interbrain connection. Such judgements are also associated with activation of the cingulate cortex[53] along with other areas of the brain (Williams *et al.*, 2005).

Contagious facial expression can lead to contagion of short-lived emotions, as I have suggested in an earlier chapter. Contagion of mood requires a longer-term adjustment to emotional reactivity, which may be a 'down regulation' with a reduction in, say, anxiety proneness; or an 'up regulation' with a greater sensitivity to anxiety. The orbitofrontal cortex and the anterior cingulate have the ability to up or down regulate the amygdala and therefore the fear response (Eippert *et al.*, 2007). One way that an interbrain connection might result in contagion of mood might therefore be through its connection to the cingulate cortex.

Attachment theory, the interbrain and the cingulate

One possible piece of evidence for the interbrain would be to demonstrate that contagion of mood, as well as contagion of emotion, does take place. Managers in care homes or nurseries know this to be true from their own experience, even if it has not been demonstrated scientifically. Calm carers or nursery nurses induce calm in their charges.

Angry or anxious ones are more likely to induce these moods. This observation is fundamental to attachment theory, but it is attributed to a metaphorical linkage, bond, or attachment, between the carer and their charge. Attachment theorists postulate that this bond can be secure, insecure, or avoidant and that these characteristics can damp down, increase, or suppress anxiety in the charge. Although attachment theories place considerable emphasis on touch and holding, the theory also gives an important place to mutual gaze as a signal of attachment (Koulomzin et al., 2002).

There are two elements to attachment theory: proximity seeking and carer–infant interaction. Proximity seeking is assumed to be an innate behaviour, often associated with specific vocalizations that call a mother to an infant. These are likely to be emergency calls, however, when mother and infant are unusually separate,[54] but proximity is probably normally maintained by smell.[55] Proximity is a requirement for much of the nonverbal communication, or interbrain communication, that I have considered in this book. It is assumed that attachment ensures that infants are more likely to be protected by their mothers against predators if they remain close to the mother's side. Oddly enough fathers are rarely involved in attachment bonds amongst mammals, which might be expected if infant protection were the main purpose of proximity. Another reason given for attachment behaviour is that infants that are close to their mother are more likely to learn from her. In people and possibly in some primates, this learning can be by instruction. But in other mammals it has to be learning by imitation—and therefore, as I have argued, mediated by the interbrain connection.

Are these brain areas affected in ASD?

Recent neuroimaging lends support to the existence of brain systems that can mediate nonverbal communication, and this may be their primary purpose although, as yet, too little attention has been given to nonverbal communication to determine this. These systems include the areas assumed to contain mirror neurones, used for reflexive imitation; the gaze direction system (inferior parietal lobule, frontal operculum, superior temporal sulcus); and the cache (orbitofrontal and ventrolateral prefrontal cortex). Arguably, an association between lesions or functional inactivity in these areas and ASD would be evidence for their importance in ASD, and therefore indirect evidence for the importance of impaired nonverbal communication and ASD, too.

Two caveats have to be applied before drawing these conclusions. The first is that ASD is unlikely to be caused by damage to an area of the brain, but to some alteration in the connection between areas (Hughes, 2007)—a connection that may sometimes involve the connection between two or more brains, not just within one brain. New methods of fMRI analysis do provide some evidence about connections (Welchew et al., 2005), as do investigations of brain activity over time using the changing electrical activity of the brain (event-related encephalography and magnetoencephalography). But these are at an early stage of development.

Another caveat is that scientists are not above being connected to the interbrain themselves. They too work within a Weltanschauung, a feeling of the time. Currently that feeling is to investigate the social brain, and recent studies of autism and fMRI have mainly focussed on the areas that have been the topic of this chapter, to the exclusion of other areas which were the topic of past investigation—the neocerebellum is one example of the latter.

Given these two caveats, it is my conclusion from reviewing the literature that there is strong evidence for a difference in the way that faces and gestures are processed in the brains of people with an ASD, and that difference is consistent with there being a defect in mirroring (Hadjikhani et al., 2007). However, there is as yet no consensus about whether or not mirror neurones do occur in the human brain and, if they do, how they might relate to the clinical deficits in imitation that are observed in people with an ASD. If there are mirror neurones, they will be located in the area in the human brain that most closely corresponds to area F5 in the macaque brain, the supplementary motor cortex. There is evidence from independent studies of abnormal connections in the supplementary motor cortex in people with an ASD (Hendry et al., 2005; Mueller et al., 2001; Rinehart et al., 2006).

There is also strong evidence for an alteration in the function of the superior temporal sulcus (Pelphrey, Morris, and McCarthy, 2005),[56] which involves the right side particularly (the side which is likely to be involved in reflexive gaze detection) although here the evidence is more complex as the superior temporal sulcus is also involved with detecting mutual gaze as a threat as well as mutual gaze as a prelude to gaze following, and attention shift. The particular area of the gaze detection system that may be implicated in disaggregating mutual gaze as an attention orientator and mutual gaze as a threat might be the inferior parietal lobule, which recent studies have also implicated in autism.

The interbrain hypothesis I have put forward assumes that gaze and other attentional shifts chunk up our experience into meaningful bits, much as frequency shifts chunk up our speech into syllables.[57] There is evidence for the superior temporal sulcus being involved in this chunking (Redcay, 2008), with the left sided sulcus being involved in language, and the right side in nonverbal communication. A study by Pelphrey *et al.* showed that the brain activity (mainly in the fusiform face area and in the amygdala) in people with Asperger syndrome look-ing at static pictures of fearful and angry faces was no different to when they were looking at dynamic pictures, but neurotypicals also activated their posterior superior temporal sulcus during dynamic picture pro-cessing, i.e. they were using the gaze direction area of their brains as well as face reading and face responding areas (Pelphrey *et al.*, 2007).

There is also evidence suggestive of altered orbitofrontal function in people with an ASD (Ashwin *et al.*, 2007; Bachevalier and Loveland, 2006; Dichter and Belger, 2007; Hiraishi *et al.*, 2007) although the reduction of empathy that I have attributed to a reduced ability to cache information is also associated with reduced orbitofrontal function in three other 'conditions': adolescence (Eshel *et al.*, 2007), antisocial behaviour (Whittle *et al.*, 2008), and attention deficit hyperactivity dis-order (Hesslinger *et al.*, 2002; Itami and Uno, 2002; Lynn and Davies, 2007; Plessen *et al.*, 2006).

Conclusion

There is an almost overwhelming amount of neuroimaging information emerging, and even if one confines one's attention to studies of people with autism, there is almost too much of it to come to grips with. The information available is outstripping the means of summarizing it, and certainly the ability of anyone to draw any definite conclusions at this stage. I have suggested that a lot of this information does support my proposal that autism is fundamentally a disorder of nonverbal communication, that nonverbal communication is different from verbal communication, and that it amounts to an interbrain connection between each of our brains which is undetectable to our minds.

Whether or not this is proven scientifically may matter less to many of the readers of this book than whether or not it helps to understand ASDs, and the difficulties of people with those disorders, better. It is to this important matter that I turn in the next chapter.

CHAPTER 6

What are the consequences of living with an impairment in nonverbal communication?

Living with an autistic spectrum disorder (ASD) may be disabling. In the survey of Sheffield residents by Myles Balfe and myself (Balfe, Chen, and Tantam, 2005) that I have mentioned previously, 70 adolescents and adults (mean age 29) with a definite (30) or a probable (40) diagnosis of Asperger syndrome provided us with detailed information about their health and social care needs. Only 14% were in unsupported paid work (amounting to 21% of those aged over 18), 59% were still living with parents, and only 58% of over 19s were living independently. There was a high level of reported psychiatric problems (affecting 61%) and 90% said that they had been bullied, which may not be unrelated to the anxiety that was the commonest psychiatric problem (affecting 53%). Our respondents rarely went into many of the public places that were popular with their age group, but restricted themselves to places, like cinemas and libraries, where there was little requirement for socialization. It has been estimated that the inability to work and the need for support, along with other difficulties requiring intervention, amount to a life-time expenditure by parents and society generally of $3.2 million for every person diagnosed in childhood with an autistic disorder (Ganz, 2007).

Suffering from an ASD may clearly be profoundly disabling; a fact that people with ASD, and their carers, do not think is sufficiently appreciated by others. One other finding in the Sheffield survey was that we had many fewer people coming forward suspecting that they had an ASD than we expected from the childhood prevalence figures, that is, the proportion of children with the disorder.

It may have been that for various reasons many people with an ASD did not wish to participate in our study. We know, for example, that some women who had an ASD and who were in a relationship did not wish their partner to know that they had any psychological difficulties. Even taking these factors into account, it seems to us that there were children who had suffered from the consequences of an ASD in childhood who had shaken them off in adulthood. They had not volunteered for our study because they had seen no reason to do so. They had not considered that they had any problem with getting on with other people any more.

I shall consider in a later chapter what might have changed the future for these children with an ASD who no longer felt imprisoned by this condition as adults. In this chapter I want to focus on what it is about having an ASD that might create the social impairment that afflicted the adults who still considered that they were disabled. But rather than focus on the diagnosis of ASD, I want to consider the fundamental impairment, the problem with nonverbal communication.

In so doing, I shall leave aside some of the causes of social impairment in ASD that are not the consequence of an impairment of nonverbal communication. These include those psychiatric problems that are not a direct consequence of the ASD, but linked genetically or in some other way. Examples of this are catatonia and cycloid psychosis, rare mental illnesses which appear to be more common in people with an ASD, and may be genetic. Bipolar disorder also appears to be more common in people with an ASD, but also in their families, suggesting another genetic link.

People with an ASD are more likely than average to have a father, a sibling or less likely a mother with an ASD. This may affect their lives without it being a consequence of their own 'offline' experience of life. Other sequelae of ASD may actually be sequelae of the linked conditions with which it may be associated in some people, like dyspraxia, language problems, or learning disability.

So this chapter will not principally be about the consequences of living with ASD, but the consequences of the interbrain, and of not connecting with it. There are some medical conditions other than an

ASD that may cause this. Some people who have had a stroke affecting the right side of their brain may show similar symptoms to those of people with an ASD, as may some people who have dementia. It is likely, too, that just as intelligence can vary between people so can the efficiency with which people can link to the interbrain. This would mean that there are times when people are distant or can connect to the interbrain by only one channel, and so only very good communicators might actually succeed in connecting. There may therefore be more people than those with an ASD who experience some of the adverse consequences of being offline from the interbrain.

Being connected to the interbrain may have, as I conceive of it, many consequences. Some of them will depend on the individual concerned, just as how being online or offline affects a computer will depend on the range of services to which that computer is subscribed. Just how the interbrain does affect people is an unknown—demonstrating this would, I imagine, be one the ways of demonstrating that my interbrain hypothesis has something to it. It is possible to see how people with an ASD suffer in comparison with neurotypicals in their social and emotional connectedness and this does, I think, give some clues about the impact of interbraining on the rest of us.

Even if the reader does not accept the interbrain idea, for which there is as yet little direct evidence, there is good evidence that I have summarized in previous chapters for there being an impairment in nonverbal communication in ASD. I have already argued that it is this breakdown in communication that leads to much of the distress and social impairment associated with an ASD. Five areas stand out as particular consequences: being victimized, for example through bullying; being marginalized, which begins in adolescence with a failure to fit into the social groupings that become particularly important then; being out of touch with one's feelings; making an identity; and thinking differently. I shall consider each of these separately.

Being connected to others is not simply an issue for people with an ASD. That neurotypicals are connected is something that we take so much for granted that we do not even realize that we are. Looking at the consequences of not being connected might therefore, I think, give a better understanding of what networking means for all of us.

Being bullied

Bullying has, quite appropriately, emerged as a major concern for educationalists and parents. This is not because it is a new phenomenon. Books about school, from *Tom Brown's Schooldays* onwards, have described bullies and bullying, and its emotional consequences. Rudyard Kipling, who was himself bullied at school, describes the sadistic, possibly sexual element of bullying in boys' public schools in *Stalky and Co.* Boys who learnt to survive public school, Kipling suggests, could survive anything that Afghan wars could throw at them (there were Afghan wars then, too).

The assumption of the general public may have been that bullying was a problem confined to schools where boys did not have the softening influence of girls, or where the pupils had strained relationships with parents who were stationed overseas. These perceptions may also have blinded educationalists to the malign influence of bullying on pupils in mainstream, state schools. Pupils who are bullied feel ashamed that they cannot escape their victimization, and so keep silence. That, too, may have contributed to keeping the problem hidden.

But possibly the main cause of schools' failure to tackle bullying was the belief that it was inevitable, and that consequently nothing could be done about it. The only explanation for this assumption that I can see is that bullying is considered normal by many and even, for some, desirable like other manifestations of coercion such as war or imprisonment. War is justified, or so many would think, if it is to redress a terrible wrong which cannot be dealt with in any other way, and the example that occurs to many is the war against the Nazis.

What could be the justification for bullying? Bullies, who rarely consider themselves as such, often describe themselves as helping someone else to see the error of their ways. Bullies believe that they are normalizing another person's behaviour. This is why, in my belief, bullies are so often drawn from people who have been bullied, or have had some concerns about their own normality. Bullies demonstrate their social conformity, and their commitment to social values, by imposing them on others.

Some of the pessimism about eradicating bullying comes, I think, from the awareness that we all have it in our natures to try to make others conform to our values and that many people, furthermore, have the capacity to resort to coercion to achieve this if persuasion fails. Most of us learn to hold this tendency in check or, rather, our participation in the social network does it for us so long as the others in our network value tolerance more than conformity.

People with an ASD who I meet in my consulting room agree with the participants in our Sheffield survey that bullying, or victimization, is a major cause of social avoidance and of distress. The bullying that a person with an ASD receives is, in my view, a consequence of the bullies' wrong-headed belief that the person with an ASD could conform, if he or she wanted to, and should be made to do so. So less able people with autism, who may be overtly handicapped, may be understood not to be able to conform and so be less bullied than people with Asperger syndrome whom bullies may think have no cause to be nonconforming. The brunt of bullying and its after-effects therefore fall on more able people with an ASD and the remainder of this section will mainly concern them.

Bullying may sometimes extend to other family members who may be given an implicit choice, to ally themselves with their own kin and risk becoming socially isolated themselves, or to maintain their social connectedness with peers at the expense of their family member. Richard's brother, John, was faced with this decision. He had defended his younger brother right through primary school, but one day in the playground his friends had seen his brother behaving, as they saw it, weirdly, and said to him, 'Your brother's a real spazz. Why do you want to hang round with him?' John realized that he had to choose, to be with his friends or to continue to stick to his brother's side and be seen as weird, too. It was a hard choice, and John chose for his friends. When I met Richard, some 15 years later, he was still angry with his brother and contact between him and John had dwindled to almost nothing.

Fathers often urge their sons to deal with bullying by 'fighting back', and their sons' inability to do so may lead fathers to blame their sons for not doing more, and their sons to think that their father has become a bully like the rest. Mothers on the other hand may side with their sons and try to act as champions for them, which can sometimes lead to mothers themselves becoming socially isolated. Additional family stress may follow on from this. Parents may split up over dis-agreements as to how firm or how supportive to be with the child who has the ASD. Fathers may overestimate their wives' attachment to them in these circumstances. Maria, the mother of Jake who had been diagnosed with Asperger syndrome in his early teens, had rowed with her husband about her husband's disciplinary attitudes towards Jake. Her husband had eventually said, 'It's either Jake or me', not expecting that Maria would choose Jake, but she did. Her husband had left to live in a flat of his own, and his contact with Jake had dwindled to almost nothing although their other child, Tricia, had ended up living with her father.

People with an ASD often do have a sense that other people are connected together, as I have been postulating. They feel that they are different from other people in that they are cut off, but also that other people, being connected, are somehow all the same. Many people with Asperger syndrome therefore experience what another person does as representative of what the whole of the neurotypical world would do. This can lead to aggression towards one person, often chosen because of their vulnerability, being justified on the basis that 'all neurotypi-cals are the same'. Some people with an ASD start to think of their neighbours being in a conspiracy against them. This seems to happen most often when people with an ASD are in their late twenties, and are living alone for the first time. Paranoid ideas like this are based on the idea that everyone else is in communication and they are passing on observations and comments on one's everyday life.

To be angry at the whole world takes a considerable amount of courage. What happens (more often) to people with an ASD is that they feel that other people are justified in their attacks. In early adolescence this may be expressed in a dissatisfaction with bodily appearance. Half of the participants in the Sheffield survey said that they felt dissatisfied on direct questioning, but few volunteer this, just as only a minority of people with an ASD tell anyone about their bullying. They may feel that they have little alternative. Very few people with an ASD have a friend that they can confide in. Very few people with an ASD know of effective means to deal with interpersonal conflict, either, except by iterating what is right and proper and, if that fails, trying to enforce it. Neither of these strategies works with bullies. The only alternative left to a person with an ASD might be to hide, both from the bullies and from the knowledge that they are impotent in the face of them.

When other people's negative opinion coincides with one's own negative opinion of oneself, and when all one can do to overcome that combination is to hide from the knowledge, then shame results. Shame is a kind of anxiety, but of a particularly mordant kind. It is often the background for the development of social phobia in adolescence. I agree with the sociologist Thomas Scheff who has argued that there is no psychic energy called 'self-esteem' and that people who are described as having 'low self-esteem' do not have a lack of something, but an excess: an excess of shame. Very few people can live in the full awareness of shame; it's just too painful. So people find ways of adjusting to it. This might be by avoidance. Many adolescents with ASD who are bullied at school find reasons not to go, or sometimes become so challenging that they are excluded. My impression is that this problem has worsened in the UK since the emphasis has been placed on 'mainstreaming', and more people with an ASD have been required to attend their local secondary schools. Many of my patients have dropped out of school at 13 or 14 and are then lost to the educational system, and my impression from talking to them is that a major reason for this is to escape bullying.

The word 'shame' is probably derived from a Germanic word meaning 'wound'. Being in a state of shame certainly seems like having a wound. Even when it seems to have healed, this may only be superficial and there may be an unhealed or festering sore under the skin. Touching a wound that has only healed on the surface is very painful. Touching on something potentially shaming can be extremely painful for someone who is shame-prone, too. So many adolescents with ASD who have been bullied can be extremely sensitive to any reference to their inadequacies of any kind or to any criticism. This can lead to considerable conflict, even physical fights, in the family home where parents try to exert some kind of oversight. Some parents try to deal with this by acceding control, and trying to go along with an adolescent with an ASD, sometimes justifying this by pleading how hard his or her life is outside the family. This approach rarely works, either. People with an ASD often have need of their parents in practical ways long after a neurotypical child might have become independent. Sometimes the consequence can be that the person with an ASD becomes a sort of tyrant in the home. Other times, it can lead to the young person allying themselves with others who end up exploiting or abusing him or her.

Tara seemed to be developing quite normally to her parents, although they worried that she seemed not to have any friends. It was only later that they found out that Tara was being bullied at school. She would have her lunch money taken, or things stolen from her locker, but most often the bullying was more subtle, as it often is with girls. Rumours would be started about her parents; she would overhear scathing remarks about her dress sense or her personal hygiene; girls who had been prepared to allow her to spend time with them at break would be courted by more popular girls and would then tell Tara to go away if she approached them. Tara had an atypical ASD, of the kind that I considered in a previous chapter, in that her nonverbal expressiveness was not obviously impaired, but she lacked empathy. This was particularly a problem for her father who was a high powered executive and was used to people fitting in with him, and not he with them. When Tara found the bullying unbearable, her behaviour at home changed from being compliant to being, as her father saw it, sulky. They had words, and her father started to impose penalties. Tara said that she hated her father, and there were more rows.

At 14, Tara told her parents that she was going to a sleepover with a friend, and her parents felt relieved that Tara had found one. The sleepovers became regular events, and sometimes Tara would be away for several days at a time. Her mother urged Tara to invite her friend to stay at her house, but Tara said that her friend had a special allergy which made this impossible. There came a day when Tara was 15 that her mother saw her by chance with two men late in the evening when Tara had said that she was staying at her friend's house. After a terrible row at home Tara admitted that there was no girl friend. She was spending nights with a boyfriend, who turned out to be an older man with a police record. Her father said that she was no better than a prostitute and locked Tara in her room, but Tara ran away. The next time that her parents saw her was in police custody, some four months later. She had been arrested for theft, but the police were concerned that she had effectively been imprisoned in the house with the boyfriend, and suspected that she had been forced to prostitute herself.

James was less of a victim than Tara. He lived in a hotel with his parents, who were the proprietors. James had become socially isolated in his last years at primary school. This only became apparent when the form teacher in his last year, who seemed to understand James, had gone off sick halfway through the year and had been replaced by a supply teacher. The supply teacher had told James' parents that he thought that James' only difficulty was that previous teachers had let him get away with bad behaviour. There had been an incident in which James had punched this teacher, and was suspended. His parents thought that the teacher's contribution to the incident had not been taken into account, and reiterated their request that James had an educational assessment. This did not happen and when he went to secondary school it was with a reputation for being a difficult and demanding pupil, but not someone who had any particular educational requirements.

James managed the first year at secondary school, but started becoming withdrawn at home during his second year and then there was a further incident in which he had tried to strangle another boy. James' parents found out that this was a boy who had also been at his primary school, and who had bullied him there. The bullying had continued at secondary school, and other people had joined in. Despite knowing this, the school said that they had no alternative but to sanction James, and suspended him for a week. At the end of the week, James refused to go back. At first, he helped around the hotel, and his parents thought that this might be a good opportunity for him to build up his self-esteem and they did not push him to go back to school.

James became fascinated with the hotel routine, and particularly with the cutlery. He asked to be allowed to check that all the cutlery had been returned to its drawer in the morning, and his parents were happy for him to take this minor chore. However, James began to claim it as his right to do this, and once hit his mother when she said that she was in a hurry and wanted to check it herself. On another occasion, James did leave the dining room, but was heard shouting and pacing in his room, and when his parents went up to check on him he was in a state of high agitation and had thrown all of his CD collection out of the window. His parents were reluctant to interfere with James' cutlery ritual after that, but the checking took longer and longer, and he would not allow his parents into the dining room where the cutlery was checked until he had counted it. It started to take James all morning, and there were occasions when the hotel had to turn away people who wanted lunch because James was still in the dining room.

Being out of touch with emotions

James had an all or nothing outlook to his relationship with his parents. They were either for him, or against him. He could not manage the kind of flexibility or give and take that is so important in relationships. One reason that is often put forward for this kind of rigidity is that it is due to weak central coherence, and the inability to combine different characteristics of another person into a composite. Another possible explanation used to be given by psychoanalysts who argued that infants think of the world around them as either wholly good or wholly bad until, after some months, infants recognize their own impact on the world, and accept that other people are good and bad, like them. A simpler explanation, derived from equilibrium theory, commends itself to me. Equilibrium theory was an explanation for the observation that couples would look at each other more if they were further away: the idea was that there was an optimum value for 'closeness' and if couples were more distant they would increase eye contact to increase closeness back to its equilibrium point or, if not at a physical distance, they would decrease eye contact to bring closeness down. There was an equilibrium because the proponents of the theory thought that there was a point at which a wish for closeness and attachment exactly equalled the strength of a countervailing wish for moving away and exploring.

Further studies have not supported equilibrium theory as it applies to nonverbal communication, but everyday experience suggests that it does apply to our emotions in relationship to others. Since emotional contagion means that I experience another's emotion to some degree, then there is an equilibrium point when another person's strong emotion balances my own weak one. So if I want to stay in and catch up with some housework, but I only want mildly to do this, and my friend strongly wants to go out with me, whether or not I do will depend on whichever action maintains my emotional equilibrium. I may sometimes act to further my own plans if my friend's disappointment, as it is propagated to me in attenuated form via the social network, is more than offset at my own satisfaction at catching up. But if my friend's disappointment is so great that even in the weakened form that it is transferred to me it outweighs my own pleasurable anticipation of staying in, then I will apparently act altruistically.

James was offline to these emotional influences and so his own emotions were unmodulated. If his parents imposed themselves on him, he did not benefit emotionally from going along with them, and vicariously enjoying their relief at his doing so. He just felt baulked, and assumed that his parents would not treat him like that unless they did not care about him. So they would, momentarily, become his enemy.

The emotions of people with an ASD have often seemed a puzzle to carers. I think that neurotypicals are so used to having direct, although weak and easily suppressed, experience of the emotions of people in their local social network that the absence of a contagious emotion is often translated as the absence of emotion at all. Sophie and Steve are examples of this. Both of them had Asperger syndrome, and both had conspicuously absent expression in their faces or voices. Both, too, had been treated with antipsychotic medication which had further reduced their facial expressiveness (this is one of the side effects of antipsychotics). Each complained of severe anxiety but this was repudiated by their professional carers who said that 'they were far too laid back to be anxious'. With reluctance Sophie's psychiatrist prescribed an antidepressant for her, and she reported considerable improvement and asked for a full dose because she thought that there was a possibility of even more improvement. He was so unwilling that he said that she was already having the maximum dose according to recommended guidelines, even though this was not true. It seemed that he, and also the community nurses and other staff involved, could not accept Sophie's report of anxiety at face value.

In the past, some people with an ASD have been diagnosed as having 'schizoid personality disorder', a condition in which a person detaches emotionally from other people, and sacrifices passion and close relationships for activities and interests which are intellectual or aesthetic. Neither James, Sophie nor Steve were like this. They had very strong antipathies and likings for others. They simply could not communicate them through the interbrain.

Another more recent theory about emotions in people with an ASD is that they are 'alexithymic'. This term was coined by two psychoanalytically trained psychiatrists, Robert Sifneos and John Nemiah. They thought that people with psychosomatic disorders had the inability to put words to feelings—hence the term—and feelings therefore found another route of expression, through bodily symptoms. This theory derives from the psychoanalytic idea that emotions represent energy which normally flows out through human relations, but if it is dammed up eventually flows out through some other route. This 'hydraulic' theory of emotions has been superseded by the observation that some people with psychosomatic illness, and also people who are addicted to drugs, do not accurately label emotions. In a small study that I carried out many years ago, I found evidence that the cause of alexithymia might not be that emotions could not be linked to words, but that people whose emotions got short-circuited into physical symptoms at an early age—I looked at adults who had eczema since infancy—were more alexithymic than adults who developed eczema in adulthood. I thought that this suggested that physical symptoms were more effective than words for communicating emotions and when the infants grew up to be children and then adults, they carried on using physical symptoms and not words.

This would not explain why many people with an ASD also seem to be alexithymic. An alternative explanation that seems more plausible to me now is that we learn emotion words in discourse with other people about our own emotions, and that so long as those other people are in our local social network, they have direct knowledge of our emotions and can therefore teach us the usual labels for them. Children with eczema will itch more if they are anxious, angry, bored, or even excited. So scratching cannot function as a contagious emotion, and is not communicated via the interbrain. Parents can learn what their child's scratching means by an observation of the context in which it occurs, but this is an intellectual recognition, rather than just knowing as they would if the emotion was a contagious one and so communicated via the interbrain. Because the emotions of children with eczema are not shared through the interbrain, the adults who name them can only do so approximately, basing this on their intellectual judgement of what the emotions are. All psychotherapists know that this is not a good way to learn about emotion. Our clients learn much more from an empathic therapist who has 'rapport', who actually feels their clients' emotions. Therapists who have a lot of emotion knowledge but can only reconstruct their clients' emotions by thinking about them are much less successful in putting words to what their clients are experiencing. Hence my suspicion that alexithymia is a consequence of being emotionally offline and therefore failing to benefit from discussing shared emotions with carers.

Similarly people with an ASD who are not connected to the interbrain are also emotionally offline and have emotions that are hidden from other people, just as Sophie's and Steve's anxiety was. So other people cannot teach them the right words for these emotions either. Feeling the same emotions as someone with an ASD may be particularly difficult for others because those emotions may be strongly vested in objects or events that neurotypicals take to be emotionally neutral. For example, the twice a year shift into, and out of, British Summer Time can be a chore and can even be unsettling for many people, but rarely leads to suicidal despair. It did however for one person with an ASD who threw himself into his local river. Jolyon's given reason was that every time a watch is changed an hour forwards or back its mechanism is a little bit damaged. This seemed to this man an unfair and unnecessary punishment to useful hard working objects like watches. A therapist like myself naturally expects that there may be more to it than this, and I do. I think that Jolyon felt he was a kind of watch, or mechanically regulated object himself. I think that he thought that society's cavalier attitude to its horological servants was the same as its attitude to him, and this made him despair.

Persuasiveness and impact

The philosopher and economist Adam Smith tried to rescue his belief in what we would now call the free market by suggesting that the power that it gave to the strong over the weak was curtailed by the sympathy that existed between people. We would now term this 'empathy' rather than sympathy, but some people might still agree with Smith that empathy is what prevents us from acting to further our own ends at the expense of other people. Empathy, many modern commentators believe, prevents us from being violent towards others even when violence would gain us something that we might otherwise want.

Adam Smith and his friend David Hume thought that sympathy resulted from fellow feeling, and this remains the view of many experts, though they would use different terms and say rather that emotional contagion is the basis of empathy. Fellow feeling—emotional contagion—is automatic, from brain to brain. It is thus, in my terms, an interbrain phenomenon. Disconnection from the interbrain in people with an ASD might be expected to reduce or even prevent emotional contagion, and therefore to reduce empathy, and the evidence suggests that it does. In people with an atypical ASD, emotional contagion may work to produce empathy for a person who is present, but, as I have argued, becomes aetiolated when a person is absent.[58] People with dementia or a right sided stroke may also lose their ability to empathize and also become socially impaired.[59]

Some of the most distressing aspects of dementia for carers are the aggressive outbursts and the lack of restraint by the feelings of others. These can be upsetting aspects of ASD, too. But the worst effects of a lack of empathy fall on the person who lacks the empathy themselves, in that we need empathy to know how to negotiate effectively with other people.

I sometimes say to people with an ASD that they lack the kind of skill that is so abundantly possessed by a successful double glazing salesman. Selling door to door has to be one of the most challenging, and dispiriting, social encounters. A salesman has to read his mark's facial expressions, know when to be forceful ('You've kept me all this time, when I could have been selling to someone else, and now you're not going to buy *anything*...'), when to be reassuring ('You need put no money down now...'), when to be rational ('It's been tested by an independent consumer organization...'), and when to be emotional ('Won't it be wonderful to have some extra time just to put your feet up...'), and so on. Salesmen may go to selling school to learn their techniques, but I suspect that really good salespeople use their excellent connection to the interbrain and are automatically guided by the principles of emotional equilibration described above. They just need to keep in mind that their mark has to be receptive, and to focus themselves on being determined to make a sale without any compunction.

International diplomats need the same skills, and the same focus on an ultimate goal, although in their case it is a signed agreement. However, diplomats and salespeople are not the only ones who have to do this. In every playground or family, people are exercising similar skills to persuade their friends to go to a late night French film rather than a blockbuster, that having a boyfriend does not mean having sex, or that Dad needs to upgrade the pocket money.

Success in these negotiations requires a single minded focus on the intended goal, plus skill in social interaction. Focus on the goal requires confidence and a belief that one is right, and that may be reduced by a lack of confidence. The nuts and bolts of the negotiation, giving in when it is appropriate and pushing when it is possible, are the result of empathy and a connection to the interbrain. People with ASD and others who lack empathy cannot do this so well, and so often lose out in these discussions. This becomes a particular problem in early adolescence when anything worth doing is done in a group. Unless one can influence activity of the group, one ends up just going along with everyone else, but even this requires a social skill. Followers need to indicate an active involvement in what their group is doing to maintain their position or risk getting dumped out of the group. And this is what almost always happens to people with an ASD unless they are willing to occupy an interesting if deviant position like the clown, or the butt of the jokes, or the risk taker, someone who can always be cadged into giving money.

Being marginalized

Many people with an ASD experience increasing marginalization in early adolescence. One reason for this is an unwitting lack of conformity with dress, taste in music, or other identifiers of the group. But a major reason, in my clinical experience, is a lack of empathy. People who are dumped out of the groups that they see around them feel powerless and they dream of having an impact on other people. People who are severely affected by ASD may have their impact through aggression. This may be rewarding because it does create such a strong reaction, which is easily interpreted even by the person with severe ASD. The aggression may take a shocking form, with attacks being sudden, upsetting (biting or hitting someone's breasts), and apparently unprovoked. Vulnerable people may be targeted selectively. More able people may find more far reaching ways of having an impact.

Celine used to go to her local shopping mall and stand at an intersection between two long, echoing lanes, and scream, and scream. Richard was so disruptive at school that he was sent to a semi-secure hostel. On his first night there, he spotted a coat in the staff cloakroom which had a bulging pocket. In the middle of the night, he went downstairs and stole the keys and was gratified to find that he had stolen the only copy of the hostel master key which opened all the doors. He was adamant that he would not tell the staff where he put them. Donald rang his favourite aunt to tell her that her husband had been killed in a traffic accident when, in fact, he was just delayed at work.

And so on.

These are instrumental ways of dealing with the world, ways that one might adopt if one was kept in a cage by aliens. Anything in that situation to upset one's captors, one might think. Being disconnected from the interbrain must be, I think, a bit like being amongst aliens and a bit like being in a cage.

Making an identity

The philosopher Heidegger devoted his life to the consideration of what being human entails. One aspect of human being was, he thought, transcendental or, as he considered it, ontological. But another aspect was ontic, or being thrown into the world of other beings. In fact, he thought that the starting point for any discussion of humanity was 'Dasein', or being there, and one aspect of Dasein was being in a social world with others (Mitsein).

Because we are thrown into the world, we are imbued with particular circumstances of biology and culture. Heidegger thought that we are able to free ourselves of these, though, by an act of perception in which we see ourselves authentically. Sartre also thought that we could have a kind of being which was beyond our actual circumstances, which gives rise to being in itself, which he calls being for itself.

These ideas are immensely seductive in a world where, on one hand, individuality is highly valued and on the other we are increasingly interdependent.

Most people on meeting someone for the first time, at a party for example, are not so direct that they say, 'Tell me what sort of person you are', but a lot of the initial conversation has that as its underlying theme. In these circumstances people do say something about themselves, something about their identity as we might say. When identifying themselves, people rarely comment on their freedoms or choices, but instead comment on what Heidegger might call their thrown-ness. They describe their occupation, or their family, or, if the gathering merits it, their hobbies, interests or beliefs. After a few glasses of something intoxicating, they may also describe their hopes or intentions. If they are talking to an advertising executive, these would be distressingly familiar since most of us share such concerns with other people in our income band, a fact that advertisers know and exploit when they plan advertising campaigns.

So although many of us aspire to the kind of freedom that existentialist writers extolled, we rarely live in this way: in fact, it may only be at moments of crisis that we do have real choices to make. Our lives, our hopes, our choice of university, our preferred family size, what we call our children, all of these are shaped by others. Not that there is often one specific influence, only a general field of influences, a field that corresponds to the kind of influence that the interbrain exerts on us (if I am right about the interbrain) rather than the kind of influence that comes from something we take in consciously as we might a philosophy or a sermon.

Because our identity is shaped in this way, we may never have to consider what kind of person we are, or what we are fit for. People with an ASD, who are not connected to the interbrain, do ask themselves these questions. I am going to argue in this section that this is because they struggle with their identity and that the reason that they struggle is precisely because they are not connected to the interbrain.

It may seem strange to argue that people with an ASD are highly individual and yet struggle with a lack of identity. One simple explanation is that identity is not just something that a person adopts. It is conferred. There is an aspect of identity that is socially prescribed. So far as the Government is concerned, my national insurance number is one important mark of my identity. Even in my family or my work, my identity is tied up with my role, the part I have been asked to play. A person with an ASD may have a very small role assigned to them, if any. So their life style may not be so constrained, but yet they may also lack one of the building blocks of identity. They would for example lack the first rejoinder at a party to the challenge, 'And so who are you?' to which most of us would answer with our role—'I'm mein Host' or 'I'm a receptionist in the office'.

There is a more radical reason that a person with an ASD lacks an identity. To understand this we need to look more closely at the identity that we create rather than the identity that society confers on us. To fall back on the metaphor of the theatre, if living is like playing a role on stage, we can choose to play that role, like actors in Japan or ancient Rome, wearing a mask. In ancient Rome this was called a persona, hence our modern terms 'person' and 'personality'. A persona may conceal our private identity, but all actors know that some of their performances get audience approval and others don't. Gradually, whatever persona we choose to adopt, we are pressured into adopting only those roles that get this approval. So although we can choose our roles, and we can adopt a persona, we find ourselves pushed towards particular roles and towards adopting particular personae that go with them, by the reaction of our audience. On the stage, this may lead to actors getting typecast. So strongly identified do some actors get with their roles that one wonders to what extent these types actually become the identity of the actors who play them. Reverting from the metaphor to everyday living, it would seem that identity might also be shaped by other people's reactions to our self-presentations, with some being effective and others getting us nowhere. These reactions are not like the considered opinions of the critics the day after. They are spontaneous automatic responses which are rarely consciously formulated. They are predominantly nonverbal responses to the nonverbal, or at least non-verbalized, elements of our social performance. They are, as I would say, mediated by the interbrain.

The greatest actors do not get typecast. They are able to change their identity to suit the part, and the public seems to accept this because the identity of the actor him- or herself does not shine through.

'It is almost as if she can become a different person', people say. Actors who are able to do this notoriously pay a high price in their private lives. It seems as if they often do not know who they really are when they are off the stage.

People with an ASD who are disconnected from the interbrain face a similar problem. They do not get shaped by social feedback. Like someone playing to an empty theatre, they are left unsure of how they come across or what sort of actor they are. So, as so often, people with an ASD fall back on their conscious selves, and adopt an identity semi-deliberately.

Interests or hobbies can often be important here. Whereas a parent may often introduce their son or daughter as being at university, or preparing for examinations, or having just qualified as something, parents of people with an ASD will often introduce their child as having an interest. For example, Mr and Mrs Smith introduced their son Conrad to me in the following way: 'Thank you for seeing us, Doctor. [turning to Conrad: Did you tell the doctor about your interest in birthdays? [turning to me] He's amazing, Doctor. He can remember everyone's birthday. Did he ask you yours? He can work out which day you were born on, like lightning. He's so intelligent.'

Less able people with an ASD may hang on to their identity through rituals, or through the clothes that they wear and are very unwilling to vary. Identity can be invested in places and objects, too. More able people with an ASD may adopt beliefs or attitudes as the corner stone of their identities. Unlike the beliefs of most neurotypical adults, these are often not nuanced and so come across as extreme or unconditional. They may be liberal or right wing, religious or atheistic, but they are typically held with conviction and provide justification for many of the activities of the person with an ASD.

On closer enquiry the beliefs, or the rituals, are quite often acquired from someone else. Many people with an ASD who memorized top 20 lists of popular music, or collect CDs of popular music, are most interested in the music that was popular when their mother was young, rather than the music of today. Other people may acquire their interests or beliefs from an admired relative. Some people with an ASD identify with other people that they consider that society has also rejected. These may include notorious murderers. One of the attractive aspects of murderers may be that they had the power to fight back, at least so far as the person with an ASD may perceive it. Other powerful figures can also provide an identification. American wrestlers are popular in this respect.

One contributor to our sense of our own identity is our sexual identity. Some people with an ASD seem to have none, and even after puberty, suppress their sexual interest in others. Other people with an ASD may pick up elements of previous experience and fabricate them into a sexual identity. Sexual fetishes—a sexual preoccupation with an object, or on an activity not normally associated with sexual consummation—may be one way of doing this. Some of these fetishes are not uncommon in the neurotypical population. Examples that people with an ASD have told me about include wearing nappies; a sexual interest in urine or faeces and in urination and defaecation; talking to women about private bodily functions; and a fascination with hair, particularly blond hair. Some fetishes are more unusual: one that stands out is getting excited thinking about a dress shirt being torn. Many of these fetishes are based on personal experience which has become elaborated.

My image for the function of sexual fetishes, hobbies, unusual dress, speaking in a foreign accent, or other kinds of adopted identifiers is that they serve as a protective coating. Like the caddis fly, whose pupa lacks the thick skin of its cousins and who therefore coats itself with small stones or other detritus that it finds around it in the pond, people with Asperger syndrome who are changing into adulthood need an identity to protect them and make one from what is available around them.

Thinking differently

Much of the research in ASD recently has focussed on cognition, and many of the current theories about the fundamental impairment in ASD are cognitive ones. What I have considered so far has turned around the emotional consequences of having an ASD. A reader might therefore be forgiven for concluding that I have not been looking at the fundamental handicap of ASD at all, but at some kind of consequence of the fundamental problem in cognition.

I have previously argued that there is strong evidence for infants who go on to get a diagnosis of an ASD showing a different style of nonverbal communication early in life. Even at a few weeks old, many such infants seem socially cut off. This suggests that social disconnection—what I would call a failure to connect to the interbrain—precedes any overt cognitive impairment. But there is something unsatisfactory in this, in that it would seem that it is necessary to posit two impairments in an ASD, the interbrain disconnect one that I have been putting forward and a cognitive one. This may not be a problem when autistic disorder is considered, as that is often associated with an additional language impairment. It could be argued that it is the language impairment, and not the offline status, that leads to the cognitive problems. This might explain some aspects of theory of mind, as I noted in a previous chapter, but not all of them.

There are intriguing interactions between movements and cognition, which might explain why people with an ASD who are also clumsy have some cognitive deficits. Many of the movements that assist cognition can also be used as gestures. Putting the tip of the tongue between the teeth is a common gesture of children and of highly engaged or disinhibited adults who are undertaking a difficult task involving insertion. It may be seen when someone is threading a needle, or driving their car through a narrow gap.

It is obvious that there is a spatial similarity between inserting the tongue between the lips, and passing a thread through an orifice. It is possible that the tongue and the lips are a model of the thread and the eye of the needle, and that the tongue movements are translated into hand movements. If this is so, then one can suppose that the person faced with this complex task concentrates on moving their tongue rather than their hands, assuming that the tongue is a kind of joy-stick, whose movements will be translated into the appropriate movements of the hands holding the thread or the steering wheel.

Sticking out one's tongue is not the only gesture that influences cognition.[60] Hand gestures, too, assist in cognitive tasks. One study found that subjects allowed to use hand gestures were more able to give the correct word corresponding to a definition than subjects whose hands were restricted. The former were also able to recall these words better when retested later. Interestingly, the tongue entered indirectly into this study, too, as hand gestures assisted subjects most to recall words which were on the 'tip of their tongue' (Frick-Horbury and Guttentag, 1998).

It feels right that gesturing to oneself can assist one with thinking, but this cannot account for what Uta Frith calls weak central coherence. Yet the phenomenon of 'not seeing the wood for the trees', a manifestation of weak central coherence, is a common and easily identifiable characteristic of ASD thinking. The weak central coherence theory cannot be dismissed lightly. Many carers and people with an ASD themselves are aware of their difficulties in seeing the wood for the trees. People with an ASD are at home with details, with facts, or with objects, and may be floored with the bottom line, or the overall trend, or the theme of an assemblage. For my interbrain hypothesis to be credible it has to explain why people with an ASD have such difficulty with the abstractions that neurotypicals of less intelligence find so obvious.

One possible explanation was given in the last chapter. Perhaps the common neurological problem that everyone with an ASD has is a relative lack of interconnectedness between neurones and populations of neurones. Abstract words are considered to be those words which link clusters of labels. So 'bat', 'pad', 'stump' are all words that label things, and in word association tests they are each likely to be followed by the word 'cricket'. Higher abstractions like 'sport' are associations of words like 'cricket', 'football', 'hockey', and so on which are each associations from labels.

Labels are also linked together with similar words. 'Bat' might be linked with the similar word 'racket', but also with the homonymous word 'bat' and through that to 'bird', 'mouse', and so on. All of these associations are thought to correspond in the brain to connections. So if there are relatively fewer connections, as there may be in the brains of people with an ASD, perhaps there will be fewer associations with abstract words.[61]

This explanation makes many assumptions. It does not seem fully satisfactory to me, either, because it assumes that word associations are created in the same way that they are stored, by learning words like 'bat' and 'stump' first and then learning that these are terms associated with 'cricket'. But the way that one learns words is as part of a social practice. A child sees people doing something strange and says to someone, 'What are they doing?' and then someone says, 'They're playing cricket'. Many children might say, 'What's cricket?' but instead of being given a definition in specific terms, the child may be given an even more abstract explanation, for example, 'It's a kind of game'. Children learn the word 'game' because they interact in a certain way with mother or father, and then in a certain way with other children, and each of these instances involve the label 'game'. Mother might say, 'That was a good game, wasn't it?' or 'Did you have a nice game with John?' What is the common feature of these social practices is not explicit, but implicit. It is a quality of the interbrain connection. This quality is given by the level of smiling, and arousal; by the intensity of the interaction, by waiting expectantly followed by rapid action, and so on. As soon as we attempt a definition, it escapes us but we know what it feels like on the interbrain when we are playing. That's how we can understand when mother calls 'peek a boo' a game, and then uses the same word when she runs after us in the shop and says, a bit frostily, 'That was a nice game you played there'.

Mother, when she is playing a game, entrains me via the interbrain into the game playing state of mind and once I have mastery of this, I can entrain others. It is this state of mind that I can use to identify an activity as a game. Sometimes I get it wrong, and mother says, 'This is not a game. I am serious'. At these moments I am probably working hard to entrain her into the game playing mode but she is resisting. I would not be having to try hard if the interbrain connection was established because mother's and my state of mind would be coupled. So mother is right: it is not a game when I have to try to make it into a game.

If mother pays particular attention to games, I might learn to pay attention too, and will pay attention as well to contexts in which the word game is used. I will quickly extend my use of the term to these contexts so long as I can recognize myself in them. For example some infants will refer to playing a trick on someone as 'playing a game with them' if they have come across 'game' used in contexts of competition by fair means, or foul. Children learning a motor skill from adults may be so linked to them via the interbrain (as I would put it)—one might also say caught up with, or identified with—that they may, wrongly, believe that it is they who performed some action and not the adult. Children who are more likely to do this also learn more (Sommerville and Hammond, 2007).

I would argue that an interbrain connection is required for me to learn abstractions like 'game' and that having an ASD might inhibit me learning abstractions of a similar kind because I would have to learn them the roundabout way, not through experiencing instances of them with others, but by learning definitions. It is consistent with this that children with an ASD may ask many questions, often about things that their parents think are 'obvious'—for example, 'Why is the sky blue?' Neurotypical children might learn the word 'sky' because when their mother looks up at the sky, and it happens to be a lovely day (perhaps that is why she is looking at it), the neurotypical child mirrors her and looks up at the sky, too. So when mother says, 'Isn't the sky blue?' the child understands that what they are looking at together is 'sky'.[62] Mother's tone of voice at that moment is likely to be calm, contented even. Nothing to make her child curious or worried. And so the question, 'But why is the sky blue?' does not arise. A child with an ASD, when mother looks up at the sky, is not likely to have either noticed or to follow her gaze. Mother, seeing this, is unlikely to say, 'Isn't the sky blue?' because that presupposes a shared experience. A person with an ASD is more likely to acquire the word 'sky' by asking what it means. This is a difficult question for a mother to answer, indeed anyone to answer, because the answer is it's what you see when you look up, out of doors. So many mothers might say, 'It's the name for all that blue right up high above the buildings and the trees'. It would be natural for a child to ask, 'Why is the sky blue?' because mother had just used it in her definition.[63]

As it happens, asking 'Why is the sky blue?' is a very good question, in that answering it requires knowing that there is an atmosphere, that white light can be split into colours by reflection or differential absorption, and that blue light is the most energetic radiation in the visible spectrum. So not taking things for granted, asking original questions, testing assumptions, and all of the other characteristics of the thought of many people with an ASD can be of considerable social value, as Hans Asperger himself pointed out. Maybe it is for that reason that Simon Baron-Cohen has found that people with an ASD seem to be drawn to science and engineering.

People with an ASD cannot be fobbed off with an answer like, 'It just is'. They persevere until they have an answer that fits with their explicit theory of how the world should be. This persistence may be of value in scientific exploration, but it can be frustrating to people in an informal setting, where it can turn into the repetitive questioning that parents dread. 'It just is' is an answer that relates to a social practice, too. 'Why are there three stumps, and not four, Dad?' or 'Why do I have to go down the snake and up the ladder, and not up the snake?' are questions that can only be understood in the context of knowing that arbitrary rules are part of the essence of games as a social practice. 'Why can you only walk on the top of the wall, Tommy, and not the pavement?' many parents have probably said, in one variant or another. Tommy's answer will usually be the same, too. 'It's part of my game, Mummy. I want to see if I can do it.'

Terminating enquiry with 'It just is' is bad science, but may be good living. 'Will Daddy bring sweets tonight?' many a child must have asked, and many mothers will have replied, 'We'll just have to see'. The real answer will be in the tone of voice, and the comfort or discomfort that comes over the interbrain. If the answer 'We'll just have to see' is associated often enough with comfort, then that answer becomes comforting. As the child gets older, mother might say, 'Worrying about it won't get Daddy home any earlier'. Again, if said in a comforting but not scolding way, that too might become a comforting answer.

Later in life, feeling a relief of discomfort by saying to oneself 'Worrying about it won't make it happen' becomes an important el-ement in what has been called 'emotional processing' of worries as compared to 'intellectual processing'. Worries are just one instance of repetitive thinking that cannot be solved by coming to an intellectual conclusion. Worrying about whether or not one's daughter will be OK out on her first date can be assuaged a bit by intellectual processing, for example by saying to oneself, 'She's a very sensible girl and she knows not to take risks'. But this is only a weak obstacle to worry and easily pushed aside by alarms like, 'There's always a first time' or 'I have no idea what sort of boy he is really'.

Worry of this kind responds best to either distraction or to emotional processing, for example saying to oneself, 'She's got to do what she had to do' or 'I just have to remember that I was young once'.

People with an ASD find comments like these derisory. They mean nothing. So when they are confronted with repetitive thoughts, which many are, frequently, only intellectual processing will do. The repetitive thoughts are often about the past, turning on whether or not someone had been fair to act the way that they did, or whether they had really meant what they said. Parents react to these with emotional processing appeals like, 'It's so long ago', 'It's all in the past', 'What's done is done' and so on. People with an ASD find these statements meaningless tautologies, as indeed they are. But they compose a great deal of everyday conversation, or chat, and in this context play an important role in emotional regulation in the group.

Not being able to use clichés in this way is what so often defeats people with an ASD about socializing. The price that many people with an ASD pay for their originality of scientific thinking is not being able to go with the flow in everyday life. Even in science, this may prove a handicap. There are few scientists who use words purely to denote facts. Like the rest of us, the connotations of words are also important. When someone in a seminar responds to an ingenious theory (about the interbrain for example) by saying 'That's hardly falsifiable' they can expect that they have weakened and possibly destroyed the likelihood that anyone will take the hypothesis seriously. How? By invoking a test that a highly influential philosopher of science, Karl Popper, said was the acid test of a science. Only hypotheses which could be tested and found false could be included in the canon of science. To put forward a nonfalsifiable hypothesis is not to be talking science at all, and so the rejoinder in the seminar, whilst making no comment on the value of the idea, tried to rule it out of court.

CHAPTER 7

*N*onverbal communication as a tool to understanding and moving forward

I and my colleagues in the Sheffield Asperger Assessment Service often ask parents and people with an autistic spectrum disorder (ASD) to tell us about the plus or minus side of their contact with this clinic within the UK National Health Service, on one occasion surveying over 70 past users of the service to get a more representative picture. We were surprised to find that diagnosis continues to be the single most valued intervention.

The child is the father to the man, says the proverb. This is usually interpreted by developmental psychologists to mean that our thinking, feeling, and acting as adults are all based on tendencies and patterns that have been established in childhood. In fact, developmental psychologists once went further than this, arguing that if some skills were not established during a critical period in childhood, they were never established at all. Language development was one of these.[64]

Critical periods are no longer seen as quite so hard and fast but there remains agreement that putting time and effort into helping a 'nonverbal' child with an ASD to speak is justified, but putting the same effort, or at least the same effort in the same direction, into helping an adult is much less likely to be crowned with success, and therefore less justifiable. This is because it does seem as if the brain's ability to support speech and language dwindles if it is not used for this purpose, even if there is no specific 'critical period'.

Nonverbal communication, and our connection to the interbrain, is not time limited in the same way. Clinical evidence suggests that a significant number of children with an ASD do develop the capacity to make an interbrain connection as they get older, and some of their ASD symptoms then disappear. It seems likely that the bandwidth of that connection remains restricted because later crises requiring substantial social or psychological adjustment may disclose the symptoms of an ASD again. But many, perhaps most, people with an ASD do not recover. In this chapter, I will consider what they can do, and what others can do for them, that will minimize the adverse effects of ASD on their lives.

Having a diagnosis

There are very few people with an ASD in whom the condition can be treated. Some people with epilepsy and ASD may show improvement in both conditions with effective treatment for the epilepsy, although this is only in a minority of cases. Diagnoses cannot be confirmed by any particular investigations. So the usual justifications for a medical diagnosis—investigations and treatment—do not apply.

We have become accustomed to medical diagnoses being considered 'mere labels' of which we should be suspicious. According to some, they are just means of extending doctors', or drug companies', hegemony over new territories. Is the fact that some women do not have an orgasm a medical problem? Giving it the name of 'female orgasmic disorder' and prescribing the same drug that is used for male impotence seems to make it so. Some would argue that this does a disservice to women. Not having an orgasm may be a reflection of dissatisfaction with one's partner, and being made into a medical condition may cover this up. Another argument against diagnosis is that the diagnostic process may be unreliable, with some doctors freely making diagnoses using one set of criteria and others, just as freely, concluding on the basis of other criteria that no diagnosis applies. This is especially a problem when there is no diagnostic test, as there is not in ASD, independent of the doctor's or psychologist's own judgement and experience. Some people argue that the apparent increase in the prevalence of ASD is due to doctors and psychologists using less and less strict criteria to diagnose it.

Other critics point to the potential harmful effects of diagnosis. 'Labelling theorists' argued that diagnosis changed other people's social expectations leading to an increasing vilification of the diagnosed person, and the development of 'secondary deviance'. Some even argued that the label could bring about the condition being labelled, a self-fulfilling prophecy. There is little evidence for this, but it has left a persistent mark on health and educational services for children. Professionals are often reluctant to 'label' children. They may cite the argument that every child is different, so singling out one child is inappropriate. They may also argue that the UK is a signatory to the Salamanca declaration which asserts that it is every child's right to a 'normal' education in their local school. If the child is anyway going to the local school, what is the value in saddling them with a label, or so goes the argument. Children's self-confidence may be easily blunted. So some would argue that giving a child a diagnosis might worsen this by making the child out to be 'damaged'. Finally, disability activists may argue that a diagnosis like one of the ASDs simply asserts that someone is disabled, and that is questionable. Is it that the person with an ASD is disabled, they would argue, or that society does not enable them?

None of these criticisms are completely unjustified, but they do not apply to every diagnosis. As I shall argue, diagnosis is of most value when it is seen as enabling and empowering, and not disabling and disempowering.

It is my practice only to make a diagnosis if the person him- or herself requests one (whether it is an ASD diagnosis or not) or if someone else who is legitimately acting as their next friend requests one. There are some difficult marginal situations when a carer desperately wants a diagnosis, and my patient denies that there is any sort of problem. I try to deal with this by addressing the patient's fears about a diagnosis. But if they are Gillick competent, I do not make a diagnosis if they are sure that having a diagnosis would be unhelpful.

Getting a diagnosis can also be seen by some people as a way of getting excused from bad behaviour. Say, for instance, that Simon hits someone at school. Some people might respond to this, and to Simon, by saying that he's not to blame; that he has an ASD and because the school doesn't really understand his difficulties, it is not surprising that he lashed out.

This last example mixes up diagnosis and justification. Simon's lashing out may have been caused by his lack of other coping strategies when he is being bullied, or his lack of empathy for other people. But neither of these things amounts to a justification. We would need to enquire further about Simon's understanding. If he knows right from wrong, if he knows and understands in particular that aggression towards other people is wrong, then his aggression can not be fully justified because we expect that other human beings exercise self-control. There may be mitigating factors that would alter our way of responding to Simon, for example that he was provoked or that he had just found that he had to move to a new classroom, but none of these take away Simon's responsibility for his actions.

Focusing down on diagnosis

Despite all of these pitfalls and shortcomings in diagnosis, people with ASD in our Sheffield survey valued diagnosis above any other interventions and this is consistent with other surveys of people with an ASD and their carers.

Their position is much simpler than the critics would suggest. They want an explanation of why they are different from other people, and they want inappropriate blame to be removed from them. Note that I have used the term inappropriate. So this is not a means of getting excused or getting off something: it is a means of not being punished or blamed for something that is out of one's control.

Imagine that you are going deaf but that is not recognized. You start to turn up the television and people tell you that you are being inconsiderate. You start to mishear what people say, and think that they are being critical when they are not. You find that you are ringing up a helpline and can't hear what is being said, which makes you panic. You do not hear comments from your colleagues or your partner, and they think that you are becoming engrossed in yourself and ignoring them. You make stupid mistakes when you respond to things that you have half heard, and people say that you are losing it.

Having a diagnosis of deafness does not solve all of these problems. It may only lead to slight remediation with a hearing aid. But it removes the problem from a domain which requires justification to one in which explanation is sufficient. 'I'm sorry I sometimes mishear', the deaf person can say, 'but I'm getting really deaf'.

The deaf person has the responsibility of dealing with their deafness appropriately. Blaming others for not speaking loudly enough, losing one's temper with frustration, or slipping into a general suspiciousness of everyone are not caused by the deafness, but are unhelpful reactions to it. They may sometimes seem partly justified by the novelty or severity of deafness, but deafness does not fully justify them.

Deafness is a major impediment to dialogue with others, and so it is not so different from the low bandwidth interbrain connection that I believe is the core impairment in the ASDs.

Getting a diagnosis right

Most of us have the experience of 'clicking' or 'meshing' with someone else. It's one consequence of a good interbrain connection. People with an ASD rarely report having that experience, again because of their low bandwidth connection. Instead they feel different, stuck behind a glass pane, not connected, left out. Getting a diagnosis correct is often experienced by people with an ASD as a kind of clicking with a problem that has been baffling and inchoate. Getting a diagnosis right means that the person being diagnosed feels recognized and understood, and not diminished or rejected.

The reason for this is that just giving a label is not enough. There needs to be an explanation of why the label has been given, what aspects of a person's difficulties it illuminates, along with an opportunity to clarify and fine tune this 'formulation', as it is sometimes called in psychiatry.

Most importantly a diagnosis needs to provide a new way of dealing with old problems. The importance of nonverbal communication is not sufficiently known by either professionals or the public for it to be recognized very often as the vital medium of social interchange, of interbrain connection, that it is. Once a person with an ASD and their carers begin to see how so many apparently disconnected problems come together as being consequences of impaired nonverbal communication, there is often a sense of having finally got a problem to deal with.

I think that ASD will become more easily recognized and its disability kept to a minimum once there is as much recognition of the importance of the interbrain for both cognition and emotion as there is currently for the importance of language. In fact, this has been my motive in writing this book.

Moving forward

Sandra was seven and had come to see me because her parents suspected that she had Asperger syndrome. I agreed with them, but what they also wanted to know was how much further improvement could be expected. Sandra had hardly spoken or interacted at all, they said, when she was little but then they had bought a Labrador, a bitch that they had called Honey. Honey had the intense Labrador wish for social contact and would not take 'no' for an answer. She wanted recognition from Sandra as from any other member of the family and so constantly requested it over weeks, that Sandra began to look at her, and then to pet her. It was some time before Sandra looked at other members of the family, but this did gradually follow. If only, Sandra's parents said, more people could have Honey therapy.

Honey had overcome Sandra's social withdrawal and apparent aversion to social contact, but had she done that by establishing an interbrain connection? The latter seems unlikely since the evidence is that even the great apes, our near cousins, cannot read human nonverbal signs well enough to be able to use them in solving a task (Tomasello and Carpenter, 2007). So a dog is even less likely to be interbraining with a human.

Other mothers have told me of their determination to get the attention of their autistic child, even to the extent of spending minutes at the beginning of any interaction with the child doing nothing but staring at the child until they felt the child's gaze on them. Martha Welch, a New York psychiatrist, developed 'holding therapy', in which mothers were taught to hold their children tightly, but safely, and stare at them until the child returned their gaze. I once observed a session of this, and it was clearly extremely aversive for the child—who was one of the many people with ASD who find other people's touch unpleasant—but the change in the child when gaze was finally returned was dramatic, almost if, as its proponents claimed, the ASD had temporarily disappeared. Holding therapy was given up because it was clearly so distressing to the child. But many mothers believed that the distress was worth it because of the improvement that the child had made.

If holding was not curing ASD, as its proponents hoped, was it simply doing nothing? Were people being duped? Over the years there have been repeated claims of cures for autism, with individuals or small groups of people making dramatic improvements. The interventions have ranged from vitamins, hormones (most recently a hormone active in the gall-bladder, secretin), sensory integration training, psychotropic medication, psychoanalytic treatment, behavioural treatment, and special educational methods. How can these dramatic improvements to these very diverse interventions be explained?

It is quite possible that there are some charlatans. It is also, regrettably, the case that interventions which start full of promise when applied to larger groups begin to fail, and this can lead to their over-application, and ultimately abuse. But none of this would explain the constancy of the reports of dramatic improvements when something new comes along in the hands of a committed and dedicated innovator.

I have argued that people with an ASD have different brains and that, as a result, they do not connect reliably to the interbrain. Putting this less controversially, I think that people with an ASD all have an impairment of their nonverbal communication which arises from a difference in brain structure (probably) or neurochemistry (possibly). It seems unlikely that these can be reversed by a few months of intervention. (Note that I am not arguing that they cannot be reversed at all, ever. I will consider evidence later in this chapter that suggests that a much higher proportion of people recover from an ASD than most of us would expect.)

So if there can be improvements, sometimes dramatic ones, what is happening? Before answering this, it is important to consider the dramatic deteriorations that occur in ASD, too. Take Fiona for example. She had mild learning difficulties and autism. She went to a special school, where she did well. She lived at home with very supportive parents, but was approaching the point where they wondered if she would be able to manage to live alone with support. She could do simple food shopping independently and could use the bus on her own, once she was familiar with the route. After leaving school, Fiona went to a day centre where she got on well, but then had to move because it was closing. After a few weeks at the second day centre, Fiona changed completely. She became withdrawn and her self-care deteriorated. Over several months she spoke less and less, and was only using a few words when I met her. There were times when she became agitated, and had on occasions bit staff at the day centre when she was approached at one of these times. Eventually her parents were told that she could not stay there any longer. Some years later, her parents discovered that a carer at the day centre had been arrested for abusing one of the attendees and they wondered if Fiona, too, had been sexually abused by this person. Fiona herself by this time was hardly using language communicatively and it was impossible to find out for sure.

There was no evidence that Fiona had developed a neurological disorder. Fiona's deterioration is unlikely to have been the consequence of a structural change in her brain. Occasionally people with an ASD do develop schizophrenia in adolescence although no more frequently than do adolescents without an ASD. Schizophrenia is probably a kind of subtle neurological disorder when it develops like that, and the deterioration that it produces is not traumatic. But Fiona had not developed schizophrenia, and the most likely explanation of her deterioration is that it was a kind of psychological trauma but expressed not as a new problem, separate to her ASD, but as a worsening of the ASD symptoms themselves.

We all of us have habits or difficulties which can get worse under stress. People with an ASD are like this, too. Someone with an ASD who has rituals will often spend more time on their rituals, or become more upset if their rituals are interrupted when they are stressed than when they are not. Fiona did not get mildly worse, in proportion to the stress that she was under, but shifted from one level of adjustment to another, from high to low functioning.

There may be other causes of deterioration than trauma, just as there are many causes of dramatic improvement apparently. The important message of Fiona's experience is not that trauma or any other specific psychological stress or intervention makes a particular contribution to ASD, but that events which have a psychological effect can cause step changes, either of improvement or deterioration, in social impairment. My own belief, based on examples such as those given above, is that the social impairment caused by an ASD is a consequence of a poor connection to the interbrain but also a consequence of how much demand is placed on what interbrain connection there is.

Honey did not need any interbrain connection to interact with Sandra. She was going to do that anyway. With a human being, even if Sandra's responses were faint or intermittent, they would still have had to be of the appropriate form, to hand-shake with the interbrain. Not with Honey. Honey reacted enthusiastically to any of Sandra's responses however idiosyncratic they were.

I don't know what Fiona experienced, but if she was indeed abused and given that she had such loving parents up until then, one might suppose that her previous expectation of being able to communicate her feelings via the interbrain was sharply disconfirmed. Perhaps this would have been enough to have produced the withdrawal and regression that then occurred. Something similar does occur to severely neglected children, whose communicative overtures are met with no response or with anger. Fiona will not have received repeated and prolonged unresponsiveness the way that some Romanian orphans have. So we have additionally to suppose that an already jeopardized interbrain connection can be weakened further by empathy failures which might not damage a neurotypical's interbrain connection and, conversely, that strengthening an interbrain connection requires more than ordinary and more than ordinarily persistent efforts of the part of others already on the interbrain.

'Catastrophe theory' is the name for the study of systems in which progressive changes in a variable produce negligible alteration in the system up to a certain point ('the cusp') but then a further small change in that variable causes a substantial alteration, or 'catastrophe'. What I am putting forward is a two variable catastrophic theory of social impairment, with one variable being the efficiency of interbrain connectedness and the other being the 'load' placed on the interbrain connection by social demand. I considered 'load' in the previous chapter, although not in this way. I covered the most salient consequences of an impairment of the interbrain, but we can put what I said there on its head, and treat that chapter as a description of the social demands that place the most load on the interbrain connection. So, if my argument is correct, people with an ASD who are bullied would be at risk of catastrophic social deterioration. My clinical experience supports this. People with an ASD whose identity is challenged would be at risk, too, and this is also my clinical experience.

Reducing interbrain demands

You are used to an excellent broadband connection, and suddenly you are back to using a modem, probably going at 1/50th the speed. What do you do? At first, if you are like me, you try to carry on as before and get increasingly frustrated. Then you start to think what you absolutely require your internet access for. Perhaps you start getting your emails only once, instead of several times, a day. You avoid surfing and, when you do, you turn off the images. You do not perform any large downloads or uploads unless these are essential. You might use alternative methods of getting information into your computer, like transferring files by memory stick rather than by email. And, of course, you try to do as much as possible offline.

Does reverting to a modem when you are used to broadband provide any useful analogies for helping people with an ASD whose connection to the interbrain is limited? Reducing the calls on interbrain connections obviously does. People with an ASD rely on receiving information explicitly, just as I might hand a memory stick to someone and say, 'The file you want is…', instead of sending an email with an attachment. We do not trust information that is really important to email attachments normally in any case because we cannot be sure that the person has received them. If we do use this method, we ask for a confirmation that the file has been read. So canny parents will normally give as much information explicitly to a child with an ASD rather than relying on it to be 'picked up' the way children often seem to do. Furthermore, they will ask some questions to check not just that the information has been received, but that it has been taken in.

People with an ASD will often wish for more time offline than most people want, spending time in their room or going for long walks. This is akin to not trying to use a modem connection except when it is essential rather than having it always running in the background, as one would with broadband. But modem connections are still of considerable utility if they are used selectively. By analogy, it is very important not to take a person with an ASD out of the loop of interbrain communication altogether. There should be some face-to-face contact, but it should be used strategically. Both people with an ASD and their carers (if they need carers) need to have some priorities for how the interbrain connection during face-to-face time will be used. If one were considering this in relation to a computer, the personal priorities of the user would be relevant. For a person who was a keen computer games player, downloading the latest game developments would be a priority. For someone else it might be emails, or new programs, or checking facts on Wikipedia. Deciding on how limited or effortful interbrain time should be used is therefore something that needs to be negotiated according to the values of the individuals concerned.

Connection to the internet might be essential for some aspects of work, too. Sharing an internet calendar might be a requirement for a work group, for example. So the involvement of a person with an ASD in domestic or work roles will need to be factored into the negotiations about how limited interbrain connection time should be used.

A person with an ASD who is a parent should spend time networking with their child. A person with an ASD who is a life partner owes it to the other person in the partnership to open themselves up to the other person's concerns and difficulties. Both of these demands do require interbraining. Many parents, and partners, consider that they are often called on to know what their child, or their partner, is thinking or feeling without them having to say. This is particularly challenging to a person with an ASD. It is challenging to all of us, sometimes. In fact, much of the time all that is required is to be receptive and to signal that receptiveness to the other person. In the counselling world, there is a well documented list of 'listening skills' that will indicate receptivity to another person. This includes looking at the other person, responding to what they say with interest, and showing that one has taken in what has been said, something that may be achievable simply by repeating the last few words of what one has been told.

Possibly the most important listening skill is, well, listening. That is, having time and not filling it up with one's own concerns, worries, or preoccupations. Interbraining is not required for this, only an interest in other people and a willingness to apply the rules of 'social exchange theory' which are that rewards should outweigh costs for a relationship to be stable. So a person with an ASD who wants other people to listen to them—a cost for the other person—needs to pay this back (or even better, pay it 'forward' or invest) by spending time listening to them.

Bandwidth

So far I have spoken of limiting the time spent interbraining. One reason for this is that many people with an ASD find connecting to other people's unspoken communications effortful, and that only a short time can be spent doing it before exhaustion supervenes.

The most important characteristic of an internet connection is not the time spent connected, but bandwidth. Bandwidth means how much information can be downloaded in unit time. Bandwidth is important because some of it is used to maintain the connection between local computer and remote computer, or server. If too much information is asked for simultaneously, the information about maintaining the connection can get lost and the connection gets broken or corrupted information is communicated.

Discrepant nonverbal communication takes up a lot of bandwidth because there is a low level of redundancy. Group situations often give rise to discrepancy because members of the group are feeling, thinking, and reacting in different ways. So one cannot afford just to concentrate on one person because their reactions can be taken as the standard of all of the others, which would be the case if there was a lot of redundant, or duplicated, information. There are exceptions. One is outrage. Some people with an ASD go through a phase, often in early adolescence, of saying or doing things that cause outrage in the people around them. One possible explanation for this is that this increases the redundancy in the communications around them and makes it easier for them to understand what is happening.

Another kind of discrepant, nonredundant communication is when people are trying to communicate several things at once. Facial expressions are often like this. We either blend different emotions into one expression—sad but resigned, for example, or angry and frightened—or we try to conceal or suppress an expression (really also a kind of blend, since an emotional expression is being blended with a neutral face). Typically, a person with an ASD will either fail to pick up the message altogether or will focus on just one element.

Discrepancy may also arise because facial expressions are discrepant with bodily postures, or with the content of what is being said. Such 'mixed messages' have been thought in the past to be so paralysing that they have been called 'double binds'. Mixed messages are challenging for everyone, and the evidence is that it is the negative element of the message, whether that is carried in the content of what is said, the facial expression, the tone of voice, or the attitude, that is the one we particularly notice.

Responding

Probably most people with a computer and an internet connection will have downloaded programs at some stage. Some downloads go like a dream. In fact, some just happen without us doing anything except confirming that we want to download an update. Others get interrupted by meaningless but threatening messages like 'Installing this module will change your registry. You are advised to set a restore point before you do this. Proceed?'

Some interbrain situations are like this, too. Someone suddenly collapsing into tears is a kind of demand for a response, as are questions like, 'You do still love me, don't you?' or 'We've done everything we can for you, haven't we?' Knowing how to respond to demands like this is something that comes from practice, and from watching other people deal with similar situations. It is not for the new user, who is just starting out to explore the internet. Similarly making these kinds of demands of someone who is not an experienced or confident interbrain user is likely to cause panic. We are much less aware of that because we assume that by the time a peer reaches adulthood, they have acquired a high level of interbraining skill and experience. But this will not be true of an adult with an ASD.

Asking for sympathy is one example of an interpersonal demand, but calling for a justification is much more common. Criticizing someone, being hostile or angry towards someone, calls for them to defend themselves and this means knowing how to do so effectively but not inappropriately.

The evoked emotion paradigm

People who suffer from schizophrenia may develop what is sometimes called a negative syndrome in which they seem to have comparable interbraining problems to people with an ASD. It has been shown that they are at risk of relapsing into acute illness if certain kinds of interpersonal demands are made of them, and these include the discrepant, nonredundant communications that I have just been describing.

Counselling carers of people with severe mental illness, such as schizophrenia, in how to make their communication less likely to provoke relapse has been developed. One of the most successful interventions is based on the notion that there is a certain level of 'expressed emotion' (actually, expressed negative emotion) in many communications, and the finding that this more likely to be high in families where the family member with a mental illness has a rapid relapse of their acute illness after successful treatment. The initial findings were made in family studies by George Brown, Michael Rutter, and Jim Birley. Julian Leff and others demonstrated that the key features of high expressed emotion were critical comments, emotional demands, and hostility. He and his co-workers developed psychological interventions to reduce the level of 'high expressed emotion', and showed that these reduced relapse (Weardon *et al.*, 2000, provide a history of the developments).

The expressed emotion paradigm has not been applied to families where there is one or more people affected by an ASD, so far as I know, but may be a helpful way of explaining to carers and others how to reduce interbrain bandwidth demands in people with an ASD. For example, John's parents were trying to help him to get up on time in the morning. John usually slept through his alarm. It was agreed that John should work towards getting himself up in the morning, and not sleeping through his alarm, but it was also agreed that interim goals needed to be set and achieved before that could happen. John's father left for work at about the time that John had to get up, and could therefore wake John up before he left at about the time that John actually needed to be getting up. His father said that he was already doing that, and so the counsellor asked how it went. His father said that he would knock on the door and when he did not hear anything inside, would go into John's room and sometimes shake him. He would then leave John, but go back to check in five minutes and would usually find that John had gone back to sleep. At this point John's father would be running late, so he would be feeling irritable. John's mother chipped in that it would be obvious that he *was* irritable as he would often shout, and tell John that he was making him (father) late. There would sometimes be a third iteration, by which time Dad was really late and he would begin to make remarks about John's character.

The counsellor pointed out that John often dealt with interpersonal stress by wanting to withdraw and sometimes he would go to bed when the stress got great. So a high EE approach such as the family had adopted would make John want to stay in bed rather than get up. Father's strategy whilst designed to serve John's interest at Dad's own expense (Dad liked to be punctual at work) was based on what would have worked with him, Dad. Dad would have wanted to avoid reproach and would have tried to get up even before his own father would have knocked for him. But John needed a different, low EE, strategy. The counsellor drew up a timetable for the hour and a half between John getting up and the taxi coming to take him to the day centre. During that time John had to dress, to shower (which because of his washing rituals took at least a half hour) and to have his breakfast. The counsellor worked backwards from 9.30, when the taxi came. It was agreed that mother, who also left the house about then, had to put away the breakfast things at 9.15 so that she could wash up. There would be no breakfast for John after that time. He needed 20 minutes to eat, so he would have had to finish his shower at about 8.50 and that meant getting in the shower at 8.20. What time would John want to get up? He said 'Eight'. What was needed to get him up? He said, 'Just knocking'. His father pointed out that there were times when John slept on despite his knocking. So it was agreed that John would have to acknowledge his father's knock, otherwise his father would come in and wake him up, shaking him if necessary. It was agreed that his father would accompany the knock with a greeting, like 'Good morning, John', and that he would not knock again or check whether John had, in fact, got up. If John was not up by 9.15 he would have to make his own breakfast and clear up after. If he was not up by the time that the taxi came, the taxi would be sent away and mother would leave and go to work (John was an adult, and safe to leave at home alone).

In the first week of trying this out, there were several mornings when it did not work well, and these were all associated with either father, or one occasion mother, losing their temper and criticizing John—sometimes in response to him swearing at them. They were encouraged to persist, and not to feel responsible for John's behaviour, only their own. Previously they had felt hopeless about John because they had felt responsible for him getting to the day centre and yet did not feel that they had the power to ensure that he got there. Hopelessness is an emotion that can lead to criticism of others and contribute to high EE, and more bandwidth demands. The counsellor anticipated this and gave the parents no option to fail. Even if John did not get up, she said, his parents would have worked out new, more effective low EE ways of dealing with problems that would stand them in good stead in the future. As it turned out, she need not have worried. In the week following this second appointment, John got up twice after his alarm went off, without his father needing to knock, and this improvement continued over the next few months.

Viruses and spam/emotional malware

Reducing the reliance on the interbrain, reducing bandwidth demands, reducing the amount of response required from a person with an ASD as a condition of using the interbrain, all of these are valuable. But they are all reductions in function. Carers often worry that reducing the social demands on the family member with an ASD too much will result in a loss of interpersonal skills, and will lead to a worsening of the situation. Sometimes this may be put in a hostile way, and a father might say, 'We shouldn't let him get away with so much'. More often the worry grows out of unalloyed caring. It is not an unreasonable worry. Honey the dog's demands on Sandra's interaction resulted in an improvement in Sandra's condition as we saw at the beginning of this chapter. Honey did not make high bandwidth demands, and expected the most minimal of responses. So the principles of reducing interbrain usage did apply to her in some respects. But if Honey had been kept away from Sandra because it might make her condition worse, Sandra would have been denied an opportunity for improvement.

I think that carers and parents are right in thinking that increasing the time spent in interbrain connection with other people *is* good for people with an ASD but only so long as the bandwidth of the connection is not exceeded. Having a time limit is important because the longer that a person with an ASD has to be on the interbrain, the more tiring that becomes and, as with any other cognitive or neurological impairment, tiredness brings anxiety and failing efficiency which brings a reduction in bandwidth.

Spending time in dialogue with others is important for people with an ASD, just as it is for all of us, but that time needs to be budgeted if it is to be used most effectively, without loss of bandwidth. Given this limited budget, scarce interbrain time should be given over to high priority activities. If I was writing about an internet connection, I would say that the priority would depend, paradoxically, on how much internet connection there was. If there were some, then keeping my virus checker and firewall up to date would be the highest priority. If I had no internet connection at all, then I would not be getting sent new viruses or malware over the internet and so it would matter less— although my computer could still get infected via a disk or memory stick from someone else's computer.

Human viruses are not really very similar to computer viruses, and we don't catch them from being on the interbrain. No-one got an actual cold by talking to someone on the telephone even if that person had a cold themselves. But they can catch an 'informational' cold, a nasty chill of bad news or a sharp dig at their self-confidence. These emotional shocks are more like the computer virus: something that hijacks the system, and may, if it is really malignant, make it crash.

I think that my extended computer analogy should not be stretched much further, and perhaps applying it to emotions is more of a distortion than an extension. Disembodied computers lack emotions of their own although they can be made to mimic them. But my clinical experience is that many emotions, particularly the ones that are often termed social emotions, are tied in closely to interbrain function.

This can be seen most clearly in relation to emotions that seem most like infections or viruses transmitted from other people. Here are two examples.

Roberta was 14 and very worried about her appearance. She tried always to look nice. Her mother always looked nice in Roberta's opinion because she took pains to do so. Roberta intended to follow in her footsteps. Roberta's parents had both gone to state schools, but her father had worked hard and made money in his building firm. He could afford to send Roberta to a private school, and he did. Roberta had always thought that her background was irrelevant in this day and age. People took people as they were, and did not take account of their families. But in this she calculated without the subtle indicators of taste that are really indicators of caste. One day she carried herself proudly into school as she always did, and overheard one of the popular girls saying, 'Here comes the tart again'. As it happened, Roberta was a very moral girl. She didn't dress to flirt with the boys, but to make herself look well done up. The remark opened up a world of malice for Roberta, and the implications of this grew and grew until Roberta became so unhappy that she wanted to leave the school. It was as if she had suddenly been injected with a nasty idea that had been able to take root, and grow.

Luke's mother had cancer. The whole family were terrified of what would happen if she died, and everyone knew that could well be some time in the next two years. His sisters had a role to play. They could comfort their mother, help her by doing some of the housework or running errands, and could take her to the doctor's. Luke had nothing that he could do. He didn't even know if he should mention the word 'cancer'. It became increasingly frustrating for him, and his rituals got worse. One particularly difficult day, his mother who was tired after a course of chemotherapy lost her patience, and he heard her say to one of his sisters, 'He'll be the death of me'. Luke took this statement at its face value. Could stress kill someone with cancer? Could living with him be that stressful? He had thought before that he should not mention 'cancer' and he was doubly sure that he should not mention his worries to anyone. But the last thing he wanted to do was to hurt his mother, let alone to kill her. The thought seemed to burrow deeper and deeper into him. For a while he blamed his sister because she had agreed with their mother, and said, 'The death of you? He will yet'. This thought festered, too, and he hit his sister out of the blue one morning. He was seen by a doctor who diagnosed depression, and arranged for him to go into hospital. No-one though knew what had really got to him: it was ruminating about whether he would one day be held up to be the murderer of the mum that he would have wanted to care for, if he only knew how.

Infectious thoughts like these, the aftertaste of social encounters that have gone wrong, misunderstandings that are not corrected, inadvertent upsets or accidents in which other people are hurt, all of these can act like emotional viruses. The more they grow, the more other beliefs they undermine, or the more that memories are changed to accommodate them, often spreading the damage further by providing new instances of mishaps or hostility to be recalled.

These unpleasant viral thoughts cannot be dealt with easily by rational argument. Luke might have told himself that it was very unlikely that he, and not his mother's cancer, would cause her death—but then he could not be certain that he would not have hastened the cancer by the worry that he caused. Emotional coping strategies, such as saying to yourself, 'That's hardly likely' or 'Plenty of other things in her life to stress her. Why pick on me?' might have been more successful, but emotional coping strategies like this don't come easily to people with an ASD.

The reason that a viral thought lodges is that it is, in some way, the truth. The best way to cope with the truth is to be able to accept it, and not deny it. The problem for Roberta in accepting that she looked like a tart was that it made her realize that her mother's taste was 'tarty' so far as her new middle class friends were concerned. Going along with that judgement meant going along with all of the other associations of 'tartiness' which Roberta knew, for sure, did not apply to her mother. She felt torn, wanting to be accepted by her friends, and wanting to continue to value her mother. Changing her mode of dressing seemed like doing harm to her mother, in her mind. Luke did not want to accept that he may have been a cause of stress to his mother, either.

Both Roberta and Luke were stuck. Accepting the truth had consequences that they saw as unacceptable. Denying the truth would not work either, because the other person's words would not go away.

In a previous book (Tantam, 2002) I have considered in detail how psychotherapists and counsellors can deal with predicaments in which every way forward seems to lead to some undesirable consequence. I argued there that the first step in dealing with the predicament was to get as close as possible to what really hurt about it, to get down to, as I called it there, the preoccupying concern. For Roberta this might have been something like, 'If I accept the tastes and values of the girls that I admire at school, will this mean that I have to turn on my mother and look down on her?' Luke's concern, as it turned out much later, was more simple but also less easily guessed at. He wanted to tell his sisters that he did not want to kill his mother, but did not know how he could make them believe him.

Most of us keep our deepest concerns to ourselves, as a safeguard until we are sure that they will not be dismissed. Finding out what is on someone's mind, what they are really concerned about, means establishing a relationship with that person which gives them confidence that what they say will be respected. For many of us, that comes about when we have a quiet time to sit with someone else without any particular task that we have to perform. It also requires that we can empathize with the other person, and they with us. Under these circumstances, a free floating discussion can begin and can be guided by emotion. Emotion in this situation is a bit like the signal from a metal detector. It alerts us to things that are hidden, and gives us some idea of what they are made of. We can excavate what is buried using the signal, and when it has come to the light of day, we can see what it really is and what we need to do with it.

People with an ASD almost always have repeated experiences of being misunderstood. They do not assume that other people will see their point of view, and do not readily volunteer deep concerns. In fact, it may be difficult for them to know what these are themselves, since many of us only find out what is really bothering us when we have a confidential talk with a friend or a family member. In the previous paragraph I suggested that empathy functions in this situation as a kind of metal detector, but tuned to concerns and not metal objects.

(This is not really a good analogy, because a metal detector emits a radio signal and detects distortions in it, but empathy is more like one Bluetooth device detecting another; both have to be radiotransmitters and receivers.) If the signal is weak or if there is limited interbrain bandwidth, as it will be for someone with an ASD, this is not a reason to give up trying to identify the buried concern, but it is a reason for making sure that every circumstance is favourable to the weak signal being picked up.

Uncovering buried emotional concerns and dealing with them can be helped by ensuring that there is a regular opportunity for quiet discussion, without making other demands which will use up bandwidth. A bit like the dodgy metal detector, which has to be recharged after every use, many people with an ASD will find this kind of interaction draining, and may have reduced interbrain bandwidth subsequently. But my experience is that this is the single most important use of empathizing and therefore should have the highest priority in the use of limited interbrain bandwidth.

Being with

Being in emotional contact in relationships is often referred to as 'quality time' or 'being close'. Many couples, and couple therapists, assume that an absence of emotional contact reduces couples' satisfaction and increases the risks of relationship breakdown. One way that this might work is if closeness enables some kind of emotional equilibriation over the interbrain even in the absence of any deliberate application of that empathy such as searching out a person's current preoccupying concern, as described above.

This kind of sharing in adults is similar to the intersubjectivity that is considered to be an indicator of mother–infant closeness. It requires not just that one person stops what they are preoccupied with to pay attention to the other, but that the other does so too, and that they pay attention to each other. Almost everyone in a close relationship with a partner will have had moments like this, and will know that there is some deeper quality in the mutual attention when it feels as if we are in contact with the other person, and they with us. It is as if we become aware of an interbrain connection being established.

That special quality of being in contact that we can all recognize is not easy for researchers to measure, and there has been little empirical research into what it is. But most people believe, judging by advice given to couples whose relationships have gone stale, that these special moments are particularly important in re-establishing closeness and, because of that, particularly relevant to mental health.

Even less research has been carried out on closeness between people with an ASD and their carers, but many carers set great store by instances of such closeness whether or not they are merely rewarding for the carer, or do have some benefits to the person with ASD too. Establishing closeness is a demand on bandwidth and the same principles apply as to the instance described above, of establishing closeness in order to explore a concern.

One factor that will drain bandwidth is fear, and therefore one of the main considerations—as older psychologists working with children with autism often pointed out—is to reduce avoidance in favour of increasing approach. Being with Tim was an illustration of this. Tim was 14, with limited understanding of speech and no use of words. He had a troubled, restless upbringing which had left him a rather detached figure, who was unusually passive and tractable and who quickly developed everyday activities into routines. When a routine was interrupted he would scream, rock, and sometimes bite. I met him for an assessment. He sat next to me at a table while I talked to his grandparents, who occasionally referred to him or asked him to run errands. I did not take much notice of him and when I did glance at him his eyes were always staring into the forward distance. There would be an occasional slight grimace on his face, but no acknowledgement of my glance. After about 30 minutes, I asked him to hold my hand, to test his grip, and he was reluctant to let it go. About ten minutes after that, Tim turned round and began to look searchingly at my face. When I looked back, I saw a person in his eyes for the first time. He grunted, as if trying to speak, and then touched the lapel of my jacket. I began to speak to him for the first time.

As this illustration shows, Tim and I did reach the point that he was making contact, but it was after a prolonged time in which we had been together but without any communicative demands being placed on him. Although he was interested in finding out about me, Tim did not show any interest in who I was, how I was feeling, or why I was there. It would have taken much more time for us to reach that point, during which I would have to have minimized the bandwidth demands that I made. This would have involved me establishing with Tim what I did and did not feel comfortable with since, like many people with an ASD, he would have been interested to touch my face or hair and would not have the bandwidth to pick up the discomfort that I might have felt about that.

Offline processes

Many psychologists see the brain as like a computer which runs complex programs, including programs for processing social stimuli—these have sometimes been called modules or components. Social impairment in ASD has been attributed to breakdown in the social cognition module, although some researchers have questioned whether there is a specific module.[65] Despite these doubts researchers who are also clinicians have developed training packages designed to remedy faults in the social module or its components, which require both training and repeated practice. The most commonly targeted components are empathy and socially appropriate behaviour. Training involves explicitly learning the skill, and repeated practice which is designed to make it automatic.[66] This is how many of us learn to do mental arithmetic or to dance the Viennese waltz, and so the rationale for it in autism is good.

The results of training do seem to bear these expectations out. Children and adults with an ASD trained to recognize emotional expressions improve, and children and adults with an ASD trained to behave more appropriately do behave more appropriately. The catch is that the evidence from most of these studies is that the improvement is only shown in the particular situation in which the skills training was being carried out. There is inadequate evidence of 'generalization' to other situations or settings (Williams, Keonig, and Scahill, 2007), and sometimes direct evidence that there is no generalization. So an adolescent who learns to identify certain phrases or facial expressions that his mother uses when she is getting upset may get better at picking up his mother's distress, but show no change in his or her ability to pick up anyone else's distress.

Getting on better with mother may be a valuable goal of training, but it falls far short of the ultimate goal, of restoring the social cognition module to something like normal function. It is possible that refinements in training may achieve this, but I don't think so. We do not, as it seems to me, take some reading of a social situation or a facial expression in, process it according to complex rules, and then output a response. Even learning the waltz is not like that after the very first few minutes when one is learning the steps. Dance teachers, for one thing, often demonstrate a step and say, 'Now imitate me'. Many of their training instructions are about interaction, too: 'Remember that you have to lead (or follow) your partner' or 'You must give your partner more room in the turn'. The instructions about specific tasks that the individual dancer has to perform are rarely at the level of the dance step, but at a very detailed element of it: 'Remember, keep your head up the whole time' or 'Always lead off on your right foot' or, even less helpfully, 'Stop looking like you want to run away'.

Actually learning the elements of the dance does not normally require, and may even be hindered by, explaining verbally what to do. But it does require that the person learning the dance knows what to look at. No-one only does one thing when they are moving. So the dance teacher may be looking in a particular direction, smiling or frowning, or performing some other action at the same time as demonstrating the step. There will also be some preparatory action and some finishing action before and after the step. None of this presents any problem for most neurotypicals, who just know what to imitate and what to ignore. People with an ASD on the other hand find imitation much more difficult, as I found in my own study carried out in the early 1980s. The difficulty is often attributed to an impairment in the link between seeing an action and performing an action that, as I discussed in a previous chapter, may be mediated by 'mirror neurones'. But this does not address the issue of knowing what to imitate.[67] This would be an almost impossible challenge to learning a new gesture, or a new dance step, if one had to work out when the gesture began or ended in isolation, without any information from the gesturer, or the dance teacher.

I think that our interbrain connection provides us with the information to know that a gesture, or a dance step, has started or ended.

That we 'get the nod' when the dance step starts is clear if we do not get the step the first time. The teacher repeats it but with a certain emphasis on when it begins. Perhaps there is a nod, or perhaps a glance at us. The step continues and then the teacher says, 'there' or perhaps just smiles, or looks up again at us. Even if the teacher is an enthusiast and carries on twirling for a little while, we know that particular step has ended. In other words, it is our connection with the dance teacher via the interbrain that enables us to 'parse' the action stream, and to know when a step begins and ends. I think that this is true of gestures, too. Not knowing this requirement is one of the things that makes the gestures of people with an ASD often seem unreadable. A hand movement begins and ends, but we do not see the glance at us or the emphasis on a word that alerts us to the fact that a gesture is beginning. Similarly the hand movement seems to an observer to tail off, without an ending being signalled as we would expect if it were a gesture.

Socially appropriate behaviour is a bit like dance. It is made up of steps. I have argued that these are not learnt explicitly but by imitation, and that imitation learning requires an interbrain connection. Explicit learning can build on the basics, but only once these have been acquired by implicit learning. Expert dancers can benefit from looking at videos of their dances, or from particular critiques of their footwork, or how they are holding their arms. Learning to dance cannot be built up in this way.

There is another reason that the interbrain is needed for an empathic or socially skilled performance. I can best illustrate this with an example. Let us suppose that I grow up in Borsetshire, where it is usual for any visitor to the local pub to be stood a round of drinks, and it is equally usual that the visitor will then stand a round back. But I move to Camfordshire, where visitors stand the locals a round first, and only after that do the locals reciprocate. I am not told this before I go to the pub for the first time in my new home. I greet several people that I recognize and I sit with them at a table. I go to the bar to order a beer. There is an awkward pause, and the barman looks at me meaningfully. I experience a feeling of heightened awareness. One of the people that I am sitting with touches his empty glass almost imperceptibly. I now experience the same feeling that I used to have when it was my turn to buy a round in Borsetshire, but I am surprised because that only occurred when someone else had bought a round first. But the silence is becoming uncomfortable, and I think, 'In for a penny, in for a pound'. So I say to my friends, 'What will you all have?' There is an audible intake of breath. I have passed the test.

My description of the happenings when I first go the pub in Camfordshire is much more drawn out than the actual event, which would be over in seconds. I might not even think of my own emotions, or pick up on the nonverbal cues around me. I might just say, 'It felt like a good thing to do' to buy a round. Buying a round is not always the right thing to do. People who are too ready to buy rounds are considered suspect, and, if they do it often enough, a bit daft. The kind of person buying the round makes a difference too. An outsider buying a round causes alarm, for instance. Getting it right matters, but it would be at the very least difficult to produce a set of rules for when buying a round of drinks for acquaintances is appropriate.

I have chosen a trivial example to demonstrate how, even for that, producing rules for when that behaviour is appropriate is next to impossible. So how much harder would it be to learn which actions are timely and appropriate in more nuanced situations? Can social rules be the way that neurotypicals choose socially appropriate behaviour? Is it sensible to teach people with ASD explicit principles or social skills as a way of overcoming their social impairment?

I have already indicated that I think that the answer to the last question is 'no', and I think that we have to assume that given that the answer to the first question is 'much, much harder' then we have to assume that it is just too hard to learn and apply rules for socially appropriate behaviour and that this cannot be the way that any of us learn how to behave. Perhaps this becomes even clearer if we consider the few situations in which we do learn explicit rules, such as being presented to the Queen or becoming a Bat Mitzvah. Being told where to stand or how to dress seems so unusual that we often feel slightly rebellious or over-awed, despite the fact that we have been standing and dressing fittingly for social occasions all of our lives.

In my example of being in an unfamiliar bar, the other people in the situation helped me to know how to behave by cuing in elements of behaviour that I had learnt in other situations and eliciting it in this new one. In other words, my connection with the interbrain was determined by choice of action rather than any set of rules. One of the leading researchers on the amygdala's contribution to social cognition comes to a similar conclusion (Adolphs, 2006) about this kind of 'situated cognition':

> We actively probe the social environment in order to glean relevant information…our brains do not store all knowledge about the world in explicit form, and do not hold comprehensive explicit models or representations of the environment. Rather, it has been argued, our brains contain recipes for seeking out that information—often rather trivially by deciding where in the environment to look (p.33).

How can people with an ASD learn implicitly?

There were two elements of buying a round of drinks in my previous example: knowing when to do it, and knowing how to phrase the offer (in the example, I say 'What will you all have?' but I could equally have said, 'What's your poison?' or 'Can I get you anything while I'm up?'). Knowing how to phrase the offer is a bit like learning to do a step better when one is dancing. It's possible to study it offline because the basics are there. I argued, though, that knowing when to make the offer is not really a kind of knowledge, but being receptive to the signals on the internet connection. So this is not something that can be learnt by offline processing.

People with an ASD can therefore refine their social skills, as we all can, once they have learnt the basics. But learning the basics requires an interbrain connection, which neurotypicals have and use, but which people with an ASD may not be able to make use of. So how do people with an ASD acquire empathic awareness or social skills in the first instance, or are they for ever blocked from doing so?

Some people with an ASD in my clinical experience remain handicapped by it throughout their lives, but some do improve and may even overcome their social impairment, at least when they are not stressed or having to deal with too great an interbrain demand. What is their secret?

There are many anecdotal experiences of recovery, and many of them attribute it to a specific medical, dietary, or social therapy. But careful testing has not so far been able to establish that any of them is curative. One feature of all of these interventions is that they are time consuming, inconvenient, and sometimes potentially dangerous. These factors may increase the size of what is sometimes called the placebo effect, that is, the response to having any treatment that gives hope irrespective of any specific value of the treatment. Another feature of many of these interventions is that they increase the amount of time that the person with an ASD spends interacting with others. Could that, too, have an effect?

I have already suggested that increasing familiarity with, and reducing anxiety at, social interaction may reduce bandwidth demands on the interbrain. So perhaps this may make some implicit learning possible. But there is another possibility. Many people with an ASD are excellent mimics, who can slip into another person's way of speaking, way of moving, and even their opinions without any resistance from any rooted identity in themselves. Could greater contact with another person lead to copying that person and could that lead to social learning?

Many children and young adolescents go through a copying period, often associated with a strong positive emotional investment or 'crush' on another person. Crushes like this can lead to lifelong patterns of interest or belief, and sometimes people do adopt mannerisms or patterns of speech, too. My experience is that at least some people with an ASD who overcome their social impairment do so by copying an admired other person and not just by copying some of their mannerisms or patterns of speech, but by almost being the other person. Contrary to expectation, copying like this seems to be easy for some people with an ASD to do. It might be expected that the lack of imagination and spontaneous role play that is often described in relation to ASD would prevent this, but many people with an ASD like being on stage and enjoy acting a part. Copying another person is a bit like acting a part. Unless one is a method actor and attempts to live the part, the part and one's own identity can remain completely separate. Unlike acting a part, copying another person who one knows well means having a memory of lots of different situations in which that person has acted, and therefore a stock of memories of how he or she has acted. Knowing how to behave in a situation therefore becomes thinking about how John or Jane, or whoever one is copying, would react.

Here is an example. Lester was bullied so badly that he tried to hide away from other people as much as possible, but that also made him identify strongly with other people who were ridiculed. He was particularly fascinated by people like comics who could rise above ridicule by laughing at themselves. He was fascinated by particular comics who were especially good at this, and followed one particular comic round the working men's clubs in which he appeared in the North of England. He would sit in the audience and mouth the comic's catchphrases with him, and after a while would change them slightly, and embellish them. Lester was fascinated by computers, and got a job in the IT industry. But instead of putting him in a technical department, he was put into sales. Lester floundered at first, but one day started to speak to a customer in the voice of the comic that had fascinated him. The customer was amused, and the sale went through. Lester did that automatically from then on, although his boss did overhear one of his sales conversations and told him to speak in a less loud and dramatic way as Lester was talking on the phone as if he was addressing an audience.

Prevention

The interbrain connection is established very early in life, perhaps from the very first day. In the majority of people with an ASD, some indications of their later full blown difficulties already become apparent early in life, too. If there were some way of detecting these very early problems, possible low bandwidth in the interbrain connection might be flagged up and that would make it feasible to try to correct it. What the value of this would be is uncertain, but there is a theoretical chance that many if not all of the developmental problems of ASD could be averted.

What could be done about the minority of people with an ASD who develop an ASD following a period of normal development is less clear, but potentially their regression could also be remedied if their interbrain connection could be strengthened.

All the evidence points to gaze at the eyes, and then gaze at the eyes when the other person's face is communicatively active, as being one of the principal first steps in interbrain connection. If the infant does not orientate to the mother's eyes, two possible strategies suggest themselves. The first is to increase looking at the mother's eyes. The second is to adopt the alternative attentional strategies used by infants with visual impairment.

To increase the infant looking at the mother's eyes requires knowing the cause of the infant not looking at them. As I discussed in an earlier chapter, there are several possible explanations, some of which are directly opposing. It may be that looking at mother's eyes causes a fear response, or it may be that looking at mother's eyes causes no response at all. Telling someone to look at your eyes may work for a while (although it has limited application in infancy) but when this was tried in someone with a brain lesion which in many ways mimicked an ASD, the person quickly forgot to keep looking.[68]

Directing an infant's attention to the eyes of the person attending to them, in the absence of an interest in looking at eyes in the infant, would require something to make the eye region of more interest. I have often wondered whether mothers wearing a kind of headband with a flashing light just in between their eyes might do the trick, but without any good evidence to persuade new mothers to do this, it is difficult to imagine anyone wanting to try it out speculatively.

Mothers with children who are visually impaired also have to find alternative strategies to gain and hold their babies' attention. The American Foundation for the Blind (2008) advises mothers: (a) not to be put off by their baby's apparently paradoxical response, but to continue to be loving and affectionate; (b) touching their baby as a way of establishing contact using a gesture that will come to be recognizable as mother; (c) giving the baby things to feel and smell as a basis for joint attention on these articles; (d) tickling, swinging, and crooning as a substitute for smiling or making silly faces as a way of engaging the baby. Although none of these procedures have been tried out in people with autism, mothers who are worried about their lack of eye contact with their children, particularly if there is a family history of an ASD, may find them worth trying as an alternative means of developing joint attention and helping their baby to 'handshake' successfully with the interbrain.

Getting gaze right by itself may not be enough. Looking at the right place and at the right moment may be only the first step. Imitation, as I have described previously, may be the second. Even if imitating is not possible, being imitated may simulate the connectedness of the inter-brain and can cause remarkable reductions in the social withdrawal of people severely affected by an ASD.[69]

But developing very early methods of intervention, whilst promising for the future, are at a very early stage. What is becoming clear is that few people with an ASD have no interbrain connection and that there is the possibility of increasing the bandwidth of the connection, or at least of using it as efficiently as possible throughout development. The interbrain is, of course, a network between brains and like the internet, its function depends on all computers in the network.

So another way of looking at prevention is to reconsider what connections neurotypical brains offer the brains of people with an ASD.

CHAPTER 8

*C*an society afford people with an ASD, revisited

I have mentioned the economics of autistic spectrum disorders (ASDs) only once, briefly, in the introduction. Because ASDs are long-lasting, sometimes having life-long impact, and because many people with an ASD are unable to obtain work, the costs to society—as health economists calculated them—are very high. The direct costs of ASD are, however, low. There are no expensive, cutting edge interventions for ASD. Those costly drugs that there are, such as secretin, are not considered to be effective and the costs are not reimbursed by third party payers. Many people with an ASD benefit from special help at school, but educational policy internationally has been towards 'main-streaming' and away from special education, and this has—perhaps deliberately or perhaps not, depending on how cynical one is—driven costs down. Classroom support of various kinds is available, but local authorities in the UK, who hold the educational budget, are reluctant to recognize special educational needs and thus make sure that spending is rationed. I have no reason to think that the UK is unique in this respect. Many of the interventions for adults that might be beneficial (www.researchautism.org lists many of these) are similarly rationed. Finally, the low rate of diagnosis means that many people with an ASD—perhaps as many as a half—do not receive any autism-specific help because they are not recognized as needing it. Since many people with an ASD are phobic of public transport, of large groups, and of unfamiliar situations, they probably receive less public money than other people who are unemployed.

Society does afford the cost of people known to have an ASD and who are in touch with services, but sometimes there is an unexpressed fear in those who are responsible for health and social care budgets that it could not afford the cost of caring for everyone with an ASD. This would have to include those who are not known, those who have been wrongly told that they do not have an ASD, and those that, despite having a diagnosis, have dropped out of contact with a service that is reluctant to keep in touch with them.

These fears are based on the expectation that everyone with an ASD needs, or even wants, costly help. What many adults with an ASD want is to be able to work, and to be more independent. A diagnosis may be the gateway to this, and not, as politicians and managers might fear, to an unending dependence on the public purse.

Can society afford to recognize people with an ASD?

The politicians and managers are right to think that greater recognition of ASD might lead to more investment in services for people with an ASD, but the investment is likely to be an investment that is to lead to a reduction, and not an increase, in cost (Jarbrink *et al.,* 2007). Measures to deal with bullying and its aftermath, counselling or mentoring, support into work, and flexible working, including schemes for working at home, might all result in a long-term saving on the indirect costs of disability and unemployment pay-outs.

So, far from being not able to afford the cost of recognizing ASD, I would say that society cannot afford the cost of not recognizing it, and not coming to the aid of those people with an ASD who might need it.

Of course, this kind of 'affording' has not been what this book has been about. I have been discussing a special use of the word, coined by the psychologist J.J. Gibson. I have argued that this kind of affordance means something like 'making room for' or even 'giving way to', much as new parents have to make a place for, or give way to, a new baby, or an orchestra has to take a new conductor 'to its heart' and an organization has to 'get behind' a new chief executive.

Why society cannot afford bullying

Human groups have a boundary which is endangered when the composition or structure of the group changes. Resisting change is one way in which this boundary is protected. To change couples, institutions, or organizations means having to overcome the conservative forces that oppose change. So affording something or someone new in an organization requires that new person to deal with opposition. Their new initiatives will be tested. One way to do that is to see how well they will stand up to criticism, or ridicule.

Perhaps this works when everyone concerned is equally tough and when they are not too personally involved in the new initiative. 'You win some, and you lose some', tough minded people can say after an unsuccessful conflict. The statement is one of those emotional distancing devices so commonly used by neurotypicals but so difficult for people with an ASD. It means, 'My emotional investment has been withdrawn from that issue, which I send to the dustbin of my personal history'. But few people with an ASD can process the past so easily. For the majority of people with an ASD, issues should be resolved and not just forgotten. 'Emotional processing'—saying to oneself that 'no-one can win them all' or 'time moves on' or 'you win some, you lose some'—comes much more easily to neurotypicals. One reason may be that the losers in a trial may still accept that it was a fair fight and may even come to acknowledge that the opposition was right, and they were wrong. This in turn is based on the assumption that conflict is a good test of ideas: it is after all the model that is the basis of democratic courts and parliaments.

Conflict has a much less reliable issue if one of the parties is a less able fighter. Then it is quite possible that excellent ideas, of potential value, are dismissed because their introducer is not able to champion them effectively. This is the situation by definition in abuse, a kind of coercive conflict when the power is all on one side. Bullying is a kind of abuse that is tolerated more than it should be because the bullies act on behalf of the conservative forces that resist change. Bullies are often themselves socially marginal, often having been bullied themselves. They hope that they will gain more social acceptance by doing the group's dirty work.

Resisting change is not wrong. Defeating new initiatives is not bad. What is wrong and bad is resisting change by the abuse of the group's power, and defeating new initiatives by targeting the initiators rather than their proposals. Bullying is therefore both wrong and bad. Why? Well, as Geoffrey Maddrell, the founder and chair of Research Autism, said at a recent meeting with UK members of parliament, 'Injustice to one person puts justice for everyone at risk'. Condoning bullying towards one person, or one group of people, increases the risk for everyone else that, finding themselves in a position of weakness, they too might be bullied.

Are people with an ASD disabled?

Bullying, like other kinds of abuse, leads to long-term harm to people with ASD, as I have already discussed. Many of them react by withdrawal, and isolating themselves from the social mainstream. Bullying, in other words, often leads to social exclusion.

Maybe some neurotypicals find this desirable. Dealing with people in public places puts, as I have indicated previously, a strain on the interbrain connection. Interbraining becomes more difficult when people differ more from each other, and so diversity increases behavioural unpredictability too. People with an ASD, who are off the interbrain network, are likely to conjure up even more anxiety in the people around them.

Affording people with an ASD requires, as I described in the last chapter, finding ways of interacting that do not place demands on the interbrain. This requires effort and thoughtfulness. Both can be economized by reifying the difference of the person with ASD, and calling it disability. People with disabilities are not fully able, by definition. To call ASD a social disability, and to treat people with an ASD as having a social disability, means reducing the extent of social interaction that one might expect to have with them. There is a cost to this, too. Well-intentioned people want to help people with disabilities, and not take advantage of them. So a certain sacrifice is required. But when many people call someone 'disabled' it is not to consider what has to be done to 'enable' them, but what they have to do to fit in or, not being able to fit in, what consolation they can be offered.

If I break my leg, I am disabled for a while and I can be consoled that, although I cannot do many of the physical activities that I did before, I am likely to recover and be able to do them again in the future. Suppose though that I have a comminuted fracture and spend months on bed rest. During this term, I put on a lot of weight. Suppose, too, that I live in a society in which obesity is increasingly being made out to be a stigma—as is arguably the case in the West currently. Would it be good or bad for me to be told that I have a weight disability? What if I discovered that seats on buses and planes had dividers which were so placed that I could no longer fit in with them? Would it be good for me to have to make a special disabled booking when I take a bus so that I can have a specially wide, disabled seat? One might argue, as indeed people do, that I can overcome obesity any time I want. I just have to eat less. People with an ASD, especially if it is of the Asperger type, might similarly be told that they just have to try harder to get on with people. Or that if they remember to take other people into account, and not talk so much about their own, special, interests, they could get on fine.

Being called 'disabled' in this latter situation is hardly consoling. It may carry with it an under-current of moral criticism, and it seals the implicit bargain between the disabled and society that disability means exclusion in exchange for special considerations.

Sometimes saying that someone with an ASD is disabled is an act of humanity, and sometimes it is in the interests of a person with an ASD to accept this status. If my broken leg never healed properly, I would almost certainly choose to be considered to be disabled although I would want to make sure that the extent of my disability was clear to everyone. I would not want to think that because I could not climb, I could not rise in status or seniority in my organization, for example.

Can society afford to exclude people with an ASD?

In the previous section, I was writing from the perspective of the person with an ASD. If I write from the perspective of Joe Public, I might say something rather different: 'Why doesn't anyone give me a break? I have to work hard, there are always problems of some kind to deal with at home, if it's not the kids, it's the older relatives. You make out my life is easy in comparison, but it's certainly not. I'd love to have someone give me the kind of breaks you're talking about. But if I don't make a sale, I can't say that it was because my interbrain connection was iffy. I just get told that I need to do better, and to accept less commission for this week. I'm not saying that I'm not sorry for people with ASD, of course I am. I'm sorry for anyone who has the cards stacked against them in life. But at the end of the day, I can only just cope with the hand of cards that I'm dealt. I'd do anything for my family, of course, and I'd do a lot for my friends. I'd give a helping hand to a stranger if I could help and if I had the time to do it. But I'm not employed to work with people with ASD. And, to be brutally frank, I wonder what's in it for me to do anything for them. I mean I can't afford the time or the money now to go to football more than twice a year.'

I have given Joe my own views about needing to reduce abstract considerations of society to what they mean to individuals although I do not share his other sentiments. To think of social action as any more than the coming together of individual actions may lead to the kind of category error in which people say, 'the Government should do something about it'. So what does Joe get for his outlay in time, effort, or understanding in working with someone with an ASD, in having more people with ASD being empowered to travel on the buses that he uses, or in people with ASD representing him in the local or national legislature?

Neurodiversity

The term that people with an ASD most often use about other people who do not have an ASD is 'neurotypical'. In so doing, they are asserting that there may be much more variation in brain organization between human beings than the 'neurotypicals' accept. 'Neurotypicals', the term suggests, do have similar brain organizations to each other, and take that type of brain as being the type by which to evaluate other brain organizations. So a person with an ASD, and their different brain organization, is not just considered to be different but 'abnormal' by a neurotypical, who takes his or her own neurotype to be the norm.

'Norm' can mean no more than average, or most common. But it usually means something more, well, 'normative'. It means setting a standard, in this case of what a human brain should be.

Suppose that genetics advanced to the point where it was possible to alter the genotype of someone who had inherited a genetic disposition to developing an ASD. Would it be desirable to alter that genotype so that the person did not develop an ASD? Would it be desirable to routinely alter all of the genotypes in this way? What if a friend says that her son with an ASD has married a girl who has the same condition, and now they want to have children? She, your friend, knows that there is a much increased chance that their children will also have an ASD (Muhle, Trentacoste, and Rapin, 2004). Should she try to dissuade her son and daughter in law from having babies?

This is the area that eugenicists made so very unpalatable. I do not want to argue, as they would have done, that people with an ASD should be automatically dissuaded from having children. In fact, I want to argue that it is advantageous that at least some of them do, or rather that we should not want to reduce human genetic diversity in this way because society gains, rather than loses, by the neurodiversity that results.

In the film *Cube*, a group of people, including one person with Asperger syndrome, is put through a series of tests by an unknown, but implacable, foe. Each test somehow finds out a particular weakness of the people being tested and at the end only the person with AS survives. He does not fall into any of the traps because he does not rely on thinking cooperatively or on team work for survival. The film may have been inspired by the many books about the wild boy of Aveyron, a child who survived exposure in the woods of 18th-century France for months and possibly years. It has been conjectured that he had autism (Creak, 1972) and that it was precisely this that enabled him to survive.

The chances of a child being exposed or simply lost in nature are too low for this to be a credible reason that society needs to retain the genetic endowment to cope with this happening, just in case. But there are other environments in which atypical human brains might function better than the neurotype. Interacting with intelligent machines is one example. Many people with an ASD seem to have more effective strategies for understanding and designing human–machine interfaces. This ability is not confined to more able people with an ASD. Children without the use of language may still be able to pick up a television controller and through apparently random button presses be able to work out how to use it, leaving their neurotypical parent well behind and trying to work all of the functions from the manual.

An increasing number of great physicists, philosophers, mathematicians, and others have been retrospectively suspected of having an ASD (Fitzgerald, 2005) and, although I do not think that it is permissible to impose our own diagnostic criteria on historical figures in this way, there are contemporary figures who have publicly acclaimed their diagnostic status and have attributed their success with computers to their ASD. Bram Cohen, the inventor of the BitTorrent file distribution system, is one example.

If our future lies more and more in collaboration with machines, then we may need more people with ASD, not less.[70]

Interbrain malware

Thinking that the neurotypical brain is not normal in any but the statistical sense, and that other human brain types exist and may in some circumstances be superior, leads to the thought that the interbrain connection may not be essential to humanity, either. So far, I have been considering the many disadvantages of not having an interbrain connection and the stigma that may result in the eyes of the majority who do have one. It is time to look at some possible advantages.

Experience with the internet has demonstrated that it has disadvantages. There are the effects of internet addiction, that is, of the repeated use of the internet as an end in itself rather than to further some real-world end. Perhaps the person who goes out clubbing night after night without any expectation of this leading to any enduring relationship would be the interbrain equivalent of this.

The internet poses problems, too, for the hardware that it links. Viruses can be downloaded and degrade hardware function. Alien programs can replicate within the computer, suborning some of the computer's systems and locking out the user, and these programs can then propagate themselves over the internet, send confidential information to a third party, track the use of the keyboard to reveal passwords and other secrets, or even allow the computer to be used by someone else for their own purposes, such as originating spam. Trojans may lurk unseen until they are ready to propagate as viruses or worms. Not all computer viruses are malware. Some, like software updates, are tolerated, much as the vertebrate cell has tolerated and used the viruses that have imported valuable genetic information into its genome over the millennia.

'Memes' are viruses of the interbrain. They too spread without conscious intervention, often by a process of imitation or identification that will be familiar to readers of earlier chapters as one of the basic operations of interbrain connection. 'Memes' may be like benign viruses, simple software upgrades, which lead us to ditch our pointed shoes ('so last year') for wedges or alert us to new intellectual currents which we seem to know about even before we have thought about them. New words often accompany these, but we may not learn what they mean until long after we have started to use them. We use them to identify ourselves with others who have used them. 'Celebs', themselves a kind of meme, are important sources of viral infection of this 'memetic' kind.

Not all memes are harmless. The 'anthrax scare' meme was an unexpected consequence of the 9/11 atrocities, and the subsequent manufacture, by probably one person suspected to be a research worker and ex-US serviceman working in a US government research laboratory, of anthrax spores which were then sent through the mail. Five people died of anthrax, and many others were infected, but infection was localized and the risk subsided after a few months. However, the attack has had a persistent effect on millions because it created a new vulnerability that cannot be uncreated. Even now, my local sorting office contains instructions about how powders are to be sealed before the UK post office will accept them for delivery.

Other memes include 'hooligan', originally applied to members of Irish gangs, but generalized into any young person acting aggressively or disruptively and therefore acting as an inspiration to others; the 'war against terror'; and, most recently, 'knifemare', or the notion that all young people have to carry a knife to protect themselves against all the others who are carrying knives. Memes like the latter are what used to be called, in another meme, 'self-fulfilling prophecies'. Memes can be self-destructive, too. Every so often contagious spread of suicide seems to occur following an incident, or series of incidents, that gets widespread attention. Goethe's *Werther* led to the widespread adoption of the dress attributed to Werther in the novel, and to copycat suicides.

Originality

'Memes' are probably responsible for the acceleration of scientific and mathematical learning in successive generations, which enable students leaving school to have achieved a level of scientific knowledge that was just achievable by the most advanced students some years ago, and well beyond that of scientists 50 years ago. Outdated technology contributes to this. Students of electronics rarely study the thermionic valve nowadays since it has largely been replaced by the transistor. But studying electronics also benefits from the familiarity of students with electronic apparatus and what it will do. Electromagnetic radiation remains as insensible to us as it did to Faraday, but every child knows about radio waves, light waves and, since the mobile phone, microwaves.

This rapid communication of knowledge comes at a cost. What I learn through memetic transfer over the interbrain ('through osmosis', some people say as if knowledge leaks into them) is hard to challenge. Finding something out for yourself helps you to learn, too, the limits of that knowledge, and what questions remain about it. Gravity was a meme once Newton's theory took hold, but it took Einstein and others like him to resist this meme and its assumption of an inverse square law and ask deeper questions about what gravity was, leading to a more general field theory in which gravity, electromagnetic radiation, and nuclear force were elements.

Did Einstein have an ASD? Many have suggested so, but true to my belief that medical diagnosis requires the presence and cooperation of the patient, I am not in a position to know. But I do think that a person with an ASD is more able to set aside what 'everyone knows'—memetic knowledge, acquired through the interbrain—to try to find out for themselves what is really the case and, in so doing, to come up with something new. Originality, as Asperger himself noted, is one of the characteristic features of people with an ASD.

Innocence

Originality is one of the reasons that society cannot afford to be without people with an ASD. It does not just apply to science, either. Graphic artists with an ASD are making an increasing reputation although perhaps because public taste has been browbeaten by non-representational artists into accepting originality of the artist's own defining. Musicians with an ASD seem to have less success.[71]

Originality is attractive even in the domestic sphere so long as it does not topple over into uncomfortable eccentricity. But it is only the few people with an ASD who combine originality with high levels of intelligence and industry who are likely to make a sufficiently salient contribution that their absence might be considered unaffordable.

Innocence is a different matter. Innocence is a quality that almost everyone values, often in direct proportion to their own lack of it. We sometimes echo the New Testament, and say that we 'treasure' the innocent. There would seem to be no argument that society must be able to afford the innocent, else where would we be?

Innocence is, in my experience, the single, most common epithet to be used of the people with ASD that I see in the clinic. This is not because these are people with an ASD who are selected for this characteristic, far from it. These are often the most troubled, and most troubling, people with it. Nor does innocence mean peacefulness. Many of the people that I see have been aggressive to others (although probably no more proportionately than a neurotypical group of similar age and proportion of males), and a few have been dangerously violent.

Lambs are innocent not so much because they are innocuous, although that may be how we experience them, but because they are pre-pubertal. Innocence may be endearing because it reminds us of a time before we were motivated by sexuality. In this sense, innocence applies better to many people with an ASD, many of whom seem to reject sexuality even though they are physically post-pubertal. But this kind of innocence certainly does not apply to everyone with an ASD.

Many adults with ASD, although not perhaps the majority, are troubled by their lack of sexual satisfaction and a small number adopt means of achieving it that are troubling to those around them.

If people with an ASD are not consistently nonviolent and asexual, why is it that 'innocence' is still imputed to them? One possibility is that we also use innocence to mean 'unself-conscious'. There is for those brought up on one of the sacred texts deriving from the Pentateuch a connotation of the state of Adam and Eve before they ate the apple in the Garden of Eden. Eating the apple brought shame into the world because for the first time they knew themselves to be naked. It also brought into being command, dominance and, in the second generation of Cain and Abel, envy, hatred, deception, and motivated aggression.

Lacan and others have suggested that the end of this pre-lapsarian phase of innocence is recapitulated in childhood development, and corresponds to the acquisition of the symbolic and the language of the father (Lacan, 1977). Developmental psychologists attribute the development of 'self-conscious' emotions like shame to the acquisition of a theory of mind, and therefore as requiring both language and the interbrain. Shame itself, the first emotion to hit Adam and Eve in the Biblical account, probably originates before language developmentally and can be accounted for, as Sartre has famously done, by silent gaze.

There is no doubt that people with an ASD are not good at using self-conscious emotions. They often feel shame, but are poor at making others ashamed. They are also much less able than neurotypicals to persuade, to seduce, to ensnare, to lie convincingly, to backbite, to scheme, to out-manoeuvre…the list of social actions which make use of our simulations of other people, and therefore of the interbrain connection, is very long. It is precisely this lack of scheming that is, I think, the source of why people who know them say that people with an ASD are innocent. You know where you stand with them; even if that can be uncomfortable, you don't worry that some trap will open up under your feet.

Does society need to be kept in mind of this kind of innocence? I would say 'Yes'. Can it afford to be without it? I think not.

Limit situations

Some years ago, the expression 'glass ceiling' was coined to describe what happened to many ambitious business women at a certain point in their career. Despite past successes, many of them felt that they got to a certain level in their companies but then stalled whilst the men around them, who had sometimes fewer apparent successes and no greater personal abilities, seemed to continue upwards. It was, these women thought, as if there was a glass ceiling above them which prevented their natural buoyancy taking them higher.

Another way of looking at this experience was provided by Karl Jaspers, who dropped out of psychiatric training to become a philosopher. Now regarded as one of the great existential philosophers of the 20th century, Jaspers' philosophy seems grounded in everyday life and not abstraction. Like other existential philosophers, he was interested in the impact of 'The ultimate situations—death, chance, guilt and the uncertainty of the world' and concluded that they 'confront me with the reality of failure. What do I do in the face of this absolute failure, which if I am honest I cannot fail to recognise?' (Jaspers, 1951, p.22). At some point, Jaspers argues, we are all confronted with some challenge that exposes our incapacity and that we can only manage by coming to terms with that incapacity. Normally, these challenges arise in middle or late adulthood when, to revert to the original metaphor, we hit some kind of glass ceiling or when we or those we love develop illnesses or other intractable problems that we cannot make go away.

People with an ASD confront their glass ceiling much earlier. It may be in their teens when they realize that they cannot influence other people around them except by aggression or bribery; or it may be when a vacuum opens up after the structure of school or university comes to an end. Getting a diagnosis makes the glass in the ceiling opaque. There is no longer an invisible obstacle to their ambitions, which one can sometimes pretend is not even there: a diagnosis makes the obstacle all too visible, and all too real.[72]

Coming to terms with this limit requires the same kind of mourning of the loss of one's ideals and one's hopes as does facing illness or loss. It means finding new sources of meaning in life, other than the usual hand me downs of getting a good job, having a family, being a person who is respected and valued. I have often been moved by the dignity and courage that people with an ASD may bring to this task.

Most neurotypicals rush on, or are rushed on, by circumstances. As I wrote at the beginning of this book, we are shackled to each other like people in a chain gang, by our desire to maintain our interbrain connection. Much of what we hold dear comes to us through this connection, but we are also tranquillized by it. Each member of a chain gang has to shuffle forwards at the same time, or risk having their leg hurt by their shackles. Going to school, changing school, leaving school, further or higher education or work, meeting the right person, perhaps having children, maybe buying a house, a car, renegotiating relationships with parents, getting promoted...the steps of our lives are entrained into a pattern created by all of those around us moving ahead, and us catching up with them, and the interbrain ensures that much of this time we are thinking about the same things, worrying about the same things, and hoping for the same things that everyone around us connected to us via the interbrain is also thinking, worrying, and hoping for.

Only when the treadmill or rather the chain gang stops can we look around us and ask ourselves what is all this activity *for*. We may be satisfied with a prosaic answer like, 'It's the only way to earn a living' or 'This is the life I was born to'. But for many people the answer to this question has to be a spiritual one. 'Why are we here?' 'Why am I here?'

It is likely that you who are reading these words will have your own ideas about this, which may be very different from mine. My own ideas are that our intimation that there is more to life than mere existence, that there is some transcendental value, comes from our participation in society. I agree with the sociologist Durkheim who wrote that 'God is society' (I think that he could equally have truly written that Satan is society, inasmuch as Satan is an intimation of transcendence of the destruction and undoing of human projects).

To know God, to be aware of transcendence, means, in my view, being momentarily able to synthesize two antithetical experiences. To feel oneself being extended beyond one's immediate person into a larger entity, which may happen through the interbrain but may also happen by imagination in nature or when losing oneself in music or in philosophy; yet at the same time to be sufficiently grounded in oneself to be conscious of being still an individual. It is often easy to allow oneself to be swept along by the interbrain or by its products in human cooperation so that one is extended in this way. We may feel some sense of it in the library, the concert hall, in our gardens, or looking at our children. It is only when we become aware of ourselves, too, perhaps of our finitude or insignificance, perhaps not, that this vague feeling intensifies into spiritual awareness—or so I believe.

I think that it is easier for people with an ASD to experience themselves as individuals than it is for neurotypicals who are shuffling along in the chain gang. I hope that people with an ASD who can identify with a neurotypical that they are close to can experience something of the extension across minds and bodies that neurotypicals achieve more readily. I would imagine so, because many people with an ASD experience neurotypicals as an undifferentiated mass. I believe that identifying with a person with an ASD can sharpen that sense of being alone but unique, even if insignificant, that marks individual awareness.

As I have just written, being able to experience both feeling extended into a greater entity and yet being able to retain an awareness of individuality is what I think is one key to spiritual awareness. Since neurotypicals are good at the former, and people with an ASD at the latter, together we have a greater chance of exploring the spiritual dimensions of human existence than they could alone.

So if I can sum up in a sentence why society can, indeed should, afford autistic spectrum disorder, I would say that it is because autistic spectrum disorder and being offline from the interbrain is to be at our most individual, and therefore closest to an awareness of the uniqueness of our minds. Neurotypicals may dominate the social world, but people with autistic spectrum disorders rank amongst the great explorers of the untrammelled mind.

*N*otes

[1] Eibl-Eibesfeldt argues that the eyebrow flash may be the most universal nonverbal signal, and that the facial hair above the eyes has been retained in Homo sapiens in order to make this signal easily recognizable (Grammer *et al.,* 1988).

[2] This section is something of a simplification and the signifier–signified relation in language is normally more complex than this: onomatopoeic words have some indexical relation to their signifieds, for example. Semantic choices are also influenced by their subject matter. A story about floods might describe the rescue attempt as being in a state of flux, whilst a story about a fire might describe the same level of disorganization as only at half heat. In a previous publication, I have described semantic choices as carrying a burden as well as conveying a content. More recently I have replaced the term 'burden' by the term 'flavour'. Whissell uses the same term for the capacity of words, even nonsense words, to arouse emotions as a result of the similarity of the articulatory movements required to produce constitutent phonemes and the movements associated with facial expressions of emotion (Whissell, 1991).

My take on this is that all communication has some arbitrary and some nonarbitrary, or motivated, signification. There are many examples of arbitrariety in nonverbal communication, from the signing systems that are completely language-like, such as British or American Sign Language, to the gestures that we learn as children but which are stylized versions of some underlying, related, indexical action: for example the eyebrow flash to indicate disapproval, which is derived from the widening of the palpebral fissure in surprise, or the rotation of the hand to indicate a lack of commitment to one position or another, which mimics the behaviour of the see-saw.

[3] The original studies of face processing by people with autism were made by Langdell (1978) and he was the first to describe the dissociation between upright and inverted face interpretation. His findings were supported by many studies, including one performed by myself and colleagues (Tantam *et al.,* 1989) but there were also many technical objections, including the possibility that the cases and controls were not adequately matched for age and IQ, something that requires selection of participants from large pools of potential participants. However, the weight of evidence is now strongly in favour of (1) an impairment in both matching and labelling facial expressions, whether presented dynamically or statically (Lindner and Rosen, 2006); (2) a particular deficit in processing upright faces associated with

a failure (Grelotti *et al.*, 2005) or delay in the development of a privileged 'gestalt' interpretative system in fusiform gyrus; and (3) a failure to develop efficient facial scanpaths which, presumably, enable this privileged processing (Pelphrey *et al.*, 2002) in the first place.

[4] Darwin argued that human facial expressions had similarly evolved from intention movements to communication, as an adaptation to living in groups. Many psychologists still consider that Darwin was correct in his supposition (Ekman, 1982). These intention movements evolve into channels: some examples are given in the chapter. Other evolutionary adaptations include the preservation of eye lashes which make blinking more salient, and in cultural evolution, the use of clothing which alters expressiveness.

Many current authors consider that a focus on channels belongs to an earlier and now outmoded stage of nonverbal communication (NVC) research (Patterson and Manusov, 2006). The reason for emphasizing them in this chapter is that they provide a useful scaffolding for the systematic observation of NVC.

'Leakage' of intentions or emotions through nonverbal behaviour has an evolutionary advantage, or so argued Darwin (1872). For example, it is undoubtedly an advantage to rabbits that they have a white tail whose upward bounce when they are startled acts as a danger signal to other rabbits. The upward movement is a consequence of a contraction of the haunches and occurs whenever a rabbit is startled in preparation for running away. It is, to use Darwin's term, an intention movement, like someone opening their mouth to get ready to speak. Certain intention movements may occur so often that they constitute signals. Both the rabbit's tail flash and a person opening their mouths are examples. In fact, the injunction to 'Keep your mouth shut' from countless gangster movies is not a convoluted way of saying, 'Don't talk', but a direct way of saying, 'Don't invite any questions'.

Darwin's point was that such regular intention movements may become elaborated by evolution into a system of communication. Suppose that primitive rabbits had tails which were the same hue as their bodies. Then along came an ur-buck with a lighter tail which caught the eye of an ur-doe. Their kittens would be more likely to have lighter tails, too. Because it is easier to see a lighter tail, especially during the times of maximum danger at dawn and dusk, the offspring of the lighter-tailed buck, feeding together in a family group as rabbits do, would be more able to see if one of their number was startled than other families, and would consequently be quicker to escape. More of the lighter-tailed rabbits would survive (and more of the does who liked lighter-tailed bucks). Eventually, under selection pressure, white-tailed rabbits would predominate. Note that this is also an argument for the preservation of the genes by evolution, and not individuals. The first buck with a lighter tail would be more visible than other bucks, and therefore more, and not less, prone to predation even though lighter tails might make the group of rabbits less prone to predation.

The purpose (if one can speak so teleologically) of the rabbit's white tail is to pass on the message 'I am startled' to other rabbits. Bobbing is not just an intention movement, but a message, whose meaning can be interpreted by other animals.

Knowingly deceiving someone may induce an emotion like shame, anxiety or excitement in the deceiver, and this may 'leak out' in a high-pitched voice or greater speech errors. Deliberate deception may also require more thought to avoid inconsistencies and other ways in which one might be caught out. This may divert cognitive capacity from other tasks leading to slower speech, or less attention on the other person, even gaze aversion (Ekman, 1997). Accomplished liars, knowing these signs of lying, will try to make themselves not do these things. It is easier to do this in the face, or in the smoothness of speech, than it is in tone of voice or the movements of hands or feet. Hence, Ekman and Friesen's use of the metaphor of leakage, implying that signs of deception leak out from the blanket that has been placed over them.

[5] There is now considerable criticism of this particular experiment (Mehrabian, 2007), and I give it mainly as an illustration.

[6] Deliberate smiling or frowning takes place in the left hemisphere (Gazzaniga and Smylie, 1990).

[7] Gestures have a three-fold relationship to speech.

Gestures may punctuate speech, their timing indicating the transition between phonemes and larger segments of speech production. In this process, gesture may be the fundamental element. It has been suggested that the use of gestures by infants may anticipate the development of a phonemic structure. This kind of gesture is not diminished when a person is speaking to an unseen listener (Alibali, Heath, and Meyers, 2001). These developments do not occur in autistic children (Mitchell *et al.*, 2006).

'Emblems' (Ekman and Friesen, 1972) are another type of gesture that is both culturally specific and learnt, but this takes the place of language. These gestures may, however, substitute for language, for example in situations where speech is not practicable such as in noisy environments—the gestures of people directing traffic are an example—or when hearing is impaired. In the latter case, there may be a whole sign language that enables English or American to be signed and not spoken.

'Illustrators', as they have been termed (Ekman and Friesen, 1972), are gestures that do increase in frequency when the listener can also see the speaker. These gestures amplify or qualify the content of what is being said. They are often outwardly directed, i.e. their movement is towards the listener, and they may be accompanied by looking at the listener as a means of emphasis. An example is the downward chopping movement that indicates, 'That's the end of it' or the one that Darwin mentions, of the outstretched palms being turned up, to indicate wonder or ignorance. Illustrators are culturally specific, and are learnt.

ASL and other sign languages are learnt just like writing, and are used just like writing. We would therefore expect their neurology to be related and indeed this is so (Hickok, Bellugi, and Klima, 1996). There are other conventional nonverbal communications which have a one-to-one correspondence with a word or phrase. The upward jerk of the eyes and the eyebrows, which indicates, 'Listen to that', is one example. As always with language, there is some slippage between the word and the symbol, but these gestures are still in register with language and can be said to be extensions of it.

American or British Sign Language are expressions of language, just as much as is speech or writing. There are no other nonverbal channels that can communicate words so fully, but there are other nonverbal expressions that can be given a verbal reading. The eye flash—a brief widening of both palpebral fissures with a lifting of the upper eyelids and the eyebrows and sometimes a backwards jerk of the head—may be the most universal facial expression (Eibl-Eiblesfeldt): it is a greeting whose origins clearly lie in the innate expression for surprise. Rubbing or touching the nose is similarly a gesture of embarrassment which probably originates in the innate nose wrinkling associated with the facial expression of disgust.

[8] Touching and grooming is an important channel of communication between carers and babies. Grooming in at least one primate, the prairie vole, triggers the release of a peptide, vasopressin, which blocks specific receptors in the part of the brain that monitors and organizes the response to threat, the amygdala. The blockade reduces the release of another peptide, corticotrophin releasing factor (CRF), and this, through a cascading pathway,

reduces circulated corticosteroids, which are sometimes called the stress hormones because high levels of them are associated with being stressed. Not only does touch therefore reduce the body's stress response, it also reduces the expression of the genes for the CRF receptors so that there are long-term changes in the body's stress response.

Mimicry and emotion: not only is there feedback from emotion expressions to experienced emotion, but there is also feed forward (Moody *et al.*, 2007).

Imitation corresponds to rapport in later life; see Lakin (2006) for a review.

[9] The assumption of a connection is the basis of the sympathetic fallacy. An example of this attaches to the mandrake plant, *Mandragora officianalis*, which has a forked root and resembles a manikin. It was therefore considered by apothecaries to be connected to humanity and this connection was assumed to be that the mandrake had a human soul. Similar ideas attach to the fruit and to the roots of the Ginseng (Chinese: 'in the image of man') plant (*Panax ginseng* is the Asian species and *Panax quinquefolius* is the American species). The fruit reportedly resembles a three day old baby and the root is also humanoid. Ginseng plants are thought to live up to 300 years and accordingly accredited with the ability to confer long life to humans with whom they are thought to be sympathetically connected.

[10] Bandura himself (1989) refers to modelling as a kind of 'observational learning' and does not make the distinction that I do between iconic imitation and the kind of reflective, symbolically processed or interpreted learning that I am calling copying.

[11] Freud gave a preeminent place to identification in his theory of identity, and the military came to his mind, too, in his most detailed discussion of this (Freud, 1922). He argued that identification in, for example, dress or manners, led to an introjection of the feelings for other people with whom I identify, and that led to a part of myself that was patterned on them, and on my feelings for them—internalization.

[12] Note the attribution of intent, or at least animism to the door handle. There is considerable evidence that people are willing to accredit intent to moving objects, even when these are simple shapes, and use their knowledge of intent as a way of solving problems using moving shapes. People with ASD are less able to do this (Klin, 2000).

[13] The suppression of mirror responses is as important as the fact that they occur. Involuntary or forced imitation, echopraxia, occurs in conditions like schizophrenia, dementia, and sometimes autism when there is impaired frontal lobe suppression of mirror or following movements.

[14] See for example this recent paper by an advocate of the componential position (Scherer and Ellgring, 2007) which should be set against classic work by Ekman and Izzard supportive of Darwin's original 1872 hypothesis.

[15] As it happens there is one muscle whose contraction is specific to smiling, and indeed specific to involuntary or 'Duchenne' smiles (Duchenne after the neurologist who first elicited them by electrical stimulation). This is the zygomatic muscle.

The evidence for the subliminal transmission of emotions between people is overwhelming. Sonnby-Borgstrom, for example, examined facial electromyographic (EMG) responses in 61 participants looking at pictures of angry or happy faces (Sonnby-Borgstrom, 2002). EMGs were recorded at 17, 56, and 2350 milliseconds after first exposure to the photographs and even at 56 milliseconds, i.e. well before any conscious processing of emotions, high empathy subjects had contractions of those muscles appropriate to emotional mimicry. Further support for the nonconscious nature of these responses was that responders did not differ from nonresponders in their reported experience of the photographs. Other teams have come to similar conclusions (Moody, *et al.*, 2007; Thunberg, 2007). The mimicry of facial expression appears to be one of the main channels for emotional contagion, and involuntary facial expressions are more likely to be mimicked by others than posed facial expressions (Surakka and Hietanen, 1998). 'Emotional contagion' (Hatfield, Cacioppo, and Rapson, 1994) is fully established by the age of two years in human infants (Hay, 1994), but there is evidence of much younger infants showing physiological reactions to their parents' mood. The disposition to emotional contagion persists throughout life. It is one of the reasons that individuality can become submerged in the emotions that sweep through a crowd.

In an extensive review, Preston and de Waal (2002) summarize the evidence for a 'Perception Action Model' according to which the perception of another's facial expression involves activation of the neurones that would produce the same expression in the self and, at least in young infants, the imitation of that expression. Although the answering imitation is extinguished, or at least concealed, in older children, the feeling that is associated with the facial expression may persist, providing a means for the contagion of emotion (see Preston and de Waal, 2002, and their commentators, for a summary of the evidence). The evidence includes recordings of mirror neurones, found in area F5 of the premotor cortex in macaques, which fire both when the monkey performs an action and when a human experimenter performs it (Gallese *et al.*, 1996; Rizzolatti *et al.*, 1996). Event-related potential studies suggest that there are similar neurones in human premotor cortex (Grezes and Decety, 2002). Gallese, Eagle, and Migone (2007) have concluded that the existence of mirror neurones accounts for our sense of 'we-ness' or intersubjectivity (Trevarthen and Aitken, 2001) that develops early in life and which intuition suggests is closely linked to empathy.

Inevitably, there are some unresolved problems with the Perception Action Model. The model has to include some sort of dual processing of movement initiation so that a subject knows that it is their own movement that is taking place, and that they are not observing another's movement (Jeannerod, 2003). Also, the supportive evidence has mainly come from the visual transmission of emotion. Whether or not it would apply to auditory, olfactory, or sensory modalities is still unclear. It is also unclear to what extent all of the primary emotions are contagious. The majority of studies have been of the contagion of fear, and commonsense experience indicates that fear is the most contagious of the emotions. There is also good evidence for disgust and embarrassment being contagious, but less agreement about whether or not anger, pleasure, or sadness are contagious. These may, to use a distinction made by Preston and de Waal, be reactions *to* another's emotions rather than reactions *with* another's emotions.

[16] This striking observation was made by Meltzoff and has been largely upheld by subsequent researchers. The evidence is summarized in a recent review (Meltzoff and Prinz, 2002).

[17] Attunement is evidence against the notion that the infant is born without any preconceptions or preadaptations to the world. This is sometimes called the 'tabula rasa' theory of the infant mind and has been attributed to the philosopher John Locke. It is often coupled with a statement attributed to William James that the newborn infant is in a state of 'buzzing, blooming confusion'. James' admirers will be relieved to know that James did not use this phrase in connection with infancy but following his version of a phenomenological reduction: 'If my reader', he writes in *Some Problems of Philosophy* (James, 1979, p.50) 'can succeed in abstraction from all conceptual interpretation and lapse back into his immediate sensible life at this very moment, he will find it to be what someone has called a big blooming buzzing confusion, as free from contradiction in its "much-at-onceness" as it is all alive and evidently there'. It is attention that 'carves out objects, which conception then names and identifies forever...' (*ibid.*).

[18] In the 19th century, the then new science of etymology was based on the transfer of meaning from one word to another by metaphor (iconic relation) or metonym (an indexical relation). Indexical relations are sometimes called pars pro toto (that is, the part that stands for the whole as in 'the crown' coming to mean not just the crown the monarch wears but the monarch him- or herself, and then the monarch plus all his or her officers). T.S. Eliot wrote about the importance of metonym (he called it synechdoche) in poetry and used it regularly himself, for example in this passage from 'The Love Song of J. Alfred Prufrock': 'I should have been a pair of ragged claws / Scuttling across the floors of silent seas.' Sigmund Freud's *Interpretation of Dreams* suggests that symptoms are linked, as are the images in dreams, by relations of displacement (his term for similarity, and typical Freud thought of hysteria) and condensation (or pars pro toto, which Freud thought was typical of symptom development in obsessive compulsive disorder).

[19] This statement leaves out the covering effect of a full beard, but that only covers the cheeks and chin. Intriguingly these are the areas that are outside the normal facial scan paths, as I consider later in this chapter.

[20] The contrast between the white sclera and the darker iris, like that between the pale or shiny face, and the hairy or dark back of the head, may also have been evolved to make gaze direction easier to discern (Ricciardelli, Baylis, and Driver, 2000).

[21] Hedge *et al.* found that gaze towards another person rarely fell within a 10 degree quadrant of the other person's eyes unless it was directly into the other person's eyes (Hedge, Everitt, and Frith, 1978) and this has been confirmed in other studies.

[22] I described the primary gaze reflex in one of the first papers to suggest that gaze might be a factor in the aetiology of autism at about the same time as similar papers by Baron-Cohen and Loveland (Baron-Cohen *et al.*, 1992; Loveland, 1991a; Tantam, 1992).

The primary gaze reflex in developmental psychology has been reviewed by Emery on several occasions (for example, Emery, 2000).

[23] David Skuse has authoritatively reviewed what is known about this recently (Skuse, 2006), arguing that there is a very rapid, extra-cortical pathway via the superior colliculus which has some limited shape processing powers and which will detect the direction of another person's gaze with unusual speed, enabling a person to turn away from mutual gaze before the fact of mutual gaze has become conscious.

[24] Current evidence about face processing suggests that there are several streams of processes. One stream processes invariant features of faces to provide information about gender and identity, and another processes dynamic features. The latter stream is actually the confluence of smaller streams processing different channels, so that gaze processing (partly in the amygdala) and facial expression processing are initially separate, but become combined in the superior temporal sulcus. Graham and LaBar (2007) provide an excellent review of these issues, and indeed many of the others covered in this section, including evidence for the gaze reflex, for the salience of direct gaze and its alerting effect, and for the primacy of judgements about approach or avoidance signals.

[25] For an interesting overview of Swammerdam's career, and his importance in European biology, see the commentary by Dr Matthew Cobb in the Times Literary Supplement No. 5472, 15 February 2008, 15–17.

[26] In a previously unpublished study, Richings, Rippon, and myself had ten people with Asperger syndrome and a group of age- and gender-matched neurotypical volunteers look at slides of a face with the eyes averted or with the gaze outwards so that it appeared to be at

the person looking at the slide. Subjects were attached to an encephalogram whose output could be averaged through a computer. EEG recordings from frontal (Fz), parietal (Pz), and cervical (Cz) leads were made and the positive responses at 300 mseconds (P300) were averaged following the first presentation of the index slide. In one series of presentations, it was the eyes averted slide that was the index or 'oddball' (the slide was interspersed by repeated presentations of a neutral slide) and in the other the eyes full front slide was the oddball. The results are shown in the endnote table. There is a significantly increased response to direct gaze in the neurotypicals (p<0.05 for Cz channel on paired, 3-tail T test) compared to their response to averted gaze, but there was no significant difference in these two responses in the participants with Asperger syndrome, probably because only about half of them showed an increased response, whilst half showed little or no response (see Table N1.1).

[27] This proposal was, I think, first made by Patterson (1976) but see also Hobson and Bishop, 2003; Janson, 1993. Children who are deaf blind have even higher prevalence of autism (Johansson *et al.*, 2006).

[28] Where phylogenetically gaze following begins is a matter of controversy. Some think that it is restricted to the great apes and others think that prosimians cannot follow gaze, monkeys can, and great apes can also infer intention from gaze direction (see review by Emery (2000). One reason for the differences may be that handling primates from birth results in accelerated cognitive development in comparison to conspecifics reared in the wild.

[29] A recent paper by Pelphrey, Morris, and McCarthy (2005) has summarized previous studies showing that people with autism do not infer intentions from gaze direction as neurotypicals do, and adds some further information from an fMRI study. In this participants in the scanner were presented with computer animated full frontal faces whose eyes were depicted as strongly deviated to the right. There were two versions of this: one in which the apparent direction of gaze was towards a checker board pattern (congruent), and one in which it was above it (incongruent). Particular attention was paid to activation of the superior temporal sulcus (STS) in this study because this area is implicated in other studies of judging the direction of gaze. There was greater activation of the STS in the incongruent condition in neurotypicals, as if they were straining to work out why the cartoon figure was looking into empty space, when there was something more interesting to look at. People with ASD however did not show any differences in the STS activation in the incongruent condition compared to the congruent one.

[30] Ape pointing may have evolved from poking fingers into things, but apes in captivity are kept, like humans, in a prolonged state of infancy. They seem to point much more than feral apes, but also, like people with an ASD, take the keeper's hand and move it to the object that is desired (Gomez, 2007).

[31] There is a good review of the development of joint attention by Tomasello, Carpenter, and Liszkowski (2007).

[32] Engagement is required before attention can be shifted (D'Entremont and Seamans, 2007).

[33] Dream interpretation plays an even more important role in shamanistic religions. Dreams of high significance may be told and re-told, and thus disseminated. Nonverbal signs, too, get disseminated although nonverbally. Many locations and cultures have their own gestures that each new generation acquires by imitation. New gestures also develop and are communicated. The high-five gesture in which a person stretches out their right arm above their heads and slaps the palm of the outstretched hand of another person is an example of a recent innovation.

Table N1.1 Unpublished data from a study
conducted by Richings, Rippon, and Tantam.

AS participants	Fz	Pz	Cz	Fz	Pz	Cz
	21	28	30	10	14	20
	21	23	18	4	13	10
	4.5	9.5	6	8	11	6
	-1	-4	3	4	-10	4
	10	7.5	9	9	9	9
	14	18	15	9	9.5	13
	*	22	23	*	19	26
	20	8	12	-2.5	-0.5	-2.5
	11	7	11	8.5	9	3.5
	0	9	6	*	12	14
	34	28	32	19	17	17

Neurotypicals	Fz	Pz	Cz	Fz	Pz	Cz
	5	7	3	-17	-2	-8
	12.5	10.5	9	-10	-14	-14
	50	56	58	38	36	40
	-6.5	-3	-5	0.5	0	-3
	*	5.2	5.2	15.5	9	6
	21	24	21	22	14	14
	25	16	21	38	42	40
	11.5	10.5	11	3.5	11.5	10
	11	15	13	3	9.5	6.5
	9.5	15.5	14	4	4	2
	19	17	19	15	14	18
	6	12	9	11	12.5	9.5
	34	30	32	18	15	16

[34] Example taken from www.anderson.ucla.edu/faculty/jason.frand/teacher/technologies/palace/datamining.htm and accessed 29 January 2008.

[35] Many people are sure that they can tell when someone is lying although studies usually indicate that most people are no better than chance when faced with the task in laboratory conditions. Most people under these conditions tend to assume that too many people are telling the truth. In fact, our most usual lie detection strategy is to compare what one person says with what other people say about the same events. Those people who think that

they are good at lie detecting often refer to a 'well known fact' about lying which is that lying is harder than telling the truth, partly because it means more care has to be paid to possible inconsistencies, leading to more 'cognitive load', and partly because it goes against the grain of what we were taught as children, leading to tension or anxiety. Moreover most people believe that they have a sure fire way of detecting either cognitive load, or emotional tension.

Gaze avoidance, a fixed gaze or gaze deviation in a particular direction are all used to detect cognitive load, as are speech dysfluencies. None of them is reliable, but all may be shown more frequently by people with an ASD.

A lack of facial expression, a lack of spontaneous movement, and a fixed smile may all be used as signs of anxiety or emotional tension. The lack of expression is also characteristic of people with an ASD who may also show a fixed smile in tense situations, but this indicates submissiveness and not the triumph or superiority to which many people attribute it and which leads them to want to 'wipe the smile off his face'. So those people who rely on emotional tension cues are also likely, in situations when the truth of what a person with an ASD is saying is in question, to misperceive them as lying.

Sometimes one meets a person with an ASD whose parents have tried to offset their social rejection by being particularly accepting themselves. These parents deliberately suppress their suspicions that their child is lying and, in these circumstances, the person with an ASD may actually use lying or deception like others do, as a way of getting away with something.

[36] Many people still speak about smelling out the truth, and many of us spend considerable sums of money on deodorants to mask the smell of our sweat. These deodorants are normally linked to sexual excitement in advertisements, which is odd since the evidence suggests that the smell of sweat is an important releaser of sexual excitement, but it may be that their main purpose is to conceal deception which, cynics might say, plays no small part in our regular use of deodorants which may be designed to suppress the cues of deception, as well as those of sexual excitement, that we might otherwise give off to other people.

[37] Knapp (2006) argues that the link between nonverbal communication and emotion was the main focus of research into nonverbal communication in the early 20th century, although before that it had been the use of nonverbal communication as a rhetorical aid.

[38] De Saussure pointed out that language was similarly structured with an utterance being composed of places such as 'verb' or 'predicate' on a string or series (he called these syntagmatic relations) and with those places being filled by the selection of one of a group of similar words, for example suitable verbs, which he termed paradigmatic relationships. Cognitively speaking the other members of a paradigmatic class are synchronously present, so that one word can 'connote' others.

[39] Examples of this are the use of gaze to disambiguate temporal expressions in speech (Hanna and Brennan, 2007) and the use of vocalizations to alter infants to elements of an action sequence that require to be copied (Brugger *et al.*, 2007). Estigarribia and Clark (2007) provide a detailed account of how infants and parents manage each other's attention in a collaborative task, in this case talking about an object.

[40] 'Reciprocal imitation training' tries to get round this problem by imitating an action of particular interest when performed by the child, giving it a name ('Now you're smiling') and then saying 'And now I'm going to...smile, in my example...and when you see me do it, I want you to do it too' (Ingersoll and Gergans, 2007).

[41] Many of the points in this section are similar to those made by proponents of the automatic processing approach to nonverbal communication (for example, Bargh *et al.*, 2001) in that they invoke automatic nonconscious or 'noncontrolled' processing. However automatic processing is not distributed between individuals which is what I am suggesting is the case for the networked processing that I am proposing. Buck and VanLear (2002) also discuss a comparable 'spontaneous and nonpropositional stream of communication' which they consider is the product of the right hemisphere of the brain.

[42] This would be consistent with behavioural ecology approaches to emotion as well as the more conventional idea that facial expressions of emotion are innate motor schemata, with one schema for each basic emotion. Behavioural ecologists argue that facial expressions can be better considered to be expressions of action tendency. Although there is a theoretical case for this, there is little empirical support except perhaps for facial expressions of anger (Horstmann, 2003). One very amiable young woman with autism and learning difficulty that I once met had developed an action tendency theory of her own which worked well amongst her family and acquaintances. If another person's face was open, then they were open to her approach (think of facial expressions which involve mouth widening, for example smiling, or the palpebral fissures widening, such as pleased surprise), but if their face was closed and scrunched up on itself (think of frowning, fear, disgust, or sadness) then she would know that person would also be closed to her approach.

[43] Extract from Crowhurst's log cited in *The Strange Voyage of Donald Crowhurst* by N. Tomalin and R. Hall (2001), Camden, Maine: International Marine.

[44] Melanie Klein, who had a notoriously poor relationship with her own daughter, the psychoanalyst Melitta Schmideberg, thought that infants were born with an already existing emotional expectation of the mothering figure and it was this that created the mother–infant bond.

[45] Sensory abnormalities in autism were reviewed by Rogers and Ozonoff recently who found that children with fragile X or who are congenitally deaf-blind show more than children with an ASD (Rogers and Ozonoff, 2008). Case reports also suggest that sensory oversensitivity may occur without other symptoms and not lead to autism (Reynolds and Lane, 2007). Hyperaesthesia may result from a lack of habituation and reflect a child's unwillingness to be held or touched rather than being an explanation of these things.

[46] For example in recent reviews in Current Biology (Dinstein *et al.*, 2008) and Developmental Review (Rajendran and Mitchell, 2007).

[47] I have other issues with DSM-IV which emerged when I was an advisor to the text revision. One of these is that categories seem to be heterogeneous and not homogeneous, as they should be. They also jumble up impairments that do not seem to be particularly connected like repetitive speech (2c) and pretend play (2d).

[48] MRI and fMRI.

In very strong magnetic fields, a surprising number of everyday substances will behave as if they contain tiny magnets which can be orientated along the lines of magnetic flux. These everyday substances include water, whose electron cloud lingers longer over the oxygen atom than the two hydrogen atoms and therefore at one end or pole of the molecule, and deoxyhaemoglobin, the form that the blood pigment adopts when it is not carrying oxygen. When a very strong magnetic field is applied (3 Tessla is common in many fMRI scanners), these tiny magnets line up according to the lines of magnetic flux—or at least most of them do. Some 'high energy' radicals (nuclei or molecules) pair up with other 'like-minded' radicals and align themselves across the magnetic flux. If they are nudged by a pulse of radio waves

('RF excitation'), the radicals lose their orientation and some get pushed into the high energy state. When the RF excitation stops, they return to their usual nonaligned state and in the process produce a perturbation in the magnetic field which can induce a small and short lived electrical pulse (magnetic resonance signal) in a receiver coil.

The realignment of the low energy radicals with the magnetic flux is termed the T1 relaxation. The fall back from a high energy to a low energy state is the T2 relaxation. T2 relaxation produces a magnetic pulse in the receiver coil that is transverse to the flux produced by the main magnet in the scanner. The T1 relaxation pulse is used to produce a static or structural picture of the brain, an MRI scan. The T2 relaxation pulse can be used to produce additional information about activity.

The energy that it takes to excite a radical from its low energy to its high energy, paired, state is a quantum. A quantum is a multiple of the frequency of oscillation which is a characteristic of the radical concerned and by applying RF excitation at this characteristic frequency, particular radicals can be selectively shifted from low to high energy states. This means that the T2 relaxation pulse or signal in the transverse receiving coil following RF excitation at the characteristic deoxyhaemoglobin frequency is mainly contributed by deoxygenated haemoglobin. This Blood-Oxygen Level Dependent or BOLD signal paradoxically falls when particular neurones are active because their activity does drain oxygen but it also produces an increase in blood flow which means that there is less, and not more, deoxygenated haemoglobin in their immediate vicinity. By superimposing the BOLD T2 relaxation signal on the structural T1 signal it is possible to provide a picture of momentary changes in small populations of neurones deep in the brain.

[49] Not surprisingly, the notion that there are particular modules of the brain that subserve higher social functions like 'theory of mind' is giving way to a distributed processing or 'manifold' model (Mitchell, 2006) in which the elements within the manifold might deal with relatively low level processes (for example the superior temporal sulcus seems to deal with many inputs which require temporal sequencing).

[50] Older ways of looking at the brain suggested that it was like the body itself, and composed of organs that had specialized functions, except that these are not clearly separated organs, but 'brain structures'. It was assumed that detailed microscopic or histological analysis would show that each structure had a particular architectural organization of its cells and fibres and that each anatomically differentiated area (the current classification was developed by Brodmann so the cerebral cortex is divided into Brodmann areas) would have a specific function. On this view there is a structure for coordinating movement, the cerebellum, and for emotional regulation, the limbic system, and within the cerebral cortex, or the newest part of the brain, there are areas with specific functions, too. This older view had the paradox that a large part of the cerebral cortex had no known function. For a long while, these 'silent' areas were thought to be redundant.

A more evolutionary view was that the brain is like a building that has been extended. McLean suggested that there had been two major extensions building on an original 'reptilian brain' or 'R complex'. This triune brain theory remains widely quoted. The reptilian brain corresponds to the anatomical area known as the brain stem; the next extension, which occurs according to the theory in the more ancient mammals, is the 'limbic system' which deals with emotions, memory, and dispositions. A last extension is the cerebral cortex, sometimes called the 'neocortex' or new cortex, which is particularly large in primates. Arguably, there is a fourth extension, at the front of the brain, with the frontal lobes becoming larger in the great apes.

As the brain becomes larger and more complex, so coordinating its activity becomes a problem. Here the analogy that often seems applicable is that of an expanding business. In a one person business, no coordination is needed. But as the business grows workers are taken on just to deal with goods in, production, or despatch. Normally they can be left just to deal with routine demands, but they have to work together for the business to function smoothly and sometimes to give up what they are doing to help someone else out. So the workers have to be supervised and redirected by a supervisor. The supervisors themselves are working to some kind of target that is handed down to them by management, and management is monitoring them and sometimes changing the targets. Lower level managers do not see the overall picture of the organization, and so will be monitored by some kind of production manager, but he or she does not necessarily see the future goals of the organization or how they will be affected by external conditions, so there are executives who are responsible for this, and who set targets and monitor target achievement throughout the whole organization.

It seems to be a law of nature that businesses take on more and more managers as they get larger, and so it is with the brain. The newer parts of the brain are disproportionately involved with management and coordination, and the newest parts of the brain with what are called, in both business and in neurology, executive functions.

There are several problems with the triune brain, not least that it is based on very basic ethology. Reptiles, far from being the kind of primitive animal that McLean imagined, have quite complex repertoires of behaviour, which can include altruism, planning, and prolonged childcare. McLean considered these to be 'higher' functions, but clearly they are not. The concept of higher is in itself problematic. Why should mammals be higher organisms than reptiles? They are certainly more recently evolved, but then so are Galapagos finches or Hebridean wrens. When evolution is described as pointing towards human beings as its 'highest' manifestation, it is the case that the more superior and rostral areas of the brain have increased disproportionately to 'lower' centres, and that each new rostral development acts as a controller of the activity of 'lower' centres. But this control is at a cost, for example the possibility of mental illness and the costs of prolonged infancy, that may not be evolutionarily advantageous in the long run. If population count is a measure of evolutionary success then human beings are less successful than some insects, or some other mammals, such as rats.

Even more misleading than this anthropocentricity is the assimilation of mind and brain in McLean and many subsequent neuroscientists. The development of a particular brain area is assumed to be equivalent to the development of a particular higher function, as if the psychological function and the brain area are really the same or at least the same but described differently as dual description monists have it. No-one thinks that there is a word processing module in my computer right now, even though I am using it as a word processor. Its word processing function is the product of the interaction of me the writer, of various cultural artefacts created by other people like an operating system and a word processing program, and hardware.

Over the years an alternative point of view of brain function has been put forward which is that psychological functions result from the connections between parts of the brain and not from specific areas. Key contributors to this connectionist approach are the 19th-century neurologists, such as Hughlings Jackson whose work was revived by the late Norman Geschwind, 20th-century psychologists like McCulloch, Pitts, Hebb, and particularly Karl Lashley.

The interbrain idea is an extension of connectionism from neural connections within the brain to connections between brains mediated by nonverbal communication.

[51] A more recent study using fMRI and direct electrical recordings from facial muscles confirmed many of the findings of the Leslie study, although the activation was principally in the inferior frontal gyrus adjacent to and possibly overlapping with the area that is often thought to contain mirror neurones, and it was the superior temporal sulcus, rather than the gyrus, where activation occurred (Lee, Dolan, and Critchley, 2008). The resolution of fMRI images is not high and small differences like these may not amount to significant differences. Lee *et al.* review the evidence for the iconic imitation hypothesis more fully than I have done, and also with some greater caution. Interested readers could look at this paper to get more background.

[52] It would be premature to locate these functions in particular areas at this stage, but if it is assumed that the distribution of mirror neurones is correlated with the areas that subserve iconic imitation, then frontal operculum, which is particularly responsive to facial expression, and inferior parietal lobule, particularly sensitive to gesture, should be added to the list (Gobbini *et al.*, 2007; Jabbi, Swart, and Keysers, 2007; Montgomery and Haxby, 2008). The frontal operculum is adjacent to, and receives innervations from, the insula, which is linked to emotional appraisal, to shame, and to empathy. The insula also projects to the orbitofrontal cortex, as does the superior temporal sulcus (Rolls, 2000). The surface anatomy of the frontal operculum and the insula are altered in children with autism, and altered but in a lesser degree in children with high functioning autism and adolescents with an ASD. The extent of the difference from controls is therefore correlated with age, but also IQ, total ADI-R score, and the frequency of repetitive behaviour (Nordahl *et al.*, 2007). None of these findings proves that these areas are the key to ASD, but they are certainly supportive.

[53] Oxytocin, a polypeptide hormone, has long been known to make the uterus contract after the birth of an infant. In fact, doctors have given injections of it for this purpose for many years. Oxytocin also triggers the attachment of ewes to lambs shortly after birth: ewes who give birth to three lambs typically only attach to the first born two. The third is not suckled (ewes have only two teats) and is ignored. UK farmers call these 'cade' lambs, and know that they have to be hand-reared if they are to survive. Oxytocin, and its closely related peptide hormone, vasopressin, is now thought to have a general mammalian role in infant attachment and, some argue, in romantic attachment, too (Marazziti and Dell'osso, 2008). Oxytocin snuff given just before playing one of the trust games described by King-Casas *et al.* increases the judgement that the other player is trustworthy, irrespective of their behaviour during the game (Baumgartner *et al.*, 2008). Oxytocin has been proposed as a treatment for autism (Opar, 2008), possibly on the assumption that autism is a disorder of attachment and that oxytocin and vasopressin are necessary for attachment behaviour. If they are, it is possible that they mediate this effect through proximity seeking (Scattoni *et al.*, 2008) rather than through the interbrain connection the proximity makes possible which, I am arguing, is where the problem in ASD lies. Many parents would, I think, agree that their child with autism is not lacking in attachment or proximity seeking, but in knowing what to do when they are close to another person. Some parents sometimes complain to me that 'he's always under my feet. He can't seem to leave me alone'.

[54] It is interesting to note that a very early study by Ricks and Wing showed that the mothers of children with autism were not able to recognize their own infant's vocalizations but mothers of neurotypical infants could tell if their child was crying even if other children were crying too (Ricks, 1975).

[55] It may not be unconnected that the cingulate cortex is in less evolved mammals part of the brain, sometimes called the rhinencephalon, that is specialized for smell processing.

[56] See also Zilbovicius for a general review (Zilbovicius et al., 2006), Garbett et al. (2008) for genetic evidence, a SPECT study showing hypoperfusion of the right superior temporal sulcus in Asperger syndrome (Anon. 2007), and a diffusion tensor imaging study providing evidence of impaired white matter connections in ASD in the temporal lobes (Lee et al., 2007).

[57] I have used the more common term syllables rather than the more correct one, phoneme. Phonemes are not meaningful units, but most units of meaning in speech, or morphemes, do actually correspond to phonemes.

[58] People with right sided parietal lesions or lesions of the prefrontal cortex show reductions in empathy (Shamay-Tsoory et al., 2004) and people who have suffered a stroke may be socially impaired as a result of impaired empathy and social cognition (Eslinger, Parkinson, and Shamay, 2002).

[59] I have suggested that this might happen when the cache gets overwritten, but another hypothesis, although one that leads to the same end result, is that seeing another person's point of view requires two processes: inferring another person's perspective and inhibiting one's own. People with typical ASD have problems with the former, but it may be that people with atypical ASD have problems with the latter. 'WBA', who had a right sided infarction of the right prefrontal and temporal areas following a cerebro-vascular accident, is reported to have been able to take another person's perspective following the infarct but not to inhibit his or her own (Samson et al., 2005).

[60] Glosser, Wiley, and Barnoski studied elderly people (1998) and found that those with dementia made as many gestures as the nondemented group, but made 'more referentially ambiguous gestures, fewer gestures referring to metaphoric as opposed to concrete contents, and fewer conceptually complex bimanual gestures'. The more the gestural impairment, the more difficulty was evinced in being able to find the appropriate word or concept. Frick-Horbury and Guttentag (1998) tested the ability of people to find the word to fit a definition that they were given. Preventing them from gesturing with their hands reduced the number of words successfully fitted to definitions (and also the number of words remembered).

[61] This kind of model has been invoked to explain the language problems of stroke patients (Crutch and Warrington, 2007).

[62] My imaginary mother–infant scenario has been emulated in the laboratory. Tomasello, Call, and Gluckman (1997) invited children of 2.5 and 3 years of age, six chimpanzees, and three orangutans to participate, on separate occasions, in a hiding game. An assistant either pointed to the hiding place, marked it with a small block, or held up a picture of it. The children all found the hiding place more quickly with the assistance of the signs, but the apes did not. The experimenters concluded that the children could understand what the helper meant by the signs, the helper's communicative intention, but the apes could not. But another and I think more plausible interpretation is that the children were connected to the interbrain of the hider but the apes were not. Bonobos who are used to playing with humans may have been able to interbrain with humans, and so performed differently (Pika and Zuberbuhler, 2007). Hand reared chimps are more likely to be able to perform joint attention tasks with humans than chimps reared by their mothers (Leavens and Hopkins, 1998).

Nonverbal exchanges between experimenter and infant influence infant search in other experiments. Repacholi and Meltzoff (2007) studied 14- and 18-month-old infants' ability to identify the target of an emotional display. In the visual task, infants were presented with two boxes. Each box contained an object that could be identified by opening the box lid and looking inside. In the tactile task, the objects had to be pulled out of the boxes before they could be seen. An experimenter expressed happiness as she looked or put her hand inside one box, and disgust as she repeated this action with the other box. Infants were then allowed to explore the boxes. Infants touched both boxes but preferred to search for the happy object. Thus, regardless of age or task, infants identified the target of each emotional display as something inside a box and not the box itself. Infants appeared to use the experimenter's attentional cues (gaze and action) to interpret her emotional signals and behaved as if they understood that she was communicating about the objects.

This kind of nonverbal exchange is less likely between infants with autism and experiments. Stone *et al.* studied 14 young children with autism and 14 matched controls (Stone *et al.*, 1997). Each child was placed in 16 situations which required the child to interact with an experimenter. The authors' conclusions were that 'Children with autism requested more often and commented less often than controls. Autistic children were less likely to point, show objects, or use eye gaze to communicate, but were more likely to directly manipulate the examiner's hand. The autistic group also used less complex combinations of behaviors to communicate'.

[63] There is considerable ongoing argument about critical periods and language, partly because some examples of the late development of speech are based on children with very abnormal developments, for example children who have been kept in cages or hutches by their parents with no interaction. In these distressing cases, it may be impossible to know if interaction did go on that was concealed from the abusive parent.

[64] A recent issue of Brain Research was dedicated to this topic (Beer, Mitchell, and Ochsner, 2006). One difficulty that many of the contributors brought up with the modular idea is that it conflates the two kinds of processing that have been called online interbrain processing and offline processing in this book. For example, Frith and Frith differentiated top down or explicit processes and bottom up or implicit ones (Frith and Frith, 2006), and contract reflexive, automatic processes with deliberative, reflective ones (Satpute and Lieberman, 2006), or automatic versus controlled processes (Todorov, Harris, and Fiske, 2006).

[65] See the distinction made between X-reflexive automatic social processing and C-reflective deliberate social processing (Satpute and Lieberman, 2006).

[66] This may be one of the reasons for the lack of consensus in the literature. There is evidence for an impairment in the ability to imitate (Smith and Bryson, 2007) but also studies showing an unimpaired ability (Bird *et al.*, 2007). The difference may be if people with an ASD know how to imitate but not what to imitate. The tasks used in the study differ in the difficulty with which the imitated action has to be separated out of a stream of actions and it may be that it is this separation process that presents the problems, as I have suggested (Leighton *et al.*, 2008). If this is correct, then this would be evidence against an abnormality in the mirror neurone system being one cause of an ASD. The exact role of mirror neurons in humans as compared to macaques remains largely uninvestigated, and it is therefore surprising that so much has been made of them as the explanation of many human faculties, like empathy and imitation. Some influential researchers have produced evidence that they interpret as showing that mirror neurones are intact in people with ASD (Hamilton, Brindley, and Frith, 2007).

[67] Recent evidence by Adolphs' group supports the importance of the amygdala in orientating to the eyes (Akiyama *et al.*, 2006), this research being stimulated by a single case study of a woman with an amygdalar lesion whose performance at detecting fear in faces improved after instructions to look at the eyes of the test materials, but who forgot to do this after the end of that block of testing (Adolphs *et al.*, 2005).

[68] Poignant examples are given in the work of Phoebe Caldwell and I am grateful to her publisher and mine, Jessica Kingsley, for drawing this to my attention. Caldwell uses elements taken from several autism theories, including sensory overload, autism as an extreme response to anxiety, as well as imitation.

[69] Similar conclusions have been drawn by Simon Baron-Cohen from his hypothesis that the 'autistic brain' is an extreme form of the male brain, and that it supports a high degree of systematic thinking which increases the skill of engineers, physicists, and others who need to use systematic thinking in their work.

[70] The Danish composer Rued Langgaard (1893–1952) may be an example. Some consider that he is one of the greatest 20th-century Danish composers, but his work is rarely performed. He was brought up in a small Danish town, Ribe, and mainly home-schooled. Whether or not this was because he could not fit into school is not known, but he did have considerable difficulty fitting in as an adult. He had precocious ability as an organist, but was relieved of his job as the organist in the local parish church after a short time. His unexpected remarks to people he knew often led to them taking umbrage. He failed to be recognized by other musicians. Yet in retrospect his music is seen to have anticipated many of the directions that classical music took after his death.

[71] Sometimes realizing that one has a child with an ASD can also be a kind of limit situation for a parent or carer, since it often means the acceptance that one's child might never be fully independent, and sometimes the acceptance that they may never have a partner, or a family of their own. However, it is rarely such a stark situation as it is for the person with the ASD. Often the parents have always known that their child was different and their projected future for the child has been constructed on this knowledge.

References

[Anonymous] (2007) [Regional cerebral blood flow changes of right parietal lobe and superior temporal gyrus in Asperger's disorder in comparison with the patients with schizophrenia]. Seishin Shinkeigaku Zasshi, 109, 50–54.

Adolphs, R. (2006) How do we know the minds of others? Domain-specificity, simulation, and enactive social cognition. Brain Research, 1079, 25–35.

Adolphs, R., Gosselin, F., Buchanan, T.W., et al. (2005) A mechanism for impaired fear recognition after amygdala damage. Nature, 433, 68–72.

Akiyama, T., Kato, M., Muramatsu, T., et al. (2006) A deficit in discriminating gaze direction in a case with right superior temporal gyrus lesion. Neuropsychologia, 44, 161–170.

Alibali, M.W., Heath, D.C., and Myers, H.J. (2001) Effects of visibility between speaker and listener on gesture production: Some gestures are meant to be seen. Journal of Memory and Language, 44, 169–188.

American Foundation for the Blind (2008) 'Bonding with your Baby.' Accessed 3 March 2008 at www.afb.org/Section.asp?SectionID=75&TopicID=340&DocumentID=3884.

Arnold, L. (2003) 'Mission statement.' Accessed 2 February 2008 at www.larry-arnold.info/Neurodiversity/Mission/index.htm.

Argyle, M., Lefebvre, L., and Cook, M. (1974) The meaning of five patterns of gaze. European Journal of Social Psychology, 4, 385–402.

Ashwin, C., Baron-Cohen, S., Wheelwright, S., et al. (2007) Differential activation of the amygdala and the 'social brain' during fearful face-processing in Asperger Syndrome. Neuropsychologia, 45, 2–14.

Bachevalier, J. and Loveland, K.A. (2006) The orbitofrontal-amygdala circuit and self-regulation of social-emotional behavior in autism. Neuroscience and Biobehavioral Reviews, 30, 97–117.

Balfe, M., Chen, T., and Tantam, D. (2005) Sheffield survey of health and social care needs of adolescents and adults with Asperger syndrome. Sheffield: School of Health and Related Research.

Bandura, A. (1989) Social cognitive theory. In Vol 6. Six Theories of Child Development (ed. R. Vasta), pp.1–60. Greenwich, CT: JAI Press.

Bargh, J.A., Gollwitzer, P.M., Lee-Chai, A., *et al.* (2001) The automated will: Nonconscious activation and pursuit of behavioral goals. Journal of Personality and Social Psychology, **81**, 1014–1027.

Baron-Cohen, S., Wheelwright, S., Hill, J., *et al.* (2001) The 'Reading the Mind in the Eyes' Test revised version: A study with normal adults, and adults with Asperger syndrome or high-functioning autism. Journal of Child Psychology and Psychiatry, **42**, 241–251.

Baumgartner, T., Heinrichs, M., Vonlanthen, A., *et al.* (2008) Oxytocin shapes the neural circuitry of trust and trust adaptation in humans. Neuron, **58**, 639–650.

Beer, J.S., Mitchell, J.P., and Ochsner, K.N. (2006) Special issue: Multiple perspectives on the psychological and neural bases of social cognition. Brain Research, **1079**, 1–3.

Bertenthal, B.I. and Longo, M.R. (2007) Is there evidence of a mirror system from birth? Developmental Science, **10**, 526–529.

Bird, G., Leighton, J., Press, C., *et al.* (2007) Intact automatic imitation of human and robot actions in autism spectrum disorders. Proceedings Biological Sciences, **274**, 3027–3031.

Brugger, A., Lariviere, L.A., Mumme, D.L., *et al.* (2007) Doing the right thing: Infants' selection of actions to imitate from observed event sequences. Child Development, **78**, 806–824.

Buck, R. and VanLear, C.A. (2002) Verbal and nonverbal communication: Distinguishing symbolic, spontaneous, and pseudo-spontaneous nonverbal behavior. Journal of Communication, **52**, 522–541.

Calder, A.J., Beaver, J.D., Winston, J.S., *et al.* (2007) Separate coding of different gaze directions in the superior temporal sulcus and inferior parietal lobule. Current Biology, **17**, 20–25.

Calder, A.J., Jenkins, R., Cassel, A., *et al.* (2008) Visual representation of eye gaze is coded by a nonopponent multichannel system. Journal of Experimental Psychology: General, **137**, 244–261.

Chesterton, G. (2007) *The Wisdom of Father Brown.* New York: Cosimo Classics.

Chiu, P.H., Kayali, M.A., Kishida, K.T., *et al.* (2008) Self responses along cingulate cortex reveal quantitative neural phenotype for high-functioning autism. Neuron, **57**, 463–473.

Clancey, W. (1997) *Situated Cognition: On Human Knowledge and Computer Representation.* New York: Cambridge University Press.

Clark, A. (2005) Intrinsic content, active memory and the extended mind. Analysis, **65**, 1–11.

Condon, W. (1996) *Sound-Film Microanalysis: A Means for Correlating Brain and Behavior in Persons with Autism,* pp.221–225. Milwaukee, WI: Autism Society of America.

Conty, L., N'Diaye, K., Tijus, C., *et al.* (2007) When eye creates the contact! ERP evidence for early dissociation between direct and averted gaze motion processing. Neuropsychologia, **45**, 3024–3037.

Creak, M. (1972) The first observations on the wild-boy of Lacaune (called 'Victor' or 'the wild-boy of Aveyron'): New documents. Annales Medico Psychologiques, **2**, 465–490.

Crutch, S.J. and Warrington, E.K. (2007) Contrasting effects of semantic priming and interference in processing abstract and concrete words. Brain and Language, **103**, 88–89.

D'Entremont, B. and Seamans, E. (2007) Do infants need social cognition to act socially? An alternative look at infant pointing. Child Development, **78**, 723–728.

Dalton, K.M., Nacewicz, B.M., Johnstone, T., *et al.* (2005) Gaze fixation and the neural circuitry of face processing in autism. Nature Neuroscience, **8**, 519–526.

Dapretto, M., Davies, M.S., Pfeifer, J.H., *et al.* (2006) Understanding emotions in others: mirror neuron dysfunction in children with autism spectrum disorders. Nature Neuroscience, **9**, 28–30.

Darwin, C. (1872) *The Expression of the Emotions in Man and Animals.* London: Murray.

de Jong, M.C., van Engeland, H., and Kemner, C. (2008) Attentional effects of gaze shifts are influenced by emotion and spatial frequency, but not in autism. Journal of the American Academy of Child and Adolescent Psychiatry, **47**, 443–454.

Deak, G.O., Walden, T.A., Kaiser, M.Y., *et al.* (2008) Driven from distraction: How infants respond to parents' attempts to elicit and re-direct their attention. Infant Behaviour and Development, **31**, 34–50.

Dichter, G.S. and Belger, A. (2007) Social stimuli interfere with cognitive control in autism. Neuroimage, **35**, 1219–1230.

Dinstein, I., Thomas, C., Behrmann, M., *et al.* (2008) A mirror up to nature. Current Biology, 18, R13–R18.

Dunbar, R.I.M. (2004) Gossip in evolutionary perspective. Review of General Psychology, **8**, 100–110.

Durkheim, E. (1970) *Suicide: A Study in Sociology.* London: Routledge and Kegan Paul

Efron, D. (1972) *Gestures, Race and Culture.* The Hague: Mouton.

Eippert, F., Veit, R., Weiskopf, N., *et al.* (2007) Regulation of emotional responses elicited by threat-related stimuli. Human Brain Mapping, **28**, 409–423.

Ekman, P. (1982) *Emotion in the Human Face* (2nd edition). Cambridge: Cambridge University Press.

Ekman, P. (1997) Deception, lying and demeanour. In *States of Mind* (eds D. Halpern and A. Voiskounsky), pp.93–105. New York: Oxford University Press.

Ekman, P. and Friesen, W. (1969) Nonverbal leakage and cues to deception. Psychiatry, **32**, 88–106.

Ekman, P. and Friesen, W. (1972) Hand movements. Journal of Communication, **22**, 353–374.

Elfenbein, H.A., Foo, M.D., Boldry, J., *et al.* (2006) Brief report: Dyadic effects in nonverbal communication: A variance partitioning analysis. Cognition and Emotion, **20**, 149–159.

Emery, N.J. (2000) The eyes have it: The neuroethology, function and evolution of social gaze. Neuroscience and Biobehavioral Reviews, **24**, 581–604.

Engell, A.D. and Haxby, J.V. (2007) Facial expression and gaze-direction in human superior temporal sulcus. Neuropsychologia, **45**, 3234–3241.

Eshel, N., Nelson, E.E., Blair, R.J., *et al.* (2007) Neural substrates of choice selection in adults and adolescents: Development of the ventrolateral prefrontal and anterior cingulate cortices. Neuropsychologia, **45**, 1270–1279.

Eslinger, P.J., Parkinson, K., and Shamay, S.G. (2002) Empathy and social-emotional factors in recovery from stroke. Curr Opin Neurol, **15**, 91–97.

Estigarribia, B. and Clark, E.V. (2007) Getting and maintaining attention in talk to young children. Journal of Child Language, **34**, 799–814.

Fairhall, S.L. and Ishai, A. (2007) Effective connectivity within the distributed cortical network for face perception. Cerebral Cortex, **17**, 2400–2406.

Fitzgerald, M. (2005) *The Genesis of Autistic Creativity.* London: Jessica Kingsley Publishers.

Freud, S. (1922) *Group Psychology and the Analysis of the Ego.* London: Hogarth Press.

Frick-Horbury, D. and Guttentag, R.E. (1998) The effects of restricting hand gesture production on lexical retrieval and free recall. American Journal of Psychology, **111**, 43–62.

Frischen, A., Bayliss, A.P., and Tipper, S.P. (2007) Gaze cueing of attention: Visual attention, social cognition, and individual differences. Psychological Bulletin, **133**, 694–724.

Frith, C.D. and Frith, U. (2008) The self and its reputation in autism. Neuron, **57**, 331–332.

Frith, C.D. and Frith, U. (2006) How we predict what other people are going to do. Brain Research, **1079**, 36–46.

Frith, U. (2003) *Explaining the Enigma* (2nd edition). Oxford: Blackwell.

Gallese, V., Eagle, M.N., and Migone, P. (2007) Intentional attunement: Mirror neurons and the neural underpinnings of interpersonal relations. Journal of the American Psychoanalysis Association, **55**, 131–176.

Gallese, V., Fadiga, L., Fogassi, L., et al. **(1996)** Action recognition in the premotor cortex. Brain, **119**, 593–609.

Ganz, M.L. (2007) The lifetime distribution of the incremental societal costs of autism. Archives of Pediatric and Adolescent Medicine, **161**, 343–349.

Garbett, K., Ebert, P.J., Mitchell, A., et al. **(2008)** Immune transcriptome alterations in the temporal cortex of subjects with autism. Neurobiological Disorders, **30**, 303–311.

Gazzaniga, M.S. (2000) Cerebral specialization and interhemispheric communication: Does the corpus callosum enable the human condition? Brain, **123 (Pt 7)**, 1293–1326.

Gazzaniga, M. and Smylie, C. (1990) Hemispheric mechanisms controlling voluntary and spontaneous smiling. Journal of Cognitive Neuroscience, **2**, 239–245.

Glosser, G., Wiley, M.J., and Barnoski, E.J. (1998) Gestural communication in Alzheimer's disease. Journal of Clinical and Experimental Neuropsychology, **20**, 1–13.

Gobbini, M.I., Koralek, A.C., Bryan, R.E., et al. **(2007)** Two takes on the social brain: a comparison of theory of mind tasks. Journal of Cognitive Neuroscience, **19**, 1803–1814.

Gomez, J.C. (2007) Pointing behaviors in apes and human infants: A balanced interpretation. Child Development, **78**, 729–734.

Graham, R. and LaBar, K.S. (2007) Garner interference reveals dependencies between emotional expression and gaze in face perception. Emotion, **7**, 296–313.

Grammer, K., Schiefenhoevel, W., Schleidt, M., et al. **(1988)** Patterns on the Face: The Eyebrow Flash in Crosscultural Comparison. Ethology, **77**, 279–299.

Greene, J.D., Sommerville, R.B., Nystrom, L.E., et al. **(2001)** An fMRI investigation of emotional engagement in moral judgment. Science, **293**, 2105–2108.

Grelotti, D.J., Klin, A.J., Gauthier, I., et al. **(2005)** fMRI activation of the fusiform gyrus and amygdala to cartoon characters but not to faces in a boy with autism. Neuropsychologia, **43**, 373–385.

Grezes, J. and Decety, J. (2002) Does visual perception of object afford action? Evidence from a neuroimaging study. Neuropsychologia, **40**, 212–222.

Hadjikhani, N., Joseph, R.M., Snyder, J., et al. **(2007)** Abnormal activation of the social brain during face perception in autism. Human Brain Mapping, **28**, 441–449.

Hamilton, A.F., Brindley, R.M., and Frith, U. (2007) Imitation and action understanding in autistic spectrum disorders: How valid is the hypothesis of a deficit in the mirror neuron system? Neuropsychologia, **45**, 1859–1868.

Hanna, J.E. and Brennan, S.E. (2007) Speakers' eye gaze disambiguates referring expressions early during face-to-face conversation. Journal of Memory and Language, **57**, 596–615.

Hartley, G. and Karinch, M. (2008) *I Can Read You Like a Book*. Franklin Lakes, NJ: Career Press.

Hatfield, E., Cacioppo, J., and Rapson, R. (1994) *Emotional Contagion*. Cambridge: Cambridge University Press.

Hay, D. F. (1994) Prosocial development. Journal of Child Psychology and Psychiatry and Allied Disciplines, **35**, 29–71.

Hedge, B., Everitt, B., and Frith, C. (1978) The role of gaze in dialogue. Acta Psychologia, **42**, 453–475.

Hendry, J., Devito, T., Gelman, N., *et al.* (2005) White matter abnormalities in autism detected through transverse relaxation time imaging. Neuroimage, **29**, 1049–1057.

Hesslinger, B., Tebartz, V.E., Thiel, T., *et al.* (2002) Frontoorbital volume reductions in adult patients with attention deficit hyperactivity disorder. Neuroscience Letters, **328**, 319–321.

Hickok, G., Bellugi, U., and Klima, E.S. (1996) The neurobiology of sign language and its implications for the neural basis of language. Nature, **381**, 699–702.

Hiraishi, H., Hashimoto, T., Mori, K., *et al.* (2007) [A preliminary fMRI study of moral judgment task in high functioning autistic children.] No to hattatsu, **39**, 360–365.

Hobson, R.P. and Bishop, M. (2003) The pathogenesis of autism: Insights from congenital blindness. Philosophical Transactions of the Royal Society of London. B: Biological Sciences, **358**, 335–344.

Horstmann, G. (2003) What do facial expressions convey: feeling states, behavioral intentions, or action requests? Emotion, **3**, 150–166.

Hughes, J.R. (2007) Autism: The first firm finding = underconnectivity? Epilepsy and Behavior, **11**, 20–24.

Hurley, S. (2008) The shared circuits model: How control, mirroring and simulation can enable imitation, deliberation, and mindreading. Behavioral and Brain Science, **0**, 1–2.

Hutchins, E. (1995) *Cognition in the Wild*. Cambridge, MA: MIT Press.

Ingersoll, B. and Gergans, S. (2007) The effect of a parent-implemented imitation intervention on spontaneous imitation skills in young children with autism. Research in Developmental Disabilities, **28**, 163–175.

Itami, S. and Uno, H. (2002) Orbitofrontal cortex dysfunction in attention-deficit hyperactivity disorder revealed by reversal and extinction tasks. Neuroreport, **13**, 2453–2457.

Jabbi, M., Swart, M., and Keysers, C. (2007) Empathy for positive and negative emotions in the gustatory cortex. Neuroimage, **34**, 1744–1753.

James, W. (1979) *Some Problems of Philosophy*. Cambridge, MA: Harvard University Press.

Janson, U. (1993) Normal and deviant behavior in blind children with ROP. Acta Ophthalmological Supplement, 20–26.

Jarbrink, K., McCrone, P., Fombonne, E., *et al.* (2007) Cost-impact of young adults with high-functioning autistic spectrum disorder. Research in Developmental Disabilities, **28**, 94–104.

Jaspers, K. (1951) *The Way to Wisdom*. New Haven, CT: Yale University Press.

Jeannerod, M. (2003) The mechanism of self-recognition in humans. Behavioural Brain Research, **142**, 1–15.

Johansson, M., Rastam, M., Billstedt, E., *et al.* (2006) Autism spectrum disorders and underlying brain pathology in CHARGE association. Developmental Medicine and Child Neurology, **48**, 40–50.

Kaffman, A. and Meaney, M.J. (2007) Neurodevelopmental sequelae of postnatal maternal care in rodents: Clinical and research implications of molecular insights. Journal of Child Psychology and Psychiatry, **48**, 224–244.

Kendon, A. (1967) Some functions of gaze direction in social interaction. Acta Psychologica, **32**, 1–25.

King-Casas, B., Tomlin, D., Anen, C. *et al.* (2005) Getting to know you: Reputation and trust in a two-person economic exchange. Science, **308**, 78–83.

Klin, A. (2000) Attributing social meaning to ambiguous visual stimuli in higher-functioning autism and Asperger syndrome: The Social Attribution Task. Journal of Child Psychology and Psychiatry, **41**, 831–846.

Knapp, M. (2006) An historical overview of nonverbal research. In *The Sage Handbook of Nonverbal Communication* (eds V. Manusov and M. Patterson), pp.3–20. Thousand Oaks, CA: Sage.

Koulomzin, M., Beebe, B., Anderson, S., *et al.* (2002) Infant gaze, head, face and self-touch at 4 months differentiate secure vs. avoidant attachment at 1 year: A microanalytic approach. Attachment and Human Development, **4**, 3–24.

Kuro5hin (2004) 'Living with Asperger's Syndrome.' Accessed 3 February 2008 at www.kuro5hin.org/story/2004/5/17/172914/576.

Lacan, J. (1977) *Ecrits.* London: Tavistock Press.

Lakin, J. (2006) Automatic cognitive processes and nonverbal communication. In *The Sage Handbook of Nonverbal Communication* (eds V. Manusov and M. Patterson), pp.59–78. Thousand Oaks, CA: Sage.

Landa, R. (2007) Early communication development and intervention for children with autism. Mental Retardation and Developmental Disabilities Research Reviews, **13**, 16–25.

Langdell, T. (1978) Recognition of faces: An approach to the study of autism. Journal of Child Psychology and Psychiatry, **19**, 255–268.

Leavens, D.A. and Hopkins, W.D. (1998) Intentional communication by chimpanzees: A cross-sectional study of the use of referential gestures. Developmental Psychology, **34**, 813–822.

Lee, J.E., Bigler, E.D., Alexander, A.L., *et al.* (2007) Diffusion tensor imaging of white matter in the superior temporal gyrus and temporal stem in autism. Neuroscience Letters., **424**, 127–132.

Lee, T.W., Dolan, R.J., and Critchley, H.D. (2008) Controlling emotional expression: Behavioral and neural correlates of nonimitative emotional responses. Cerebral Cortex, **18**, 104–113.

Lee, T.W., Josephs, O., Dolan, R.J., *et al.* (2006) Imitating expressions: emotion-specific neural substrates in facial mimicry. Social Cognitive and Affective Neuroscience, **1**, 122–135.

Leibniz, G. (1991) *Discourse on Metaphysics and Other Essays.* Indianapolis, IN: Hackett Publishing Company Inc.

Leighton, J., Bird, G., Charman, T., *et al.* (2008) Weak imitative performance is not due to a functional 'mirroring' deficit in adults with autism spectrum disorders. Neuropsychologia, **46**, 1041–1049.

Lepage, J.-F. and Théoret, H. (2007) The mirror neuron system: grasping others' actions from birth? Development Science, **10**, 513–529.

Leslie, K.R., Johnson-Frey, S.H., and Grafton, S.T. (2004) Functional imaging of face and hand imitation: Towards a motor theory of empathy. Neuroimage, **21**, 601–607.

Lindner, J.L. and Rosen, L.A. (2006) Decoding of emotion through facial expression, prosody and verbal content in children and adolescents with Asperger's syndrome. Journal of Autism and Devopmental Disorders, **36**, 769–777.

Loveland, K. (1991a) Social affordances and interaction: Autism and the affordances of the human environment. Ecological Psychology, **3**, 99–119.

Loveland, K. (1991b) Social affordances and interaction II. Autism and the affordances of the human environment. Ecological Psychology, **3**, 99–119.

Loveland, K. (1993) Social affordances and interaction: Autism and the affordances of the human environment. In *The Perceived Self: Ecological and Interpersonal Sources of Self-knowledge* (ed U. Neisser), pp.237–253. Cambridge: Cambridge University Press.

Loveland, K. A., Pearson, D. A., Tunali-Kotoski, B., et al. (2001) Judgments of social appropriateness by children and adolescents with autism. Journal of Autism & Developmental Disorders, 31, 367–376.

Lynn, P.M. and Davies, W. (2007) The 39,XO mouse as a model for the neurobiology of Turner syndrome and sex-biased neuropsychiatric disorders. Behavioural Brain Research, **179**, 173–182.

Manjaly, Z.M., Bruning, N., Neufang, S., et al. (2007) Neurophysiological correlates of relatively enhanced local visual search in autistic adolescents. Neuroimage, **35**, 283–291.

Marazziti, D. and Dell'osso, M.C. (2008) The role of oxytocin in neuropsychiatric disorders. Current Medicinal Chemistry, **15**, 698–704.

Mehrabian, A. (2007) *Nonverbal Communication*. New Brunswick, NJ: Aldine Transaction.

Meltzoff, A.N. and Prinz, W. (2002) *The Imitative Mind*. New York: Cambridge University Press.

Mitchell, J.P. (2006) Mentalizing and Marr: An information processing approach to the study of social cognition. Brain Research, **1079**, 66–75.

Mitchell, S., Brian, J., Zwaigenbaum, L., et al. (2006) Early language and communication development of infants later diagnosed with autism spectrum disorder. Journal of Developmental and Behavioral Pediatrics, **27**, S69–S78.

Montgomery, K.J. and Haxby, J.V. (2008) Mirror neuron system differentially activated by facial expressions and social hand gestures: A functional magnetic resonance imaging study. Journal of Cognitive Neuroscience.

Moody, E.J., McIntosh, D.N., Mann, L.J., et al. (2007) More than mere mimicry? The influence of emotion on rapid facial reactions to faces. Emotion, 7, 447–457.

Mueller, R.A., Pierce, K., Ambrose, J.B., et al. (2001) Atypical patterns of cerebral motor activation in autism: A functional magnetic resonance study. Biological Psychiatry, **49**, 665–676.

Muhle, R., Trentacoste, S.V., and Rapin, I. (2004) The genetics of autism. Pediatrics, **113**, e472–e486.

Nordahl, C.W., Dierker, D., Mostafavi, I., et al. (2007) Cortical folding abnormalities in autism revealed by surface-based morphometry. J Neurosci, **27**, 11725–11735.

O'Connor, N. and Hermelin, B. (1967) The selective visual attention of psychotic children. Journal of Child Psychology and Psychiatry, **8**, 167–179.

Opar, A. (2008) Search for potential autism treatments turns to 'trust hormone'. Nature Medicine, **14**, 353.

Patterson, M. and Manusov, V. (2006) Nonverbal communication: Basic issues and future prospects. In *The Sage Handbook of Nonverbal Communication* (eds M. Patterson and V. Manusov), pp.522–532. Thousand Oaks, CA: Sage.

Patterson, M.L. (1976) An arousal model of interpersonal intimacy. Psychological Review, **83**, 235–245.

Pelphrey, K.A., Morris, J.P., and McCarthy, G. (2005) Neural basis of eye gaze processing deficits in autism. Brain, **128**, 1038–1048.

Pelphrey, K.A., Morris, J.P., McCarthy, G., et al. (2007) Perception of dynamic changes in facial affect and identity in autism. Social Cognitive and Affective Neuroscience, **2**, 140–149.

Pelphrey, K.A., Sasson, N.J., Reznick, J.S., et al. (2002) Visual scanning of faces in autism. Journal of Autism and Developmental Disorder, **32**, 249–261.

Pelphrey, K.A., Viola, R.J., and McCarthy, G. (2004) When strangers pass. Processing of mutual and averted social gaze in the superior temporal sulcus. Psychological Science, **15**, 598–603.

Pfeifer, J.H., Iacoboni, M., Mazziotta, J.C., *et al.* **(2008)** Mirroring others' emotions relates to empathy and interpersonal competence in children. Neuroimage, **39**, 2076–2085.

Phan, K.L., Wager, T., Taylor, S.F., *et al.* **(2002)** Functional neuroanatomy of emotion: A meta-analysis of emotion activation studies in PET and fMRI. Neuroimage, **16**, 331–348.

Pika, S. and Zuberbuhler, K. (2007) Social games between bonobos and humans: Evidence for shared intentionality? American Journal of Primatology, **70**, 207–210.

Plessen, K.J.M., Bansal, R.P., Zhu, H.P., *et al.* **(2006)** Hippocampus and amygdala morphology in attention-deficit/hyperactivity disorder. Archives of General Psychiatry, **63**, 795–807.

Polezzi, D., Daum, I., Rubaltelli, E., *et al.* **(2008)** Mentalizing in economic decision-making. Behavioural Brain Research, **190**, 218–223.

Preston, S.D. and de Waal, F.B.M. (2002) Empathy: Each is in the right—hopefully, not all in the wrong. Behavioral and Brain Science, **25**, 1–71.

Rajendran, G. and Mitchell, P. (2007) Cognitive theories of autism. Developmental Review, **27**, 224–260.

Redcay, E. (2008) The superior temporal sulcus performs a common function for social and speech perception: Implications for the emergence of autism. Neuroscience Biobehavioral Reviews., **32**, 123–142.

Repacholi, B.M. and Meltzoff, A.N. (2007) Emotional eavesdropping: infants selectively respond to indirect emotional signals. Child Development, **78**, 503–521.

Reynolds, S. and Lane, S.J. (2008) Diagnostic validity of sensory over-responsivity: A review of the literature and case reports. Journal of Autism and Developmental Disorders, **38**, 526–529.

Ricciardelli, P., Baylis, G., and Driver, J. (2000) The positive and negative of human expertise in gaze perception. Cognition, **77**, 1–14.

Ricks, D. (1975) Verbal communication in pre-verbal normal and autistic children. In *Language, Cognitive Deficits, and Retardation* (ed. N. O'Connor), pp.75–85. London: Butterworths.

Rinehart, N.J., Tonge, B.J., Bradshaw, J.L., *et al.* **(2006)** Movement-related potentials in high-functioning autism and Asperger's disorder. Developmental Medicine Child Neurology, **48**, 272–277.

Rizzolatti, G., Fadiga, L., Gallese, V., *et al.* **(1996)** Premotor cortex and the recognition of motor actions. Cognitive Brain Research, **3**, 131–141.

Rizzolatti, G., Ferrari, P.F., Rozzi, S., *et al.* **(2006)** The inferior parietal lobule: Where action becomes perception. Novartis Foundation Symposium, **270**, 129–140.

Rodman, R. (ed.) (1987) *The Spontaneous Gesture-Selected Letters of D.W. Winnicott.* Cambridge, MA: Harvard University Press.

Rogers, S.J. and Ozonoff, S. (2005) Annotation: What do we know about sensory dysfunction in autism? A critical review of the empirical evidence. Journal of Child Psychology and Psychiatry, **46**, 1255–1268.

Rolls, E.T. (2000) The orbitofrontal cortex and reward. Cerebral Cortex, **10**, 284–294.

Rourke, B. (1988) The syndrome of non-verbal learning disabled children. Clinical Psychologist, **2**, 293–330.

Rourke, B.P. and Tsatsanis, K.D. (2000) Syndrome of nonverbal learning disabilities and Asperger syndrome. In *Asperger Syndrome* (eds A. Klin, F. Volkmar, and S. Sparrow), pp.231–246. New York: Guilford.

Rousseau, J.-J. (1962) *Du Contrat Social.* Paris: Editions Garnier Freres.

Samson, D., Apperly, I.A., Kathirgamanathan, U., *et al.* (2005) Seeing it my way: A case of a selective deficit in inhibiting self-perspective. Brain, **128**, 1102–1111.

Sartre, J.-P. (1969) *Being and Nothingness*. London: Routledge.

Satpute, A.B. and Lieberman, M.D. (2006) Integrating automatic and controlled processes into neurocognitive models of social cognition. Brain Research, **1079**, 86–97.

Scattoni, M.L., McFarlane, H.G., Zhodzishsky, V., *et al.* (2008) Reduced ultrasonic vocalizations in vasopressin 1b knockout mice. Behavioural Brain Research, **187**, 371–378.

Scherer, K.R. and Ellgring, H. (2007) Multimodal expression of emotion: Affect programs or componential appraisal patterns? Emotion, **7**, 158–171.

Schultz, R.T., Grelotti, D.J., Klin, A., *et al.* (2003) The role of the fusiform face area in social cognition: Implications for the pathobiology of autism. Philosophical Transactions of the Royal Society of London. Series A: Mathematical and Physical Sciences, **358**, 415–427.

Selfe, L. (1977) *Nadia: A Case of Extraordinary Drawing Ability in an Autistic Child*. New York: Academic Press.

Shafritz, K.M., Dichter, G.S., Baranek, G.T., *et al.* (2008) The neural circuitry mediating shifts in behavioral response and cognitive set in autism. Biological Psychiatry, **63**, 974–980.

Shamay-Tsoory, S.G., Tomer, R., Goldsher, D., *et al.* (2004) Impairment in cognitive and affective empathy in patients with brain lesions: anatomical and cognitive correlates. Journal of Clinical and Experimental Neuropsychology, **26**, 1113–1127.

Skuse, D. (2006) Genetic influences on the neural basis of social cognition. Philosophical Transactions of the Royal Society B: Biological Sciences, **361**, 2129–2141.

Smith, I.M. and Bryson, S.E. (2007) Gesture imitation in autism. II. Symbolic gestures and pantomimed object use. Cognitive Neuropsychology, **24**, 679–700.

Snyder, A., Bahramali, H., Hawker, T., *et al.* (2006) Savant-like numerosity skills revealed in normal people by magnetic pulses. Perception, **35**, 837–845.

Sommerville, J.A. and Hammond, A.J. (2007) Treating another's actions as one's own: children's memory of and learning from joint activity. Developmental Psychology, **43**, 1003–1018.

Sonnby-Borgstrom, M. (2002) [The facial expression says more than words. Is emotional 'contagion' via facial expression the first step toward empathy?] Lakartidningen, **99**, 1438–1442.

Stapledon, O. (1999) *Last and First Men*. London: Victor Gollancz.

Stone, W.L., Ousley, O.Y., Yoder, P.J., *et al.* (1997) Nonverbal communication in two- and three-year-old children with autism. Journal of Autism and Developmental Disorders, **27**, 677–696.

Surakka, V. and Hietanen, J.K. (1998) Facial and emotional reactions to Duchenne and non-Duchenne smiles. International Journal of Psychophysiology, **29**, 23–33.

Tantam, D. (1986) Eccentricity and autism: A clinical and experimental study of 60 adult psychiatric patients, including 46 able autistic adults, with a social disability attributable to personality or developmental disorder. Thesis from the University of London.

Tantam, D. (1988) Lifelong eccentricity and social isolation. I. Psychiatric, social, and forensic aspects. British Journal of Psychiatry, **153**, 777–782.

Tantam, D. (1991) Asperger's syndrome in adulthood. In *Autism and Asperger's syndrome* (ed. U. Frith), pp.147–183. Cambridge: Cambridge University Press.

Tantam, D. (1992) Characterizing the fundamental social handicap in autism. Acta Paedopsychiatrica, **55**, 83–91.

Tantam, D. (2002) *Psychotherapy and Counselling in Practice: A Narrative Framework.* Cambridge: Cambridge University Press.

Tantam, D., Monaghan, L., Nicholson, H., *et al.* (1989) Autistic children's ability to interpret faces: A research note. Journal of Child Psychology and Psychiatry, **30**, 623–630.

Tantam D, Holmes D, and Cordess C. (1993) Nonverbal expression in autism of Asperger type. Journal of Autism and Developmental Disorders, **23**, 1, 111–33

Tessari, A., Canessa, N., Ukmar, M., *et al.* (2007) Neuropsychological evidence for a strategic control of multiple routes in imitation. Brain, **130**, 1111–1126.

Thunberg, G., Ahlsen, E., and Sandberg, A. D. (2007) Children with autistic spectrum disorders and speech-generating devices: communication in different activities at home. Clinical Linguistics and Phonetics, **21**, 457–479.

Todorov, A., Harris, L.T., and Fiske, S.T. (2006) Toward socially inspired social neuroscience. Brain Research, **1079**, 76–85.

Tomasello, M. and Carpenter, M. (2007) Shared intentionality. Developmental Science, **10**, 121–125.

Tomasello, M., Call, J., and Gluckman, A. (1997) Comprehension of novel communicative signs by apes and human children. Child Development, **68**, 1067–1080.

Tomasello, M., Carpenter, M., and Liszkowski, U. (2007) A new look at infant pointing. Child Development, **78**, 705–722.

Trevarthen, C. and Aitken, K.J. (2001) Infant intersubjectivity: Research, theory, and clinical applications. Journal of Child Psychology and Psychiatry and Allied Disciplines, **42**, 3–48.

van Deurzen, E. (2002) *Existential Counselling in Practice.* London: Sage.

Viskontas, I.V., Possin, K.L., and Miller, B.L. (2007) Symptoms of frontotemporal dementia provide insights into orbitofrontal cortex function and social behavior. Annals of the New York Academy of Sciences, **1121**, 528–545.

Weardon, A.J., Tarrier, N., Barrowclough, C., et al. (2000) A review of expressed emotion research in health care. Clinical Psychology Review, **20**, 633–666.

Welchew, D.E., Ashwin, C., Berkouk, K., *et al.* (2005) Functional disconnectivity of the medial temporal lobe in Asperger's syndrome. Biological Psychiatry, **57**, 991–998.

Whissell, T. (1991) Phonoemotional profiling: A description of the emotional flavour of English texts on the basis of the phonemes employed in them. Perceptual and Motor Skills 2000, 617–648.

Whittle, S., Yap, M.B.H., Yucel, M., *et al.* (2008) Prefrontal and amygdala volumes are related to adolescents' affective behaviors during parent-adolescent interactions. Proceedings of the National Academy of Sciences, **105**, 3652–3657.

Williams, J.H., Waiter, G.D., Perra, O., *et al.* (2005) An fMRI study of joint attention experience. Neuroimage, **25**, 133–140.

Williams, W.S., Keonig, K., and Scahill, L. (2007) Social skills development in children with autism spectrum disorders: A review of the intervention research. Journal of Autism and Developmental Disorders, **37**, 1858–1868.

Yirmiya, N. and Ozonoff, S. (2007) The very early autism phenotype. Journal of Autism and Developmental Disorders, **37**, 1–11.

Zentall, T. (2001) Imitation in animals: Evidence, function and mechanisms. Cybernetics and Systems, **32**, 53–96.

Zilbovicius, M., Meresse, I., Chabane, N., *et al.* (2006) Autism, the superior temporal sulcus and social perception. Trends in Neurosciences, **29**, 359–366.abstractions 172, 174

Subject Index